S0-BFB-731

SpringBoard®

English Language Arts

Grade
7

ABOUT THE COLLEGE BOARD

The College Board is a mission-driven not-for-profit organization that connects students to college success and opportunity. Founded in 1900, the College Board was created to expand access to higher education. Today, the membership association is made up of over 6,000 of the world's leading educational institutions and is dedicated to promoting excellence and equity in education. Each year, the College Board helps more than seven million students prepare for a successful transition to college through programs and services in college readiness and college success — including the SAT® and the Advanced Placement Program®. The organization also serves the education community through research and advocacy on behalf of students, educators, and schools.

For further information, visit www.collegeboard.org.

ISBN: 1-4573-0219-5
ISBN: 978-1-4573-0219-0

© 2014 The College Board.

College Board, Advanced Placement Program, AP, AP Central, AP Vertical Teams, College Ed, connect to college success, Pre-AP, SAT, SpringBoard, and the acorn logo are registered trademarks of the College Board. College Board Standards for College Success and English Textual Power are trademarks owned by the College Board. PSAT/NMSQT is a registered trademark of the College Board and National Merit Scholarship Corporation. Microsoft is a registered trademark of Microsoft Corporation. All other products and services may be trademarks of their respective owners.

3 4 5 6 7 8   15 16 17 18 19
Printed in the United States of America

ACKNOWLEDGMENTS

The College Board gratefully acknowledges the outstanding work of the classroom teachers and writers who have been integral to the development of this revised program. The end product is testimony to their expertise, understanding of student learning needs, and dedication to rigorous and accessible English Language Arts instruction.

Pat Bishop
Writing Coach (Retired)
Hillsborough Schools
Tampa, Florida

Julie Manley
English Teacher
Bellevue School District 405
Bellevue, Washington

Susie Challancin
English Teacher
Bellevue School District 405
Bellevue, Washington

Le'Andra Myers
English Teacher
Pasco School District
Pasco, Washington

Bryant Crisp
English Teacher
Charlotte Mecklenburg Schools
Charlotte, North Carolina

Stephanie Sharpe
English Teacher
Hillsborough Schools
Tampa, Florida

Paul DeMaret
English Teacher
Poudre School District
Fort Collins, Colorado

Susan Van Doren
English Teacher
Douglas County School District
Minden, Nevada

Michelle Lewis
Curriculum Coordinator
Spokane Public Schools
Spokane, Washington

SPRINGBOARD ENGLISH LANGUAGE ARTS DEVELOPMENT

Betty Barnett
Executive Director
Content Development

Doug Waugh
Senior Director
Product Management

Joely Negedly
Instructional Specialist

Nina Wooldridge
Senior Director
Professional Development

JoEllen Victoreen
Senior Instructional Specialist

RESEARCH AND PLANNING ADVISORS

We also wish to thank the members of our SpringBoard Advisory Council and the many educators who gave generously of their time and their ideas as we conducted research for both the print and online programs. Your suggestions and reactions to ideas helped immeasurably as we planned the revisions. We gratefully acknowledge the teachers and administrators in the following districts.

ABC Unified
Cerritos, California

Albuquerque Public Schools
Albuquerque, New Mexico

Amarillo School District
Amarillo, Texas

Bellevue School District 405
Bellevue, Washington

Broward County Public Schools
Ft. Lauderdale, Florida

Clark County School District
Las Vegas, Nevada

District School Board of Collier
County
Collier County, Florida

Denver Public Schools
Denver, Colorado

Frisco ISD
Frisco, Texas

Garland ISD
Garland, Texas

Gilbert Unified School District
Gilbert, Arizona

Grand Prairie ISD
Grand Prairie, Texas

Hillsborough County Public
Schools
Tampa, Florida

Hobbs Municipal Schools
Hobbs, New Mexico

Houston Independent School
District
Houston, Texas

Irving Independent School
District
Irving, Texas

Kenton County School District
Fort Wright, Kentucky

Lee County Public Schools
Fort Myers, Florida

Newton County Schools
Covington, Georgia

Noblesville Schools
Noblesville, Indiana

Oakland Unified School District
Oakland, California

Orange County Public Schools
Orlando, Florida

Peninsula School District
Gig Harbor, Washington

Polk County Public Schools
Bartow, Florida

Quakertown Community School
District
Quakertown, Pennsylvania

Rio Rancho Public Schools
Rio Rancho, New Mexico

Ronan School District
Ronan, Montana

St. Vrain School District
Longmont, Colorado

School District of Palm Beach
County
Palm Beach, Florida

Scottsdale Public Schools
Phoenix, Arizona

Seminole County Public
Schools
Sanford, Florida

Southwest ISD
San Antonio, Texas

Spokane Public Schools
Spokane, Washington

Spring ISD
Houston, Texas

Volusia County Schools
DeLand, Florida

Contents

Unit 1   The Choices We Make

Activities

Unit 2 What Influences My Choices?

Activities

Unit 3   Choices and Consequences

Activities

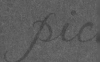

Unit 4 How We Choose to Act

Activities

*Texts not included in these materials.

To the Student

Welcome to the SpringBoard program. The College Board publishes SpringBoard to help you acquire the knowledge and skills that you will need to be prepared for rigorous English Language Arts coursework. Developing proficient reading, writing, language, and speaking and listening skills is important to your success in school, in college, and in a career. Preparing you to develop these skills is the primary purpose of this program.

As you complete middle school and prepare for high school, these skills will also be valuable if you decide to take an Advanced Placement course or another college-level course. Not every student will take an Advanced Placement course in high school, but through SpringBoard you can acquire the knowledge and skills you will need to be successful if you do decide to enroll in AP Literature or AP Language Arts.

We hope you will discover how SpringBoard can help you achieve high academic standards, reach your learning goals, and prepare you for success in your study of literature and language arts. This program has been created with you in mind: the content you need to learn, the tools to help you learn, and the critical thinking skills that help you build confidence in your ability to succeed academically.

STANDARDS-BASED LEARNING

This SpringBoard edition was developed to help you achieve the expectations of being college and career ready. Rigorous standards outline what you should learn in English Language Arts in each grade. See pages xiii–xvi for the complete standards for Grade 7.

The SpringBoard program provides instruction and realistic activities that help you achieve the learning expected by rigorous college and career readiness standards. With this program, you will focus on developing the following skills:

- Close reading and analysis of texts
- Effective communication in collaborative discussions in which you use your textual analysis to share ideas and make decisions with peers
- Fluency in writing narratives, explanations, and arguments based on purpose and audience
- Vocabulary and language skills
- Reading and interpreting film while comparing it to a related print version
- Media literacy

By learning these skills, you will enhance your ability to understand and analyze any challenging text, to write with clarity and voice, to speak and listen in order to communicate and work effectively with others, and to view media with a critical intelligence.

LEARNING STRATEGIES

Some tools to help you learn are built into every lesson. At the beginning of each activity, you will see suggested learning strategies. Each of these strategies is explained in full in the Resources section of your book. These strategies range from **close reading** and **marking** texts to **drafting** and **revising** written work. You will also encounter collaborative strategies in speaking and listening like **debate** and **Socratic Seminar**. Finally, SpringBoard uses a variety of pre-AP strategies like **SOAPSTone** and **TP-CASTT** to help you deeply analyze text; collect evidence for your writing; and critically think about issues, ideas, and concepts. As you learn to use each strategy, you will decide which strategies work best for you!

AP CONNECTIONS

When you reach high school, you may have an opportunity to take Advanced Placement (AP) classes or other rigorous courses. When the time comes to make that decision, we want you to be equipped with the kind of higher-order thinking skills, knowledge, and behaviors necessary to be successful in AP classes and beyond. You will see connections to AP in the texts that you read, the strategies you use, and the writing tasks throughout the material.

Having connections to AP Language and Literature will help you:

- Close read a text to determine literary elements.

- Write with an attention to textual evidence and chose organizational patterns.

- Identify and write rhetorical appeals.

- Understand strong relationships among author's purpose, use of literary/stylistic devices, and desired effect.

- Analyze and synthesize information from a variety of texts to respond to an AP style prompt.

- Write to interpret, evaluate, and negotiate differing critical perspectives in literature.

THE SPRINGBOARD DIFFERENCE

SpringBoard is different because it provides instruction with hands-on participation that involves you and your classmates in daily discussions and analyses of what you're reading and learning. You will have an opportunity to:

- Discuss and **collaborate** with your peers to explore and express your ideas.

- Explore multiple perspectives by reading a **variety of texts** – both fiction and nonfiction – that introduce you to different ways of thinking, writing, and communicating.

- Examine writing from the perspective of a **reader and writer** and learn techniques that good writers use to communicate their message effectively.

- Gain a **deep understanding** of topics, enabling you to apply your learning to new and varied situations.

- Take **ownership** of your learning by practicing and selecting strategies that work for you.

- **Reflect** on your growth as a reader, writer, speaker, and listener, and showcase your best work in a working portfolio.

MIDDLE SCHOOL AT A GLANCE
Grade 6

SpringBoard Grade 6 is developed around the thematic concept of **change**. During the year, you will learn how writers use that theme to tell stories in poetry, short stories, and nonfiction texts. Among the many texts that you will read are works by Langston Hughes, a famous writer who was part of the Harlem Renaissance. Sharon Creech explores change resulting from the loss of a parent in her novel, *Walk Two Moons*. John Steinbeck takes you on a trip around the country with his dog, Charley. Scenes from one of William Shakespeare's plays take you into the world of drama. As you read these texts and make connections to experiences in your own life, you will begin to see how writers use the details of everyday life to create stories that we all enjoy.

Reading and writing go hand-in-hand, and Grade 6 gives you opportunities to write your own stories (narrative), explain information (expository), and create an argument to persuade an audience. Specific strategies for writing and revising support your writing efforts from planning to drafting, revising, and editing. Writing opportunities include a personal narrative and a short story, essays in which you share your ideas about a fictional story and a real-life story, and an argumentative letter to persuade others to support you position on an issue.

You will also be asked to research topics and deepen your understanding using film. In this grade you will view a video biography of Temple Grandin while also reading about her life and how she has coped with autism.

Grade 7

In SpringBoard Grade 7, you will investigate the thematic concept of **choice**. All of us make choices every day. Some of those choices have a short-term impact (like what to have for lunch), while others have a greater impact (like whether to study in school or to goof off!). You will learn about Nelson Mandela's choice to fight segregation—even though it meant going to jail—in South Africa by reading from his autobiography. A famous poem by Robert Frost, the novel *Tangerine*, Sojourner Truth's famous speech on slavery, and a drama by Shakespeare all show you the choices that real and imaginary characters make and how those choices affect their lives. Close reading strategies will help you to determine what each text says explicitly and to make logical inferences from what it does not say explicitly.

Writing and speaking will focus on text-based evidence. For example, you and your peers will write a literary analysis of a novel and include findings from research to produce a multimedia biographical presentation. Much like in 6th grade, you will be asked to write in argumentative, informational, and narrative modes.

You will also look at print texts and then examine how those same texts are portrayed in film. Dramas are like a film done on stage, and you will get to star in a performance of a scene from another of Shakespeare's plays.

Grade 8

In SpringBoard Grade 8, units of study focus on the theme of **challenges**. Among the many texts that you will read are an essay about Civil War heroes, narratives about the Holocaust, a novel and short story by Ray Bradbury, Elie Wiesel's Nobel Prize acceptance speech, poetry by Walt Whitman, and a play by Shakespeare. These texts take you into the world of heroes—both everyday heroes and extraordinary ones—who face challenges and take actions to overcome them. You will learn about an archetype of a hero, which is a model that writers follow in creating stories about heroes.

Writing and speaking opportunities are varied and engaging. For example, you will write a hero's journey narrative about a hero of your choice, along with essays and an argument that presents your position on an issue in a compelling way. Using research on an issue of national or global significance, you will create an informative multimedia presentation.

Viewing film is also a part of researching and analyzing what authors are communicating. As part of studying comedy and Shakespeare, you will analyze scenes from the play *A Midsummer Night's Dream* and then view those scenes in film to determine how and why a film director may have changed the scenes.

PERFORMANCE PORTFOLIO

If you were asked to introduce yourself in a visual way to your classmates, you might show them pictures of yourself. Another way to introduce yourself is through your writing. You are unique as a writer, and how and what you write is a way of showing yourself.

When you collect your writing assignments over a period of time, you can see how your writing skills are changing as you learn new writing techniques.

Presenting yourself through a portfolio also provides direction as you revisit, revise, and reflect on your work throughout the year. Your teacher will guide you as you include items in your portfolio that illustrate a wide range of work, including examples of reading, writing, oral literacy, and collaborative activities. As you progress through the course, you will have opportunities to revisit prior work, revise it based on new learning, and reflect on the learning strategies and activities that help you be successful. The portfolio:

- Gives you a specific place to feature your work and a means to share it with others.

- Provides an organized, focused way to view your progress throughout the year.

- Allows you to reflect on the new skills and strategies you are learning.

- Enables you to measure your growth as a reader, writer, speaker, and performer.

- Encourages you to revise pieces of work to incorporate new skills.

As you move through each unit, your teacher will instruct you to include certain items in your portfolio. Strong portfolios will include a variety of work from each unit, such as first drafts, final drafts, quickwrites, notes, reading logs, audio and video examples, and graphics that represent a wide variety of genre, forms, and media created for a variety of purposes.

Your teacher will also instruct you about preferences for your portfolio. For example, your portfolio may be organized in one of these ways:

- In a 3-ring binder with dividers to separate the work for each unit.

- Chronologically, beginning with the first unit and moving to the last.

- With periodic reports on assessments with your reflections on your progress.

- With multiple drafts of an activity (where applicable).

- With a table of contents that lists each activity in your portfolio.

We hope you enjoy using the SpringBoard program. It will give you many opportunities to explore your own and others' ideas about becoming effective readers, writers, and communicators.

College and Career Readiness Standards

READING STANDARDS FOR LITERATURE

Key Ideas and Details

1. Cite several pieces of textual evidence to support analysis of what the text says explicitly as well as inferences drawn from the text.
2. Determine a theme or central idea of a text and analyze its development over the course of the text; provide an objective summary of the text.
3. Analyze how particular elements of a story or drama interact (e.g., how setting shapes the characters or plot).

Craft and Structure

4. Determine the meaning of words and phrases as they are used in a text, including figurative and connotative meanings; analyze the impact of rhymes and other repetitions of sounds (e.g., alliteration) on a specific verse or stanza of a poem or section of a story or drama.
5. Analyze how a drama's or poem's form or structure (e.g., soliloquy, sonnet) contributes to its meaning.
6. Analyze how an author develops and contrasts the points of view of different characters or narrators in a text.

Integration of Knowledge and Ideas

7. Compare and contrast a written story, drama, or poem to its audio, filmed, stages, or multimedia version, analyzing the effects of techniques unique to each medium (e.g. lighting, sound, color, or camera focus and angles in a film).
8. (Not applicable to literature)
9. Compare and contrast a fiction portrayal of a time, place, or character and a historical account of the same period as a means of understanding how authors of fiction use or alter history.

Range of Reading and Level of Text Complexity

10. By the end of the year, read and comprehend literature, including stories, dramas, and poems, in the grades 6–8 text complexity band proficiently, with scaffolding as needed at the high end of the range.

READING STANDARDS FOR INFORMATIONAL TEXT

Key Ideas and Details

1. Cite several pieces of textual evidence to support analysis of what the text says explicitly as well as inferences drawn from the text.
2. Determine two or more central ideas in a text and analyze their development over the course of the text; provide an objective summary of the text.
3. Analyze the interactions between individuals, events, and ideas in a text (e.g., how ideas influence individual or events, or how individuals influence ideas or events).

Craft and Structure

4. Determine the meaning of words and phrases as they are used in a text, including figurative, connotative, and technical meanings; analyze the impact of a specific word choice on meaning and tone.
5. Analyze the structure an author uses to organize a text, including how the major sections contribute to the whole and to the development of the ideas.
6. Determine an author's point of view or purpose in a text and analyze how the author distinguishes his or her position from that of others.

Integration of Knowledge and Ideas

7. Compare and contrast a text to an audio, video, or multimedia version of the text, analyzing each medium's portrayal of the subject (e.g., how the delivery of a speech affects the impact of the words).
8. Trace and evaluate the argument and specific claims in a text, assessing whether the reasoning is sound and the evidence is relevant and sufficient to support the claims.
9. Analyze how two or more authors writing about the same topic shape their presentations of key information by emphasizing different evidence or advancing different interpretations of facts.

Range of Reading and Level of Text Complexity

10. By the end of the year, read and comprehend literary nonfiction in the grades 6-8 text complexity band proficiently, with scaffolding as needed at the high end of the range.

WRITING STANDARDS

Text Types and Purposes

1. Write arguments to support claims with clear reasons and relevant evidence.

   a. Introduce claim(s), acknowledge alternate or opposing claims, and organize the reasons and evidence logically.

   b. Support claim(s) with logical reasoning and relevant evidence, using accurate, credible sources and demonstrating an understanding of the topic or text.

   c. Use words, phrases, and clauses to create cohesion and clarify the relationships among claim(s), reasons, and evidence.

   d. Establish and maintain a formal style.

   e. Provide a concluding statement or section that follows from and supports the argument presented.

2. Write informative/explanatory texts to examine a topic and convey ideas, concepts, and information through the selection, organization, and analysis of relevant content.

   a. Introduce a topic clearly, previewing what is to follow; organize ideas, concepts, and information, using strategies such as definition, classification, comparison/contrast, and cause/effect; include formatting (e.g., headings), graphics (e.g., charts, tables), and multimedia when useful to aiding comprehension.

   b. Develop the topic with relevant facts, definitions, concrete details, quotations, or other information and examples.

   c. Use appropriate transitions to create cohesion and clarify the relationships among ideas and concepts.

   d. Use precise language and domain-specific vocabulary to inform about or explain the topic.

   e. Establish and maintain a formal style.

   f. Provide a concluding statement or section that follows from and supports the information or explanation presented.

3. Write narratives to develop real or imagined experiences or events using effective technique, relevant descriptive details, and well-structured event sequences.

   a. Engage and orient the reader by establishing a context and point of view and introducing a narrator and/or characters; organize an event sequence that unfolds naturally and logically.

   b. Use narrative techniques, such as dialogue, pacing, and description, to develop experiences, events, and/or characters.

   c. Use a variety of transition words, phrases, and clauses to convey sequence and signal shifts from one time frame or setting to another.

   d. Use precise words and phrases, relevant descriptive details, and sensory language to capture the action and convey experiences and events.

   e. Provide a conclusion that follows from the narrated experiences or events.

Production and Distribution of Writing

4. Produce clear and coherent writing in which the development, organization and style are appropriate to task, purpose, and audience.

5. With some guidance and support from peers and adults, develop and strengthen writing as needed by planning, revising, editing, rewriting, or trying a new approach, focusing on how well purpose and audience have been addressed. (Editing for conventions should demonstrate command of Language standards 1–3 up to and including grade 7 on page 52.)

6. Use technology, including the Internet, to produce and publish writing and link to and cite sources as well as to interact and collaborate with others including lining to and citing sources.

7. Conduct short research projects to answer a question, drawing on several sources and generating additional related, focused questions for further research and investigation.

8. Gather relevant information from multiple print and digital sources, using search terms effectively; assess the credibility and accuracy of each source; and quote or paraphrase the data and conclusions of others while avoiding plagiarism and following a standard format for citation.

9. Draw evidence from literary or informational texts to support analysis, reflection, and research.

   a. Apply grade 7 reading standards to literature (e.g., "Compare and contrast a fictional portrayal of a time, place, or character and a historical account of the same period as a means of understanding how authors of fiction use or alter history").

b. Apply grade 7 reading standards to literary nonfiction (e.g., "Trace and evaluate the argument and specific claims in a text, assessing whether the reasoning is sound and the evidence is relevant and sufficient to support the claims").

Range of Writing

10. Write routinely over extended time frames (time for research, reflection, and revision) and shorter time frames (a single sitting or a day or two) for a range of discipline-specific tasks, purposes, and audiences.

SPEAKING AND LISTENING STANDARDS

1. Engage effectively in a range of collaborative discussions (one-on-one, in groups, and teacher-led) with diverse partners on grade 7 topics, texts, and issues, building on others' ideas and expressing their own clearly.

   a. Come to discussions prepared, having read or researched material under study; explicitly draw on that preparation by referring to evidence on the topic, text, or issue to probe and reflect on ideas under discussion.

   b. Follow rules for collegial discussions, track progress toward specific goals and deadlines, and define individual roles as defined.

   c. Pose questions that elicit elaboration and respond to others' questions and comments with relevant observations and ideas that bring the discussion back on topic as needed.

   d. Acknowledge new information expressed by others and, when warranted, modify their own views.

2. Analyze the main ideas and supporting details presented in diverse media and formats (e.g., visually, quantitatively, orally) and explain how the ideas clarify a topic, text, or issue under study.

3. Delineate a speaker's argument and specific claims, evaluating the soundness of the reasoning and the relevance and sufficiency of the evidence.

Presentation of Knowledge and Ideas

4. Present claims and findings, emphasizing salient points in a focused, coherent manner with pertinent descriptions, facts, details, and examples; use appropriate eye contact, adequate volume, and clear pronunciation.

5. Include multimedia components (e.g., graphics, images, music, sound) and visual displays in presentations to clarify information.

6. Adapt speech to a variety of contexts and tasks, demonstrating command of formal English when indicated or appropriate.

LANGUAGE STANDARDS

Conventions of Standard English

1. Demonstrate command of the conventions of standard English grammar and usage when writing or speaking.

   a. Explain the function of phrases and clauses in general and their function in specific sentences.

   b. Choose among simple, compound complex, and compound-complex sentences to signal differing relationships among ideas.

   c. Place phrases and clauses within a sentence, recognizing and correcting misplaced and dangling modifiers.

2. Demonstrate command of the conventions of standard English capitalization, punctuation, and spelling when writing.

   a. Use a comma to separate coordinate adjectives (e.g., *It was a fascinating, enjoyable movie* but not *He wore an old[,] green shirt*).

   b. Spell correctly.

Knowledge of Language

3. Use knowledge of language and its conventions when writing, speaking, reading, or listening.

   a. Choose language that expresses ideas precisely and concisely, recognizing and eliminating wordiness and redundancy.

   b. Maintain consistency in style and tone.

4. Determine or clarify the meaning of unknown and multiple-meaning words and phrases based on grade 7 reading and content, choosing flexibly from a range of strategies.

   a. Use context (e.g., the overall meaning of a sentence or paragraph; a word's position or function in a sentence) as a clue to the meaning of a word or phrase.

   b. Use common, grade-appropriate Greek or Latin affixes and roots as clues to the meaning of a word (e.g., *belligerent, bellicose, rebel*).

   c. Consult general and specialized reference materials (e.g., dictionaries, glossaries, thesauruses), both print and digital, to find the pronunciation of a word or determine or clarify its precise meaning or its part of speech.

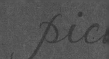

d. Verify the preliminary determination of the meaning of a word or phrase (e.g., by checking the inferred meaning in context or in a dictionary).

5. Demonstrate understanding of figurative language, word relationships, and nuances in word meanings.
   a. Interpret figures of speech (e.g., literary, biblical, and mythological allusions) in context.
   b. Use the relationship between particular words (e.g., synonym/antonym, analogy) to better understand each of the words.
   c. Distinguish among the connotations (associations) of words with similar denotations (definitions) (e.g., *refined, respectful, polite, diplomatic, condescending*).

6. Acquire and use accurately grade-appropriate general academic and domain-specific words and phrases; gather vocabulary knowledge when considering a word or phrase important to comprehension or expression.

The Choices
We Make

Visual Prompt: You may have heard the saying "A picture is worth a thousand words." What story does this picture tell? What makes you say this? What do you predict you will learn in this unit?

Unit Overview

This unit introduces the year-long focus on "choices," using a variety of genres to investigate this theme. You will examine texts that present characters who, for personal or cultural reasons, have made choices about the way they live their lives. You will analyze fiction and nonfiction texts and create and present original works that express the concept of choice. In creating these original texts, you will engage in the writing process, including collaborating with your peers in writing groups.

The Choices We Make

GOALS
* To analyze genres and their organizational structures
* To examine the function of narrative elements
* To apply techniques to create coherence and sentence variety in writing
* To apply revision techniques in preparing drafts for publication

ACADEMIC VOCABULARY
effect
effective
consequences
coherence
internal coherence
external coherence
theme
metaphor
objective
subjective

Literary Terms
genre
denotation
connotation
stanza
narrative
sensory details
figurative language
characterization
myth
plot
symbol
symbolism
objective camera angle
subjective camera angle

Contents

Activities

Texts not included in these materials.

Language and Writers Craft

- Verb Tenses (1.5)
- Creating Coherence and Sentence Variety (1.6)
- Analogies (1.7)
- Coherence (1.7)
- Punctuating Coordinate Adjectives (1.9)
- Pronouns and Antecedents (1.14)

Previewing the Unit

LEARNING STRATEGIES:
QHT, Collaborative Groups,
Summarizing

My Notes

_____

_____

_____

_____

_____

ACADEMIC VOCABULARY
Effect and **effective** are words you will encounter often in academic courses. When we talk about the **effect** of changes or the effect of a metaphor, we are referring to the way one thing acts upon another. So we are asking you to be able to describe how one thing influences another. The adjective **effective** refers to something that is successful in producing a desired or intended result.

_____

_____

_____

_____

INDEPENDENT READING LINK
The first half of this unit will focus on personal narratives. Choose from the genres of memoir, biography, or autobiography to read during this unit. Select a book that looks interesting to you and seems manageable.

Learning Targets
- Preview the big ideas and vocabulary for the unit.
- Identify and summarize the knowledge and skills necessary to complete Embedded Assessment 1 successfully.

Making Connections
In this unit, you will read a variety of genres, including poetry, autobiography, memoir, myth, and fable. You will also learn more about personal narratives and will write and revise one of your own. By the end of the unit, after studying myths and fables, you will also write and illustrate a myth. Before starting the unit, answer the Essential Questions that follow.

Essential Questions
Based on your current knowledge, how would you answer these questions?

1. How do authors use narrative elements to create a story?
2. What are the elements of **effective** revision?

Developing Vocabulary
Look again at the Contents page and use a QHT strategy to analyze and evaluate your knowledge of the Academic Vocabulary and Literary Terms for the unit.

Unpacking Embedded Assessment 1
Read the assignment below for Embedded Assessment 1: Revising a Personal Narrative about Choice on page 44. While reading, underline or highlight key skills and knowledge you will need to be successful with the assignment.

> Your assignment is to revise the personal narrative with the reflection you previously drafted. Use the revision techniques you have learned in this unit, including meeting in a writing group, to improve the beginning, middle, and end of your narrative. You will also write a text explaining the revisions you made to improve your first draft and the effect of the changes on the final piece.

Paraphrase what you will need to know to complete this assessment successfully. With your class, create a graphic organizer to represent the skills and knowledge you will need to complete the tasks identified in the Embedded Assessment.

Exploring the Concept of Choice

Learning Targets
- Paraphrase and analyze quotes related to choices.
- Consider choices for independent reading.

Paraphrasing Ideas

1. In the graphic organizer below, paraphrase each quote in the first column and write a personal response to the quote in the second column. Remember that to paraphrase means to put information in your own words.

Read and Paraphrase What is the author saying?	Personal Response To what extent do you agree or disagree with what the author is saying about choice?
1. "Life is the sum of all your choices." — Albert Camus	
2. "While we are free to choose our actions, we are not free to choose the consequences of our actions." — Stephen R. Covey	
3. "The strongest principle of growth lies in human choice." — George Eliot	
4. "The last of the human freedoms is to choose one's attitude." — Victor Frankl	
5. "The ultimate measure of a man is not where he stands in moments of comfort and convenience, but where he chooses to stand at times of challenge and controversy." — Dr. Martin Luther King, Jr.	
6. "I believe the choice to be excellent begins with aligning your thoughts and words with the intention to require more from yourself." — Oprah Winfrey	

Exploring the Concept of Choice

LEARNING STRATEGIES:
Brainstorming, Paraphrasing

Literary Terms
A literary **genre** is the category or class to which a literary work belongs; epic poetry, mythology, and science fiction are all examples of literary genres.

My Notes

Your Choices as a Reader

One choice that you will make is what you will read in your own time. Respond to the following questions in your Reader/Writer Notebook.

2. Think about the content of your favorite books.
   - What have you enjoyed reading in the past?
   - What is your favorite book, favorite type of book, or favorite author?

3. Think about the manageability of the texts you have enjoyed reading in the past
   - How do you feel about long books?
   - Do you like a novel with short chapters or longer sections?
   - What was the last book you read from cover to cover?
   - Do you usually read a book in one or two days or does it take you longer to finish a book?

4. Do you have a favorite genre?

Preview the book you've selected.
- What do the front and back cover show you?
- What type of visual is shown?
- What types of fonts and colors are used?
- Are there awards or brags? What do they say?
- What do these elements tell you about the book?

Read the first few pages.
- Does this seem interesting?
- Does the text make sense so far?
- Does this seem too hard, too easy, or just right?

After considering the content and purpose of the independent reading in this unit, do you want to continue reading the book you chose or choose something else?

5. Create an **independent reading plan** for the text you have chosen.
   - I have chosen to read

     by

     because
   - I will create time to read by
   - I should finish this text by

As you read, think like a writer; notice the way the author tells his or her own story (in a memoir or autobiography) or the story of the subject (in a biography). Your teacher may ask you to respond to your reading by asking you specific questions about your text. You may also have the opportunity to apply a specific skill or strategy you've practiced in class to your independent reading.

Your Choices as a Writer

6. What types (genres) of texts do you enjoy writing the most?

7. What types (genres) of texts do you enjoy writing the least?

8. Do you choose to write outside of school? Explain.

9. Examine the chart on the next page.
   - Why is writing a process?
   - What part(s) of the writing process are you most familiar with?
   - What part(s) of the writing process are you least familiar with?

My Notes

Exploring the Concept of Choice

Writing as a Process

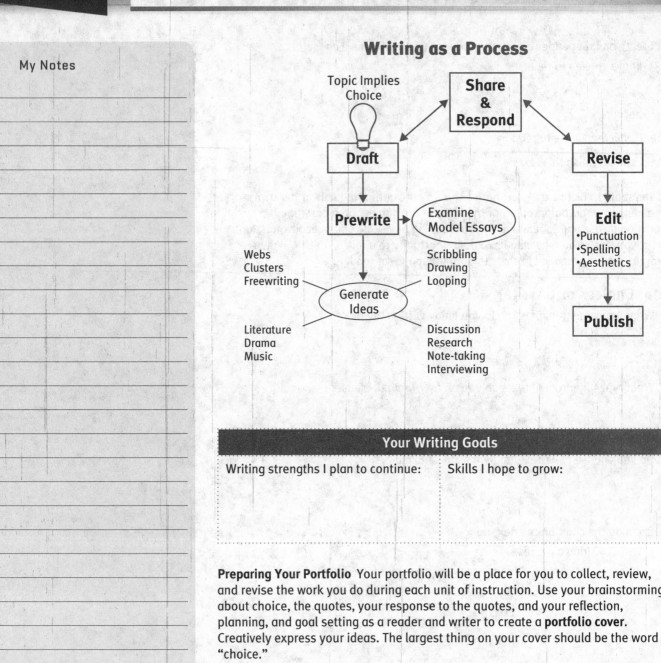

Topic Implies
Choice

Share & Respond

Draft

Revise

Prewrite → Examine Model Essays

Edit
•Punctuation
•Spelling
•Aesthetics

Webs
Clusters
Freewriting

Scribbling
Drawing
Looping

Generate
Ideas

Publish

Literature
Drama
Music

Discussion
Research
Note-taking
Interviewing

Your Writing Goals

Writing strengths I plan to continue:	Skills I hope to grow:

Preparing Your Portfolio Your portfolio will be a place for you to collect, review, and revise the work you do during each unit of instruction. Use your brainstorming about choice, the quotes, your response to the quotes, and your reflection, planning, and goal setting as a reader and writer to create a **portfolio cover**. Creatively express your ideas. The largest thing on your cover should be the word "choice."

Choices and Consequences: Paired Poetry

Learning Targets
- Analyze choices and consequences presented in a text.
- Analyze and compare diction choices in two different texts on the same topic.

Before Reading

1. In the poem you will be reading, the narrator comes to a "fork in the road." This is an example of **figurative**, not **literal**, language, as the phrase does not refer to an eating utensil in a driving lane. How would you describe a "fork in the road"?

LEARNING STRATEGIES:
Activating Prior Knowledge, Webbing, Marking the Text, Close Reading, Brainstorming, Drafting

2. In your Reader/Writer Notebook, create a web titled "My Choices" to brainstorm the choices you have faced and decisions you have made in your life. Think about large and small choices from the past and in the present. You will return to this web throughout the unit.

   Add these ideas to the second section of your **portfolio cover**. Use words, phrases, or pictures, and then label this section "personal choices."

3. Poetry is a literary form you probably have had experience with as a reader or writer or both. What do you know about poetry as a literary form? How is it different from prose writing?

My Notes

Literary Terms

A word's **denotation** is its exact, literal meaning. **Connotation** is the suggested or implied meaning or emotion associated with a word, beyond its literal definition.

A **stanza** describes a division of lines into equal groups. Robert Frost's "The Road Not Taken" is divided into four stanzas of five lines each.

Like narratives, poetry is written from a point of view. Remember that *first-person point of view* is written from a character's point of view and uses words like "I," "me," and "mine." *Third-person point of view* is written from a narrator's point of view and uses works like "he," "she," and "they."

During Reading

4. Mark the text by highlighting or underlining unfamiliar words. Marking the text helps you engage in close reading and organize your textual evidence after reading. During your second reading, paraphrase each **stanza**. It is also important to examine both **denotation** and **connotation** of unfamiliar words as a part of close reading.

WORD CONNECTIONS

Roots and Affixes

Narrative comes from the Latin word *narrare*, which means "to tell" or "to make known." The root *-narra-* appears in the English words *narrate*, *narration*, and *narrator*.

Choices and Consequences: Paired Poetry

GRAMMAR & USAGE
Punctuation

Writers use punctuation in poetry to cluster ideas and communicate meaning for the reader.

- A *period* ends a thought and creates dramatic effect.
- An *exclamation point* adds emphasis.
- The *semicolon* combines two like ideas without adding the finality of a period.
- The *comma* marks a pause and may build on or clarify something previously stated.
- The *dash* indicates anticipation of something to follow.

KEY IDEAS AND DETAILS
Summarize each stanza of the poem, and then explain how the poem's meaning is developed through the progression of the four stanzas.

My Notes

_____
_____
_____
_____
_____
_____
_____
_____
_____
_____
_____

ABOUT THE AUTHOR
Robert Frost (1874–1963) was one of America's most popular twentieth-century poets. For much of his life, he lived on a farm in New Hampshire and wrote poems about farm life and the New England landscape. His apparently simple poems, however, have many layers of meaning.

Poetry

The Road Not Taken

by Robert Frost

Two roads diverged in a yellow wood,
And sorry I could not travel both
And be one traveler, long I stood
And looked down one as far as I could
5 To where it bent in the undergrowth;

Then took the other, as just as fair,
And having perhaps the better claim
Because it was grassy and wanted wear,
Though as for that the passing there
10 Had worn them really about the same,

And both that morning equally lay
In leaves no step had trodden black.
Oh, I marked the first for another day!
Yet knowing how way leads on to way
15 I doubted if I should ever come back.

I shall be telling this with a sigh
Somewhere ages and ages hence:
Two roads diverged in a wood, and I,
I took the one less traveled by,
20 And that has made all the difference.

ABOUT THE AUTHOR

Nikki Giovanni is a popular poet and professor of English. Over the years, she has won numerous writing awards. Her writing often focuses on individuals and their choices to make a difference.

Poetry

Choices

by Nikki Giovanni

if i can't do
what i want to do
then my job is to not
do what i don't want
5 to do

it's not the same thing
but it's the best i can
do

if i can't have
10 what i want … then
my job is to want
what i've got
and be satisfied
that at least there
15 is something more
to want

since i can't go
where i need
to go … then i must … go
20 where the signs point
though always understanding
parallel movement
isn't lateral

when i can't express
25 what i really feel
i practice feeling
what i can express
and none of it is equal
i know
30 but that's why mankind
alone among the animals
learns to cry

My Notes

KEY IDEAS AND DETAILS
Examine Giovanni's diction. Notice the choice of the word *job*. Use resources to look up the denotation of this word, and then think about the connotation of the word. How does it add to a sense of Giovanni's tone or attitude?

KEY IDEAS AND DETAILS
Notice how each stanza is set up in a similar way, beginning with an adverbial clause (*if I can't … ; since I can't … ; when I can't …*) followed by a "then … " phrase.

Summarize each stanza to show their similarities in meaning.

Choices and Consequences:
Paired Poetry

My Notes

After Reading

5. Use the graphic organizer to compare and contrast the two poems.

"The Road Not Taken"	"Choices"
List examples of connotative diction and implied meaning/emotion.	List examples of connotative diction and implied meaning/emotion.
What do you notice about how the speaker responds to "choice" in this poem?	What do you notice about how the speaker responds to "choice" in this poem?
Theme: What is the message about life implied in this poem?	Theme: What is the message about life implied in this poem?

Check Your Understanding

Writing Prompt: Use evidence from the text and your analysis to complete the sentence starter below. Be sure to:

- Use precise language when referring to the poems.
- Start your paragraph with a topic sentence that finishes the sentence starter.

My attitude about "choices" is most like the speaker from (Frost's poem "A Road Not Taken" or Giovanni's poem "Choices") because ...

Choices and Consequences

Many choices have **consequences**. Create a web to explore the meaning of *consequences*. What synonyms do you know? Consult a dictionary or thesaurus to help you find synonyms.

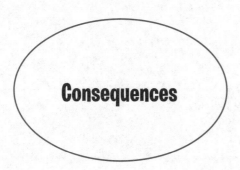

Go back to your "My Choices" web and add the consequences for the choices you labeled. Some choices may have several consequences. Add just the most important ones that resulted from your choice.

My Notes

ACADEMIC VOCABULARY
When discussing the **consequences** of an action, you are referring to something that logically or naturally follows from an action or condition. But if you say "money is of no consequence to me," you are using the word to mean "importance" or "relevance."

Exploring the Personal Narrative

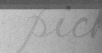

LEARNING STRATEGIES:
Activating Prior Knowledge,
Graphic Organizer, Note-taking,
Metacognitive Markers

My Notes

Literary Terms

A **narrative** tells a story or
describes a sequence of
events in an incident.

Learning Targets

- Identify the components that provide the organizational structure of a personal
  narrative.
- Write a narrative that includes an incident, a response, and a reflection.

Before Reading

1. Complete the graphic organizer below to explore your prior knowledge about
   personal narratives. You have read **narratives** in earlier grades. A personal
   narrative tells a story about something that happened in the writers' life.

Exploring Personal Narratives	
With what kinds of narrative texts are you familiar?	
What are some of your favorite narratives? Explain what makes reading a narrative enjoyable.	
What elements would you expect to find in a good story?	
What is the purpose of a narrative?	

Introducing the Strategy: Metacognitive Markers

Using metacognitive markers involves marking the text with symbols to reflect the thinking you are doing as you read. After reading, you can scan the text and use your metacognitive markers to quickly find evidence when you are talking or writing about a text. Here are the markers:

? Use a question mark for questions you have about the text.

! Use an exclamation point for a reaction to what you are reading.

* Use an asterisk for a comment about the text.

_ Use an underline to identify a key idea or detail in the text.

During Reading

2. As you read "Staying Fat for Sarah Byrnes," use metacognitive markers to interact with the text.

ABOUT THE AUTHOR

Chris Crutcher grew up in Idaho and now lives in Washington State. A highly respected writer of novels for young adults, Crutcher has won awards for his fiction, much of which takes place against sports backgrounds. He likes to place characters in realistic and difficult situations and explore what drives these characters as they are forced to make tough choices.

Novel

From **Staying Fat**
for Sarah Byrnes

by Chris Crutcher

Chunk 1

When I got to the field for our first game, I was so excited I thought I would throw up. I hadn't slept a wink the night before and spent the entire day throwing my baseball against the side of the garage, grossly exaggerating the speed of the grounders, dribbling back as I snapped them into the merciless trap of my glove and threw the runner out.

I didn't catch one ball in warm-ups. They dropped to the right of me. They dropped to the left of me. They hit my arms and fell harmlessly to the grass. But I was just so happy to be there, to belong with these other kids with 'Junior Oilers' across their chests that it didn't matter.

Chunk 2

When coach called us into a huddle before the umpire yelled, "Batter up!" he went over our positions and the batting order one last time, but he didn't need to for my sake because I had memorized those things from the first practice. I batted ninth. I played right field. I knew what that meant. I knew I was the very worst hitter on the team and the very worst fielder. But I didn't care, because I had a new glove and a green-and-gold uniform and I belonged.

GRAMMAR & USAGE
Conventions

A dash is used:

- to mark a parenthetical thought

- to indicate an unfinished sentence

- to show an abrupt change in thought when a period is too strong and a comma is too weak

My Notes

_____

_____

_____

_____

_____

_____

_____

_____

KEY IDEAS AND DETAILS
Summarize the events leading up to the point when the narrator says "Just that quick I _didn't_ belong ... "

_____

_____

_____

_____

_____

_____

_____

_____

_____

We were the home team and batted the bottom half of the inning, so we touched our gloves together in the middle of the huddle and yelled, "Go Oilers!" and broke to take our position. I was _so_ proud. But before I got even to the baseline, Coach's hand was on my shoulder, and when I turned around, Ronnie Callendar stood next to him. And he said, "I want you to give Ronnie your glove."

I said, "What for?"

He said, "He doesn't have one."

Chunk 3

Coach watched my face fall—I know he did—and I think he knew how I felt because he was very kind, but he said, 'Cindy, if we're going to win this, Ronnie has to have a mitt. A shortstop has to have a mitt, that's just all there is to it.' I looked at the glove on my hand; I bit my lower lip while I read Warren Spahn's name, and I handed it over. Coach told me to play as far back in right field as I could so no balls could get over my head—that I could run faster forward than backward—and sent me on my way. I walked so far back I almost disappeared into the playground swings beyond the field.

Just that quick I _didn't_ belong, and I remember thinking something always has to spoil it. I was hurt and embarrassed and I wanted to go back to being invisible me again, but I couldn't because I had on the green shirt and cap, and all of a sudden that uniform was my enemy. I remember hating Ronnie Callendar for being poor, and I hoped his father never got a job and they'd have to move away.

Every game after that was miserable. I couldn't quit because we would have only eight players and all the kids would hate me. Coach didn't always take my glove; in fact, I don't know that he ever took it again. But each time I walked down that hot, dusty summer road toward the playing field, I knew he _might_, that I didn't really belong because they could take my glove.

After Reading

3. During class discussion, use the graphic organizer on the next page to take notes on the key parts of a personal narrative. Describe the incident in this selection. Find textual evidence to support your ideas. Remember to use your metacognitive markers to find evidence in the text.

4. Locate the narrator's response to the incident. What does she say about her feelings? Use textual evidence (a quote or a paraphrase) to support your ideas.

Incident (what happened)	Response (your feelings and thoughts about people involved at the time)	Reflection (the lesson you learned from this experience)	Reflection (how you will use this lesson in the future)

5. Summarize the reflection in this selection. Looking back, how does the speaker understand the incident? Find textual evidence to support your ideas. How is the reflection different from the response?

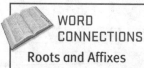

WORD CONNECTIONS

Roots and Affixes

Reflection comes from the Latin prefix *re-* ("back") and the root *-flectere-* ("to bend"), so it carries the meaning of "bending or turning back." When you reflect, you turn your thoughts back to think again about a subject.

6. Have you thought of additional choices since the last activity? Add them to your "My Choices" graphic organizer.

7. Select a choice and freewrite about it as a way to explore the topic. Be prepared to share in a collaborative group. Be sure to:

• Explain the incident. (What was the choice? What took place when the choice presented itself?)

• Fully discuss your response. (What did you choose? How did you react?)

• Communicate your reflection. (What did you learn from this choice and its consequences?)

Check Your Understanding

Write a definition of a personal narrative.

My Notes

Analyzing Incident, Response, Reflection

LEARNING STRATEGIES:
Activating Prior Knowledge,
Graphic Organizer, Note-
taking, Metacognitive Markers,
Revisiting Prior Work, Webbing,
Drafting, Looping

Learning Targets
- Analyze a narrative work using incident, response, and reflection.
- Analyze the organizational structure of a personal narrative.

Before Reading
1. **Quickwrite:** Recall an early memory from childhood that stands out to you. Think about stories that your family has shared about you growing up. For example, what were some milestones (your first toy, bike, or game) or a significant celebration or family event? Write freely to explore your memory while thinking about any choices you made.

During Reading
2. Use metacognitive markers to make mental notes as you read. Pay particular attention to any words or phrases that stand out to you as confusing, powerful, or interesting.

ABOUT THE AUTHOR
Born in 1891, Zora Neale Hurston was an American anthropologist and writer. Hurston grew up in the small town of Eatonville, Florida, the first incorporated black township. Hurston's idyllic childhood was interrupted by the death of her mother when Hurston was only 13. She struggled to finish high school, which she still had not accomplished by age 26. Despite her early struggles, Hurston went on to graduate from Barnard College in 1928. She wrote several short stories and novels. *Their Eyes Were Watching God* is considered her master work. She died in 1960.

My Notes

Autobiography

From
Dust Tracks on a Road

by Zora Neale Hurston

But nine months rolled around, and I just would not get on with the walking business. I was strong, crawling well, but showed no inclination to use my feet. I might remark in passing, that I still don't like to walk. Then I was over a year old, but still I would not walk. They made allowances for my weight, but yet, that was no real reason for my not trying.

They tell me that an old sow-hog taught me how to walk. That is, she didn't instruct me in detail, but she convinced me that I really ought to try.

It was like this. My mother was going to have collard greens for dinner, so she took the dishpan and went down to the spring to wash the greens. She left me sitting on the floor, and gave me a hunk of cornbread to keep me quiet. Everything was going along all right, until the sow with her litter of pigs in convoy came abreast of the door. She must have smelled the cornbread I was messing with and scattering crumbs about the floor. So, she came right on in, and began messing around.

GRAMMAR & USAGE
Verb Tenses

Verb tenses show time. **Progressive tenses** describe a continuing action. You form the progressive tenses with a form of the verb *be* and the **present participle** of the verb.

For example, Hurston uses the past progressive tense to indicate an ongoing action in the past:

"Everything *was going* along all right ... "

"I *was messing* with ... "

My mother heard my screams and came running. Her heart must have stood still when she saw the sow in there, because hogs have been known to eat human flesh. But I was not taking this thing sitting down. I had been placed by a chair, and when my mother got inside the door, I had pulled myself up by that chair and was getting around it right smart.

As for the sow, poor misunderstood lady, she had no interest in me except my bread. I lost that in scrambling to my feet and she was eating it. She had much less intention of eating Mama's baby, than mama had of eating hers.

With no more suggestions from the sow or anybody else, it seems that I just took to walking and kept the thing a-going. The strangest thing about it was that once I found the use of my feet, they took to wandering. I always wanted to go. I would wander off in the woods all alone, following some inside urge to go places. This alarmed my mother a great deal. She used to say that she believed a woman who was an enemy of hers had sprinkled "travel dust" around the doorstep the day I was born. That was the only explanation she could find. I don't know why it never occurred to her to connect my tendency with my father, who didn't have a thing on his mind but this town and the next one. That should have given her a sort of hint. Some children are just bound to take after their fathers in spite of women's prayers.

After Reading

3. Work in a collaborative group to analyze the narrative's organizational structure and mark the text.

- Underline the passages that show what happened, who was involved, and when and where the incident took place.
- Highlight the parts that show the narrator's response to the incident.
- Bracket [ ] the passage where the narrator reflects on why this is a memorable incident for the speaker.
- Explain in the margin how this event deals with the concept of choice.

4. Return to your quickwrite. Compare your childhood memory to Hurston's. Have you thought of any new ideas about significant incidents and choices in your life? If so, add them to your "My Choices" web.

Check Your Understanding

Write your response to the Essential Question: How do authors use narrative elements to create a story?

KEY IDEAS AND DETAILS
What is Hurston's attitude toward the event she describes; that is, what is her tone? Identify specific diction that supports the tone you identify.

My Notes

GRAMMAR & USAGE
Verb Tenses

Perfect tenses show completed actions. You form the perfect tenses of verbs with the past participle of the verb and the helping verbs *have*, *has*, or *had*.

Hurston uses both the present perfect and past perfect tenses in this story. For example:

Present perfect (passive): "hogs *have been known* ..." (expresses an action continuing from the past into the present)

Past perfect: "I *had pulled* myself up ..." (expresses an action completed before another action in the past occurs)

In your writing, use the correct tense to indicate the timing of events and actions. Then, keep your tenses consistent: use verbs in the same tense to express events occurring at the same time.

Analyzing Incident, Response, Reflection

Language and Writer's Craft: Verb Tenses

Verb tenses (present, past, and future) show time. You form the **progressive tenses** with a form of the verb *be* and the **present participle** of the verb. Hurston uses the past progressive tense to indicate an ongoing action in the past: Everything *was going* along all right ..., ... I *was messing* with ...

In your writing, use progressive tenses when you want to describe a continuing action.

You form the **perfect tenses** of verbs with the **past participle** of the verb and the helping verbs *have*, *has*, or *had*. Hurston uses perfect tenses to show completed actions. For example:

Present perfect (passive voice):

... hogs *have been known* ... (expresses an action continuing from the past into the present)

Past perfect:

I *had pulled* myself up (expresses an action completed before another action in the past occurs)

In your writing, use the correct tense to indicate the timing of events and actions. Then, keep your tenses consistent: that is, use verbs in the same tense to express events occurring at the same time.

Analyzing Language

Learning Targets
- Analyze the language of a personal narrative to determine how language shapes character and events.
- Analyze for multiple incidents and responses to determine effect.

Before Reading

1. **Quickwrite:** What choices do you make at school? Brainstorm the types of choices you make at school and the types of consequences you can face as a result of your choices .

2. What are **sensory details**? What do the terms "sensory" and "details" make you think? Can you provide any examples?

3. Some types of **figurative language** you already know are *simile*, *metaphor*, and *personification*. Can you provide any examples of these three types?

During Reading

4. Mark the text for examples of sensory details and figurative language the author uses for **characterization**. Think about how the author's language choices help develop the characters, setting, and events.

   In addition, in this narrative you will find multiple incidents and responses. Mark the text to note the multiple incidents and responses. Put a number 1 for an incident and a number 2 for the narrator's response to that incident.

ABOUT THE AUTHOR
Walter Dean Myers has been writing since he was a child. He published his first book, *Where Does the Day Go?*, in 1969. He has since written many books for children and young adults, two of which—*Scorpions* and *Somewhere in the Darkness*—have received Newbery Honors. His stories focus on the challenges and triumphs of growing up in a difficult environment. His memoir, *Bad Boy*, reveals how he overcame racial challenges and his own shortcomings to become a very successful author.

LEARNING STRATEGIES:
Shared Reading, Marking the Text, Graphic Organizer, Summarizing, Brainstorming, Drafting

My Notes

Literary Terms
Sensory details are language that appeals to one or more of the five senses—sight, hearing, touch, taste, and smell.

Figurative language is language used in an imaginative way to express ideas that are not literally true. It is used for effect, such as with personification, simile, metaphor, and hyperbole.

Characterization is the methods a writer uses to develop characters; for example, through description, actions, and dialogue.

Analyzing Language

WORD
CONNECTIONS
Roots and Affixes
The word *fanatic* comes from
the Latin word *fanum* which
means "temple." A fanatic was
someone "in the temple" or
"inspired by divinity."

My Notes

Memoir

From **Bad Boy**

by Walter Dean Myers

1 By September and the opening of school I was deep into sports and became
a baseball fanatic. Along with the pleasure of playing baseball there was the joy of
identifying with the ballplayers. I loved the Dodgers. Maybe it was because Mama
loved the Dodgers and especially Jackie Robinson. All summer long, kids playing
punchball—hitting a pink "Spaldeen" ball with your fist and then running bases
drawn in chalk on the streets—had tried to steal home to copy Robinson. We even
changed the rules of stoop ball, of which I was the absolute King of the World, to
include bases when more than one kid played. You played stoop ball by throwing
the ball against the steps of a brownstone. The ball coming off the steps had to
clear the sidewalk and land in the street. If it landed before being caught, you could
run the bases. My speed and ability to judge distances made me an excellent fielder.
We did occasionally play actual baseball, but not enough kids had gloves to make a
good game.

2 My new school was Public School 43 on 128th Street and Amsterdam Avenue,
across from the Transit Authority bus terminal. Mrs. Conway was my teacher, and
it took me one day to get into trouble with her.

3 In the elementary grades I attended, reading was taught by having kids stand
up one at a time and read aloud. Mrs. Conway had us up and reading as soon as the
readers had been handed out. When it came to be my turn, I was anxious to show
my skills. I read quickly, and there was a chorus of laughter in response. They were
laughing at my speech.

4 "Slow down and try it again," Mrs. Conway said.

5 I slowed my speech down and started reading from the top of the page. Johnny
Brown started laughing immediately. Johnny always had something to say to make
the class laugh. I threw the book sidearm and watched it hit his desk and bounce
across the room.

6 "Don't you dare throw a book in my classroom!" Mrs. Conway, red-faced,
screamed. "Into the closet! Into the closet!"

7 I had to stand in the closet for the rest of the morning. That afternoon
Mrs. Conway divided the class into reading groups. I was put into the slowest
group. I stayed there until the next week, when the whole class was given a spelling
test and I scored the highest grade. Mrs. Conway asked me to read in front of the
class again.

KEY IDEAS AND DETAILS
From what point of view is
this text written? How do
you know?

8 I looked at Johnny Brown as I headed for the front of the class. He had this glint in his eye, and I knew he was going to laugh. I opened my mouth, and he put his hand across his mouth to hold his laugh in. I went across to where he sat and hit him right on the back of the hand he held over his mouth. I was sent to the principal's office and had to stay after school and wash blackboards. Later in the year it would be Johnny Brown who would be in Mrs. Conway's doghouse for not doing his homework, with her screaming at him that he couldn't be a comedian all his life. He went on to become a television comedian and is still doing well.

9 Being good in class was not easy for me. I had a need to fill up all the spaces in my life, with activity, with talking, sometimes with purely imagined scenarios that would dance through my mind, occupying me while some other student was at the blackboard. I did want to get good marks in school, but they were never of major importance to me, except in the sense of "winning" the best grade in a subject. My filling up the spaces, however, kept me in trouble. I would blurt out answers to Mrs. Conway's questions even when I was told to keep quiet, or I might roll a marble across my desk if she was on the other side of the room.

10 The other thing that got me in trouble was my speech. I couldn't hear that I was speaking badly, and I wasn't sure that the other kids did, but I knew they often laughed when it was my turn to speak. After a while I would tense up anytime Mrs. Conway called on me. I threw my books across that classroom enough times for Mrs. Conway to stop my reading once and for all.

11 But when the class was given the assignment to write a poem, she did read mine. She said that she liked it very much.

12 "I don't think he wrote that poem," Sidney Aronofsky volunteered.

13 I gave Sidney Aronofsky the biggest punch he ever had in the back of his big head and was sent to the closet. After the incident with Sidney, Mrs. Conway said that she had had quite enough of me and that I would not be allowed to participate in any class activity until I brought my mother to school. I knew that meant a beating. That evening I thought about telling Mama that the teacher wanted to see her, but I didn't get up the nerve. I didn't get it up the next day, either. In the meantime I had to sit in the back of the room, and no kid was allowed to sit near me. I brought some comic books to school and read them under my desk.

14 Mrs. Conway was an enormously hippy woman. She moved slowly and always had a scowl on her face. She reminded me of a great white turtle with just a dash of rouge and a touch of eye shadow. It was not a pretty sight. But somehow she made it all the way from the front of the room to the back, where I sat reading a comic, without my hearing her. She snatched the comic from me and tore it up. She dropped all the pieces on my desk, then made me pick them up and take them to the garbage can while the class laughed.

My Notes

KEY IDEAS AND DETAILS
How does the author's use of vivid language that appeals to the senses (*glint*, *blurt*) help you understand what is happening in the story?

KEY IDEAS AND DETAILS
What is the metaphor in paragraph 14? How does it help to characterize Mrs. Conway and show her relationship to the narrator?

Analyzing Language

My Notes

15 Then she went to her closet, snatched out a book, and put it in front of me.

16 "You are," she sputtered, "a bad boy. A very bad boy. You cannot join the rest of the class until your mother comes in." She was furious, and I was embarrassed.

17 "And if you're going to sit back here and read, you might as well read something worthwhile," she snapped.

18 I didn't touch the book in front of me until she had made her way back to the front of the class and was going on about something in long division. The title of the book was *East o' the Sun and the West o' the Moon*. It was a collection of Norwegian fairy tales, and I read the first one. At the end of the day, I asked Mrs. Conway if I could take the book home.

19 She looked at me a long time and then said no, I couldn't. But I could read it every day in class if I behaved myself. I promised I would. For the rest of the week I read that book. It was the best book I had ever read. When I told Mrs. Conway I had finished, she asked me what I liked about the book, and I told her. The stories were full of magic events and interesting people and witches and strange places. It differed from *Mystery Rides the Rails*, the Bobbsey Twins, and a few Honeybunch books I had come across.

20 I realized I liked books, and I liked reading. Reading a book was not so much like entering a different world—it was like discovering a different language. It was a language clearer than the one I spoke, and clearer than the one I heard around me. What the books said was, as in the case of *East o' the Sun*, interesting, but the idea that I could enter this world at any time I chose was even more attractive. The "me" who read the books, who followed the adventures, seemed more the real me than the "me" who played ball in the streets.

21 Mrs. Conway gave me another book to read in class and, because it was the weekend, allowed me to take it home to read. From that day on I liked Mrs. Conway.

22 I still didn't get to read aloud in class, but when we had a class assignment to write a poem, she would read mine. At the end of the year I got my best report card ever, including a glorious Needs Improvement in conduct.

23 It was also the golden anniversary of the school, and the school magazine used one of my poems. It was on the first page of the Jubilee Issue, and it was called "My Mother." When I saw it, I ran all the way home to show Mama.

Mr. Irwin Lasher

1 My new school, the new P.S. 125, was quite close to my house. It was located on 123rd Street, right across from Morningside Park between Morningside and Amsterdam Avenues. The school was ultramodern for the day, with table and chairs that could be arranged any way the teacher wanted instead of the rigid desks nailed to the floor we had been used to having. I was in class 6–2 and had my first male teacher, Mr. Irwin Lasher.

2 "You're in my class for a reason," he said as I sat at the side of his desk. "Do you know what the reason is?"

3 "Because I was promoted to the sixth grade?" I asked.

4 "Because you have a history of fighting your teachers," he said. "And I'm telling

KEY IDEAS AND DETAILS
What is Mrs. Conway's response to Walter's reading comic books? How is her response significant to her relationship with Walter?

KEY IDEAS AND DETAILS
Explain what you notice about how the dialogue is punctuated.

you right now, I won't tolerate any fighting in my class for any reason. Do you understand.

5 "Yes."

6 "You're a bright boy, and that's what you're going to be in this class."

7 My fight with Mr. Lasher didn't happen until the third day, and in a way it wasn't really my fault. We were going up the stairs, and I decided that, when his back was turned, I would pretend that I was trying to kick him. All right, he paused on the staircase landing before leading us to our floor and the kick that was supposed to delight my classmates by just missing the teacher hit him squarely in the backside. He turned quickly and started toward me. Before I realized it, I was swinging at him wildly.

8 Mr. Lasher had been in World War II and had fought in the Battle of the Bulge. He didn't have much trouble handling me. He sat me in a corner of the classroom and said that he would see me after class. I imagined he would send a note home, and that my mother would have to come to school. I was already practicing what I would say to her when I gave her the note. But instead of sending a note home, he came home with me! Down the street we came, my white teacher and me, with all my friends looking at me and a few asking if it meant I was going to get a beating. I thought it probably would, but I didn't give them the satisfaction of an answer. Mama was sitting on the park bench across from our house when I came down the street with Mr. Lasher firmly holding my hand.

9 "Mrs. Myers, I had a little problem with Walter today that I think you should know about," he said, sitting next to her on the bench.

10 He called Mama by my last name, not knowing that I was an informal adoptee. Her last name was Dean, of course, but she didn't go into it. Mr. Lasher quietly explained to my mother that all the tests I had taken indicated that I was quite smart, but that I was going to throw it all away because of my behavior.

11 "We need more smart Negro boys," he said. "We don't need tough Negro boys."

12 Mr. Lasher did two important things that year. The first was that he took me out of class one day per week and put me in speech therapy for the entire day. The second thing he did was to convince me that my good reading ability and good test scores made me special.

13 He put me in charge of anything that needed a leader and made me coach the slower kids in reading. At the end of the year I was the one student in his class whom he recommended for placement in a rapid advancement class in junior high school.

14 With Mr. Lasher my grades improved significantly. I was either first or second in every subject, and he even gave me a Satisfactory in conduct. As the tallest boy in the sixth grade, I was on the honor guard and was scheduled to carry the flag at the graduation exercises, an honor I almost missed because of God's revenge …

My Notes

KEY IDEAS AND DETAILS
What are the most significant choices each of the main characters in this pair of narrative chapters make?

KEY IDEAS AND DETAILS
What expectations do both Walter and Mr. Lasher have about Walter's behavior?

What expectation does Mr. Lasher have of Walter that Walter does not have of himself?

Analyzing Language

After Reading

5. What were the consequences of the choices the characters in this narrative made?

6. Complete the graphic organizer.

Organization	Sequence of Events Using Transitions of Time	Character Traits or Attitudes the Choices Reveal	Textual Evidence for the Character Traits
Incident	In the beginning of the story,		
Response	Then,		
Reflection	Finally,		

7. How did paying attention to the use of sensory language in this narrative help you better visualize and understand the characters and events?

Language and Writer's Craft: Creating Coherence and Sentence Variety

One way to vary sentence types is to add **transitions**. In narrating a story, the transitions usually help the reader understand a change in time or place.

1. Examples of transitions to signal change in time are used in the second column of the graphic organizer on the previous page. What do you notice about the transitions, and how they are punctuated?

2. Brainstorm transitions you could use in a narrative and write them here or in your Reader/Writer Notebook.

In addition to using transitions to create sentence variety, consider using **parallel sentence structure**. Parallel sentence structure uses the same pattern of words to show that two or more ideas have equal importance.

3. Look for the parallelism, or patterns of words, in these sentences:
   • I walked back to the corner, searched for the owner, and considered what to do.
   • I threw my backpack, coat, and hat down on the chair.
   • Sam enjoys walking, jogging, and running.
   • Then she went to her closet, snatched out a book, and put it in front of me.
   • At the beginning of the story, Walter is impulsive, isolated, and inattentive.

4. Finish the sentence using parallel structure:
   By the end of the story, Walter ...

Check Your Understanding

Narrative Writing Prompt: Return to the list of school choices you brainstormed, or think of an idea generated from reading *Bad Boy*. Select a time you had to make a choice at school. From your point of view, describe the incident. Include your response, and provide a meaningful reflection about the incident. Be sure to:
• Use transitions to organize the incident, response, and reflection.
• Use sensory details and/or figurative language.
• Incorporate parallel sentence structure and dialogue.

INDEPENDENT READING LINK
In your Reader/Writer Notebook, note the incidents, responses, and reflections you've noticed in your independent reading text. Also, look for examples of sensory details and figurative language and think about how they develop the plot and the characters.

My Notes

Timed Writing: Choosing a Topic and Drafting a Personal Narrative

LEARNING STRATEGIES:
Marking the Text, Writing
Groups

Learning Targets
- Analyze the elements of, and respond to, a writing prompt.
- Identify and apply the roles within a writing group while sharing and responding to draft texts.

Writing Groups

During the writing process, you can get feedback for revision in a writing group. All members of a writing group work collaboratively to respond to one another's writing and to help each other through the revision process by asking clarifying questions. Writing groups use sharing and responding as a revision strategy to communicate with another person or a small group of peers about suggestions in order to improve writing. It is the responsibility of the members of the writing group to help each other develop quality writing.

Roles of the Participants in Writing Groups		
Job	**Guidelines**	**Response Starters**
The reader: Reads the text silently, then aloud. Begins the conversation after reading.	The reader's purpose is to share an understanding of the writer's words. The reader sees the physical structure of the draft and may comment on that as well. The reader follows all listeners' guidelines as well.	Reader's and listeners' compliments: • I liked the words you used, like … • I like the way you described … • This piece made me feel … • This piece reminded me of …
The listeners: Take notes and prepare open-ended questions for the writer or make constructive statements.	The listeners begin with positive statements. The listeners use "I" statements and talk about the writing, not the writer. The listeners make statements and must provide reasons.	Reader's and listeners' comments and suggestions: • I really enjoyed the part where … • What parts are you having trouble with? • What do you plan to do next? • I was confused when …
The writer: Listens to the draft, takes notes, responds to questions, and asks the writing group questions.	As the work is being read aloud by another, the writer gets an overall impression of the piece. The writer takes notes on what might need to be changed. The writer asks questions to get feedback that will lead to effective revision.	Writer's questions: • What do you want to know more about? • What part doesn't make sense? • Which section of the text doesn't work?

Preparing for Writing to a Prompt

Tip 1: Address all aspects of the prompt. Make sure you understand what the prompt is asking you to do.

- Circle the key verbs in the prompt. The verbs identify what you will do.
- Underline the nouns. The nouns identify what you will write about.
- List the verbs next to the nouns. This list prioritizes what you have to do when you write in response to this prompt. You can use this list as a checklist to ensure that you have addressed all aspects of the prompt.

Tip 2: Pace yourself. You will have _____ minutes to write your essay. How many minutes will you use for each phase?

_____ Prewrite: Plan my essay and generate ideas.

_____ Draft: Put my plan into action and get my narrative on paper.

_____ Revise/Edit: Make sure my narrative is as clear as possible for my readers.

Tip 3: Plan your essay. Look back at your portfolio cover and at your choices/consequences/reflection web. Select one incident in which you made a choice.

Use a prewriting strategy to create a plan for your draft. Consider creating a web, a plot diagram, or an outline.

Writing Prompt: Write a multi-paragraph narrative about an incident on your "choices" graphic organizer. Include information about the choice you made and the consequences of your action. Be sure to:

- Include the elements of incident, response, and reflection.
- Use transitions to connect ideas for your reader.
- Include insights about the effects and consequences of the choice.

Language and Writer's Craft: Analogies

An analogy shows a relationship between words and is often written with colons.

Example: sleeve : jacket :: shift key : keyboard.

The relationship between *sleeve* and *jacket* is the same as that between *shift key* and *keyboard*. Think of the relationship between *leaf* and *tree*. Then write the word that has the same relationship to *finger*.

Leaf is to tree as finger is to_____.

My Notes

Timed Writing: Choosing a Topic and Drafting a Personal Narrative

ACADEMIC VOCABULARY
Coherence is the clear and orderly presentation of ideas in a paragraph or essay.
Internal coherence refers to coherence within a paragraph.
External coherence refers to coherence between the paragraphs and relates to the entire essay.

My Notes

Language and Writer's Craft: Coherence

When responding to a writing prompt, it is important to consider the coherence of your writing. **Transitions** within and between paragraphs create coherence.

Transitions that you might use to move from idea to idea include: *then, next, later, after that, toward the end, in the end, additionally, nevertheless, in addition, however, finally, moreover*. There are many additional transitions you might use. Create a bank of transition words and phrases in your Reader/Writer Notebook as a reference.

When reading for **internal coherence**, make sure that each paragraph is organized and clearly written using transitions and parallel structure. When reading for **external coherence**, check that the entire text uses transitions to move smoothly from one major idea to another in a logical way.

Revising Your Essay

Review your notes from your writing group. Based on the feedback you received, create a revision plan by responding thoughtfully to the following:

- After rereading your draft and meeting with your writing group, what do you like best about your personal narrative? Why?
- At this point, what do you think could be improved? Why?
- What do you plan to change, and how will those changes improve the draft?
- After reading my draft, I realize that in the next draft I should revise

  _____ because _____.

You will revisit this draft for Embedded Assessment 1.

Check Your Understanding

1. Describe how to respond to a writing prompt.
2. Explain how a writing group can help you improve writing.

Once Upon a Time: Revising the Beginning

Learning Targets
- Analyze the effectiveness of narrative openings.
- Revise opening paragraphs to enhance effectiveness.

LEARNING STRATEGIES:
Summarizing, Close
Reading, Graphic Organizer,
Rereading, Revisiting Prior
Work

Writing and Revision

1. Read this quotation about revision: "If a teacher told me to revise, I thought that meant my writing was a broken-down car that needed to go to the repair shop. I felt insulted. I didn't realize the teacher was saying, 'Make it shine. It's worth it.' Now I see revision as a beautiful word of hope. It's a new vision of something. It means you don't have to be perfect the first time. What a relief!"
—*Naomi Shihab Nye*

Summarize what Naomi Shihab Nye means about revision. What does this quote make you think about writing and revision?

In the Beginning

2. Many writers struggle with how to begin their writing with an interesting lead. A lead, or hook, comes at the beginning. Its purpose is to encourage your reader to keep reading. Review these types of leads, or hooks. Mark the important words in the definitions of the "Type of Lead" column.

Type of Lead	Examples From Published Authors
Reaction: Some writers choose to open a narrative with a character thinking about or reflecting on the event.	"The Jacket," by Gary Soto My clothes have failed me. I remember the green coat that I wore in fifth and sixth grade when you either danced like a champ or pressed yourself against a greasy wall, bitter as a penny toward the happy couples.
Dialogue: Some writers choose to show the reader a key event, using dialogue between characters.	*Charlotte's Web* by E. B. White "Where's papa going with that ax?" said Fern to her mother as they were setting the table for breakfast. "Out to the hoghouse," replied Mrs. Arable. "Some pigs were born last night." "I don't see why he needs an ax," continued Fern, who was only eight.
Action: Some writers choose to open a narrative with the main character doing something; this type of lead puts the reader right in the middle of the action.	*Thank You, M'am* by Langston Hughes She was a large woman with a large purse that had everything in it but a hammer and nails. It had a long strap and she carried it slung across her shoulder. It was about eleven o'clock at night, and she was walking home alone, when a boy ran up behind her and tried to snatch her purse. The strap broke with the single tug the boy gave it from behind. But the boy's weight and the weight of the purse combined caused him to lose his balance, so instead of taking off full blast as he had hoped, the boy fell on his back on the sidewalk and his legs flew up. The large woman simply turned around and kicked him right square in his blue-jean sitter. Then she reached down, picked up the boy by his shirt front, and shook him until his teeth rattled.

Once Upon a Time: Revising the Beginning

3. Revisit the openings from texts you have read in this unit to examine how published authors hook readers with effective leads.

Text	Kind of Lead	Why is this lead effective? How does it "hook" readers and leave them wanting to read more?
Bad Boy, by Walter Dean Myers (Activity 1.6)		
Staying Fat for Sarah Byrnes, by Chris Crutcher (Activity 1.4)		
My own selection from Independent Reading		

Revision of Narrative Lead

4. Review your narrative draft and revise your opening using one or more of the lead techniques: action, reaction and reflection, dialogue. Your goal is to open with a strong lead that engages readers, encouraging them to continue reading your personal narrative.

5. Effective writers also reflect upon the changes they make in order to become more aware of specific techniques they use during the writing process. Describe how you have changed your opening. How did your change make your opening more engaging for your reader?

Kind of lead used:

Changes I made:

Revision reflection:

Learning Targets
- Identify effective use of sensory and figurative language.
- Revise a narrative draft by adding descriptive language.

Before Reading

1. Teachers often use the phrase "show, don't tell" to encourage students to use sensory details in their descriptions. Dramatist, short story writer, and novelist Anton Chekhov suggests, "Don't tell me the moon is shining; show me the glint of light on broken glass." Respond to this quote.

ABOUT THE AUTHOR
Imma Achilike is a student writer. She wrote this story as a student at Naaman Forest High School in Garland, Texas.

Personal Narrative

why couldn't i have been named ashley?

by Imma Achilike

1   "Ashley!" exclaimed Mrs. Renfro, and simultaneously three heads whipped around at attention towards the perturbed[1] teacher. At the same time, all three Ashleys proudly replied, "Yes, ma'am?"

2   When I was a fourth grader, I remember sitting in class that day just before the bell rang for dismissal. I remember thinking of all the names in the world, how I could have possibly been stuck with such an alien one. I thought about all the popular kids in the class. I figured that I wasn't popular because of my weird name. I put some things together in my mind and came up with a plausible[2] equation: COOL NAME = POPULARITY. The dismissal bell rang. As I mechanically walked out to catch my ride, I thought to myself, "Why couldn't I have been named Ashley?"

3   I was born, on July 7th, 1986, at Parkland Hospital of Dallas, Texas. I was the first American-born Nigerian in both of my parents' families. I was my parents' first joy, and in their joy, they gave me the name that would haunt me for the rest of my life, Immaculeta Uzoma Achilike.

4   The first time I actually became aware of my name was on the first day of first grade. I went to school loaded with all my school supplies and excited to see all of my old kindergarten friends. I couldn't wait to see who my new teacher was. As I walked into the classroom, all my friends pushed up to me, cooing my name: "Imma, Imma I missed you so much." The teacher walked in with the attendance sheet. She told everyone to quiet down so she could call roll. Before she started, she said something I thought would have never applied to me. She said, "Before I call

[1] **perturbed:** troubled or disturbed
[2] **plausible:** credible or believable

LEARNING STRATEGIES:
Marking the Text, Shared Reading, Chunking the Text, Discussion Groups, Summarizing, Paraphrasing, Adding

GRAMMAR & USAGE
Compound-Complex Sentences

A compound-complex sentence is one that has two or more independent clauses and one or more dependent clauses.

Example: I was my parents' first joy, and in their joy, they gave me the name that would haunt me for the rest of my life, Immaculeta Uzoma Achilike.

KEY IDEAS AND DETAILS
What kind of lead is used to hook the reader? Give textual evidence.

KEY IDEAS AND DETAILS
What two words in paragraph 3 are used to show the narrator's conflicting feelings about her name?

My Notes

Can You Sense It? Revising the Middle

roll, I apologize if I mispronounce anyone's name" with a very apologetic look on her face. She looked down at the attendance sheet, paused for a minute, and then looked up with an extremely puzzled look on her face. I remember thinking that there was probably some weird name before mine; although, my name was always the first name to be called in kindergarten. Suddenly, my palms started sweating and then she began to hopelessly stutter my name, "Im-Immaculet Arch-liki, I mean, Achei...." Here, I interrupted. My ears burned with embarrassment and droplets of perspiration formed on my nose. "Did I say it right?" she said with the same apologetic look on her face. Before I responded, the laughs that the other kids in class had been holding back suddenly exploded, like a volatile³ vial of nitroglycerin, into peals of laughter. One kid thought it was so funny his chubby face started turning red and I could see a tear gradually making its way down his face. I found myself wishing I could sink into the ground and never come back. I hated being the laughing stock.

5   I never really recovered from the shock of that day. From that day forward, the first day of school was always my most feared day. I didn't know what to do; all I could do was to tell my teachers, "I go by Imma."

6   I felt so alone when all the other girls in my class had sparkly, pink pencils with their names printed on them. You know, the ones they sell in the stores along with name-embossed⁴ sharpeners, rulers and pencil pouches. Every year I searched through and rummaged around that rack at the store, but I could never find a pencil with my name on it.

7   The summer of my seventh-grade year, my family and I took a vacation to our "home" in Nigeria, where my parents were born. My cousin and I were playing cards, talking girl talk, and relating our most embarrassing moments. Each tried to see whose story could top whose. I told one story of how I wet the bed at a sleepover, and she told me how she had farted in class during a test. That was a hoot. Then, I told her the story of how I was laughed at because of my weird name. I thought it was pretty funny, but she didn't laugh. She had the most serious look on her face, then she asked me, "Immaculeta Uzoma Achilike, do you know what your name means?" I shook my head at her and that's when she started laughing. I thought she was making fun of me, and as I started to leave she said: "Immaculeta means 'purity', 'Uzoma' means 'the good road' and ... " Having heard her words, I stopped walking away and turned around in amazement. What does Achilike mean?" I asked. After a long pause she calmly said, "Achilike means 'to rule without force.'" I was astonished and pleased. I never knew what my name meant.

8   My name is Immaculeta Uzoma Achilike. I am the daughter of first-generation Nigerian immigrants. I am the daughter of hardworking and brave parents. My name means "to rule without force." My grandfather was a wealthy man of generous character. When I say my name in Nigeria, people know me as the granddaughter of a wealthy man of generous character. They know me by my name. There my name is not embossed on any pencil or vanity plate. It is etched in the minds of the people.

My name is Immaculeta Uzoma Achilike.

KEY IDEAS AND DETAILS
Give an example of visual sensory language or figurative language used in paragraph 4 to make the incident more vivid.

KEY IDEAS AND DETAILS
The narrator has two distinctly different reactions to her name. How are they different, and what is the cause of her feelings?

GRAMMAR & USAGE
Commas

Commas in prose signify a pause. Writers use commas:

* to separate items in a series
* after introductory words, phrases, and clauses in sentences
* to set off parenthetical phrases (which can be omitted from the sentence without changing its meaning)
* to separate quoted material.

---

³ **volatile:** unstable, explosive
⁴ **embossed:** raised above the surface

After Reading

2. Complete the graphic organizer to analyze the organization and use of language in "Why Couldn't I Have Been Named Ashley?"

	Incident	Response	Reflection
Paraphrase each part of the narrative and mark the text for specific textual evidence.			
Record textual evidence of language use in each part of the narrative (sensory details, figurative language, precise words or phrases).			

3. Use language that "shows" by describing the photographs that follow, both literally and figuratively.

Picture	Literal Description	Description Using Sensory Images, Figurative Language, or Precise Diction
Example:	A horse is drawing an old-fashioned carriage.	The caramel-colored horse pulls a tourist-laden carriage, with its fringed top and colorfully costumed driver, past the quaint buildings.
Picture 1		
Picture 2		

Picture 3

Introducing the Strategy: Looping

You may be familiar with the revision strategies of adding and deleting words or phrases, replacing or rearranging ideas, and combining sentences. Another way to improve a draft is to revise by looping.

Looping is a revision strategy in which you underline an important sentence and then add two sentences of additional elaboration. Use looping to add additional information to images, using sensory details or figurative language.

4. Practice looping with the sentences below.

- I could not imagine a more beautiful fall day.
- Just then the professor turned and, with an odd smile on his face, threw open the door to his laboratory.

INDEPENDENT READING LINK
Look back to your independent reading plan from Activity 1.2. Reflect on your progress. Do you need to revise your plan? Communicate any struggles you are having with your text to your teacher.

My Notes

Language and Writer's Craft: Punctuating Coordinate Adjectives

Coordinate adjectives are two or more words that equally modify the same object. Use commas to separate coordinate adjectives in a sentence.

Example: The pulsing, bass-heavy beat of the music flowed from the speakers.

In this sentence, *pulsing* and *bass-heavy* are coordinate adjectives. You can identify coordinate adjectives with a simple test. Try to:

• reverse the order of the adjectives, and

• put *and* between the adjectives.

If you can do both of these things, the adjectives are coordinate and require a comma. Adjectives that give information about size, shape, age, color, material, religion, or nationality are not coordinate adjectives and need not be separated with commas.

Which of the sentences below have coordinate adjectives? Add commas where necessary.

    a. Our internship program accepts only ambitious, dedicated students.

    b. My little French music box now lay smashed on the floor.

    c. The rolling, pitching, tossing motion of the ship quickly made Elsie seasick.

    d. New York City's bustling, teeming sidewalks and streets were unlike any in the small town Gary had come from.

    e. Grandma knitted the baby a blue wool sweater for her birthday.

5. Review your narrative draft and use looping to add sensory details and figurative language. Look for opportunities to replace nondescript words with more precise diction. Then check that you have properly added commas to coordinate adjectives.

Check Your Understanding

Describe how you have changed the middle of your draft. Reflect on your use of looping to improve your draft.

Tie It Together: Revising the Ending

Learning Targets
- Analyze and evaluate narrative endings.
- Apply an understanding of the purpose of the ending by revising a narrative ending.

LEARNING STRATEGIES:
Marking the Text, Shared Reading, Chunking the Text, Discussion Groups, Graphic Organizer, Summarizing, Paraphrasing, Adding

Narrative Endings

1. Read this quote by Henry Wadsworth Longfellow: "Great is the art of beginning, but greater is the art of ending." What makes a great ending to a narrative?

2. Revisit the endings of these texts you have read to examine how published authors provide effective endings.

Text	Length of Ending	Summarization of the Ending	Author's Purpose in Using This Ending
Bad Boy, by Walter Dean Myers (Activity 1.6)			
Staying Fat for Sarah Byrnes, by Chris Crutcher (Activity 1.4)			
"Why Couldn't I Have Been Named Ashley?" by Imma Achilike (Activity 1.9)			
Dust Tracks on a Road, by Nora Neale Hurston (Activity 1.5)			

Tie It Together: Revising the Ending

INDEPENDENT READING LINK
What have you noticed about the ending of the book you are reading independently? How did it end? What did you think about the ending? If you were the author, how would you change the ending?

My Notes

Revising Your Narrative Ending

3. Use the following questions to help generate ideas for the reflective ending for your narrative:

   • What did I learn from the experience?

   • Why does this matter?

   • Can I revisit a concept or idea from my lead or an image in the middle to create coherence?

4. Review your narrative draft and revise your ending; use sharing and responding in a writing group.

Check Your Understanding

Describe how you have changed your ending. How did your change make your ending more effective for your reader?

Revising a Personal Narrative About Choice

Assignment

Your assignment is to revise the personal narrative with the reflection that you drafted earlier in the unit. Use the revision techniques you have learned in this unit to improve the beginning, middle, and end of your narrative. You will also write a text explaining the revisions you made to improve your first draft and the effect of the changes on the final piece.

Planning and Prewriting: Meet with your writing group to share and refine your revision ideas.

- How will you present and discuss your draft and revision plan (Act. 1.8, 1.10) with your writing group?

- How will you apply the revision strategies in Activities 1.9–1.10 to your draft to revise organization, coherence, and narrative elements?

- How will reading and discussing your group members' drafts and revision plans help your efforts to revise?

Revising: Review your plan and revise your narrative.

- How will you incorporate your group's suggestions and ideas into your revision plan?

- How can the Scoring Guide help you evaluate how well your draft meets the requirements of the assignment?

Checking and Editing: Confirm that your final draft is ready for publication.

- How will you check for correct spelling and grammatical accuracy?

- How can your writing group assist you with the editing and proofreading?

- How will you prepare a final draft for publication?

Reflecting on Writing: Write an explanation of your revision process.

- What were the most significant changes that you made to your original draft?

- Why did you make these changes, and what was your intended effect on the reader?

- How did your peers help you with the writing process?

Reflection

After completing this Embedded Assessment, think about how you went about accomplishing this task and respond to the following:

- Explain how the activities in this unit helped prepare you for success on the Embedded Assessment.

- Which activities were especially helpful, and why?

Technology TIP:

As you prepare for publication, don't forget to use spelling and grammar tools provided by your word processing program.

Revising a Personal Narrative About Choice

SCORING GUIDE

Scoring Criteria	Exemplary	Proficient	Emerging	Incomplete
Ideas	The narrative • skillfully describes an incident, a choice made, and thoroughly reflects on the lesson learned • shows clear evidence of skillful revision to improve meaning, clarity, and adherence to narrative style • includes thoughtful reflection with explanations for changes.	The narrative • describes a choice, explains the consequences of the decision made, and reflects on the lesson learned • outlines and implements an appropriate revision plan that brings clarity to the narrative • includes reasons for the changes made.	The narrative • is missing one or more elements of an effective personal narrative (the incident, the choice, the consequences, and/or the reflection) • includes no clear outline or implementation of a plan for revision • is minimal and/or unclear.	The narrative • does not describe or develop a personal incident • shows little or no evidence of revision to improve writing, communication of ideas, or transitions to aid the reader • no reflection about or explanation of changes made.
Structure	The narrative • has an engaging beginning that hooks the reader and reveals all aspects of the incident • has a middle that vividly describes the series of events in the incident as well as the narrator's feelings, thoughts, and actions • has a reflective ending that examines the consequences of the choice.	The narrative • includes a clear and purposeful beginning that introduces the incident • includes a middle that adequately describes the incident and the narrator's feelings, thoughts, and actions • provides an ending that examines the consequences of the choice.	The narrative • creates a limited or unfocused introduction to the central incident. • includes a middle that merely retells a series of events • provides an ending with minimal reflection and closure.	The narrative • begins unevenly with no clear introduction of the incident • fails to describe the incident and/or the narrator's feelings about it • has an inconclusive ending that does not follow from the incident or the narrator's choices.
Use of Language	The narrative • effectively uses sensory details and figurative language to vividly "show" the incident • contains few or no errors in spelling, punctuation, or capitalization.	The narrative • uses sensory images and details to make the incident clear • contains spelling, punctuation, and capitalization mistakes that do not detract.	The narrative • describes the incident in general terms without sensory images and details • contains some mistakes that make meaning and/or readability challenging.	The narrative • use no sensory details to enhance the telling of the incident • contains multiple mistakes that detract from meaning and/or readability.

Previewing Embedded Assessment 2: Expanding Narrative Writing

Learning Targets
- Identify the knowledge and skills needed to complete Embedded Assessment 2 successfully, and reflect on prior learning that supports the knowledge and skills needed.
- Identify narrative elements and the purpose of myths.

Making Connections
In the first part of this unit, you learned how to create a personal narrative to relate an incident, a response to the incident, and a reflection about the impact of the incident. In this half of the unit, you will expand on your narrative writing skills by creating an original myth.

Developing Vocabulary
1. Use the graphic organizer below to do a new QHT sort with these words from the first half of this unit:

Academic Vocabulary	Literary Terms
effect	genre
effective	denotation
consequences	connotation
coherence	stanza
internal coherence	narrative
external coherence	sensory details
	figurative language
	characterization

Remember that when using a **QHT**, think about how well you know each term and then label each word with a letter:

Q: words you have questions about

H: words you've heard before, but aren't sure about the meaning

T: words you could teach

Q	H	T

My Notes

Previewing Embedded Assessment 2: Expanding Narrative Writing

INDEPENDENT READING LINK
Find mythology from a culture you are interested in learning more about for your new Independent Reading text. Remember to consider the content, manageability, and purpose of your reading.

My Notes

2. Reflect on your experience with the Academic Vocabulary and Literary Terms so far in this unit.
   - Which terms could you now teach that you didn't know at the start of the unit?

   - What strategies, lessons, or activities helped you learn these terms?

   - Which terms will you need to focus on during the rest of the unit?

Essential Questions

3. How has your understanding of the Essential Questions changed? How would you respond to these ideas now?
   - How do authors use narrative elements to create a story?

   - Why is storytelling an important aspect of a culture or society?

4. Share your latest responses to the Essential Questions in a collaborative group. Discuss how your latest responses have changed from your first thinking.
   - What questions can you ask your classmates about their responses?
   - What connections can you make between their responses and your responses?

Unpacking Embedded Assessment 2

Read the assignment below for Embedded Assessment 2: Creating an Illustrated Myth on page 42:

> Your assignment is to work with a partner to create an original myth that explains a belief, custom, or natural phenomenon through the actions of gods or heroes. Be sure that your myth teaches a lesson or a moral and includes illustrations that complement the myth as it unfolds.

In your own words, paraphrase what you will need to know to complete Embedded Assessment 2 successfully.

The Stories and Folklore of Myth

Folklore and **myth** are genres that begin with the oral tradition of telling stories to share them with people. They were often stories meant to make meaning of the world and to teach important lessons about life. You are probably familiar with many types of folklore, such as **fairy tales** or **fables** or **legends**. These stories often have morals, or lessons, to teach us about human weaknesses such as greed, pride, recklessness, and thoughtlessness.

The characters of myth and folklore often are ordinary people in extraordinary situations. Usually, the actions of the characters in folklore have consequences that change the life of an entire culture or help explain what seems unexplainable.

Human beings have told stories throughout the ages to entertain, to teach, and to explain the mysteries of the world. Maybe you will create a story that will live on long after you.

Review the Elements of a Short Story

5. What do you remember about the elements of a short story? Match the element to the definition.

ELEMENT	DEFINITION
1. Plot	a. the time and place in which a story takes place
2. Character	b. a struggle, problem, or obstacle in a story
3. Conflict	c. the sequence of events that make up a story
4. Setting	d. a writer's central idea or main message about life
5. Theme	e. people, animals, or imaginary creatures that take part in a story

6. Review the elements of the **plot structure** of most narratives:

- **Exposition:** Background information or events necessary to understand a story. Often includes an introduction to characters and setting (place and time story takes place).
- **Rising Action:** The conflicts and complications that develop a story
- **Climax:** The peak of the action; the most intense or suspenseful moment. Often represents a turning point in the story.
- **Falling Action:** The events after the climax (often the consequences of the climax) that lead to the resolution of the story.
- **Resolution:** The end result or conclusion; "tying up any loose ends." In a personal narrative, the resolution may include a reflection.

WORD CONNECTIONS

Roots and Affixes

The word *fable* comes from the Latin word *fabula*, meaning "tale." Other English words derived from this word are *fabulous*, *affable*, and *confabulate*.

Literary Terms
Myths are traditional stories that explain beliefs, customs, or natural phenomenon through the actions of gods or heroes.

Plot is the sequence of related events that make up a story.

My Notes

My Notes

Check Your Understanding

Place the elements of plot structure on the plot diagram below.

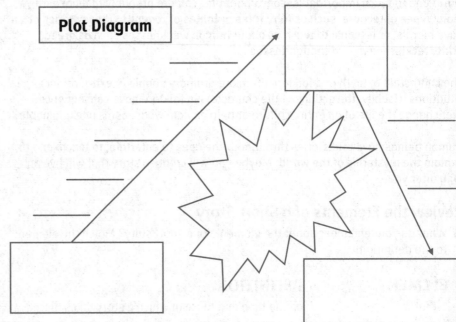

Plot Diagram

Poor Choices: "Phaethon"

Learning Targets
- Identify key plot elements of conflict and climax.
- Analyze how character is developed through words and actions.

Before Reading
1. Review elements of a short story, especially plot. This review will help you label all the parts of the plot of "Phaethon" on a plot diagram after reading the story.

During Reading
2. As you read "Phaethon," mark the text, noting especially the conflict of the story and the climax of the action of the plot. Remember, the climax is the turning point in the story in which the plot could go either way. In addition, pay attention to how the major characters are developed through dialogue and action.

ABOUT THE AUTHOR
Bernard Evslin wrote many books for young people and is best known for his adaptations of tales from Greek mythology. *Heroes, Gods and Monsters of the Greek Myths,* his best-known work, has sold more than 10 million copies worldwide and has been translated into 10 different languages. Evslin's work has won a number of awards, and his book *The Green Hero* was nominated for a National Book Award.

LEARNING STRATEGIES:
Previewing, Predicting, Close Reading, Marking the Text, Questioning the Text, Word Map

My Notes

My Notes

_____
_____
_____
_____
_____

KEY IDEAS AND DETAILS

The dialogue between the two characters is indicated by quotation marks; however, in this section, the speaker is not always named. Decide who is speaking within each set of quotation marks: the yellow-haired boy or the black-haired one. How do you know? Mark your text to show who is speaking.

_____
_____
_____
_____
_____
_____

GRAMMAR & USAGE
Pronoun and Antecedents

A pronoun takes the place of a noun or another pronoun, called its antecedent. Look at paragraph 7 on this page. The pronoun *he* is used twice. Who is *he*? The antecedent, Zeus, is not in this paragraph, but it is stated at the beginning of the text so readers know that *he* (and *father*) refers to Zeus.

When using pronouns in your writing, make sure you have clearly stated the nouns to which your pronouns refer.

Myth

Phaethon

by Bernard Evslin

Chunk 1

1 Long ago, when the world was very new, two boys were racing along the edge of a cliff that hung over a deep blue sea. They were the same size; one boy had black hair, the other had yellow hair. The race was very close. Then the yellow-haired one spurted ahead and won the race. The loser was very angry.

2 "You think you're pretty good," he said. "But you're not so much. My father is Zeus."[1]

3 My father is Apollo," said the yellow-haired boy, whose name was Phaethon.[2]

4 "My father is the chief god, king of the mountain, lord of the sky."

5 "My father is lord of the sun."

6 "My father is called the thunderer. When he is angry, the sky grows black and the sun hides. His spear is a lightning bolt, and that's what he kills people with. He hurls it a thousand miles and it never misses."

Chunk 2

7 "Without my father there would be no day. It would always be night. Each morning he hitches up his horses and drives the golden chariot of the sun across the sky. And that is day time. Then he dives into the ocean stream and boards a golden ferryboat and sails back to his eastern palace. That time is called night."

[1] **Zeus** [züs]: King of the gods in Greek mythology
[2] **Phaethon** [fā´ə thon]

8   "Sometimes I visit my father," said Epaphus,[3] the other boy. "I sit on Olympus[4] with him, and he teaches me things and gives me presents. Know what he gave me last time? A little thunderbolt just like his—and he taught me how to throw it. I killed three vultures, scared a fishing boat, started a forest fire. Next time I go, I'll throw it at more things. Do you visit your father?"

9   Phaethon never had. But he could not bear to tell Epaphus. "Certainly," he said, "very often. I go to the eastern palace, and he teaches me things too."

10   "What kind of things? Has he taught you to drive the horses of the sun?"

11   "Oh, yes. He taught me to handle their reins and how to make them go and how to make them stop. And they're huge horses. Tall as this mountain. They breathe fire."

12   "I think you're making it all up," said Epaphus. "I can tell. I don't even believe there is a sun chariot. There's the sun, look at it. It's not a chariot."

13   "Oh, what you see is just one of the wheels," said Phaethon. "There's another wheel on the other side. The body of the chariot is slung between them. That is where the driver stands and whips his horses. You cannot see it because your eyes are too small, and the glare is too bright."

14   "Well," said Epaphus, "Maybe it is a chariot, but I still don't believe your father lets you drive it. In fact, I don't believe you've been to the palace of the sun. I doubt that Apollo would know you if he saw you. Maybe he isn't even your father. People like to say they're descended from the gods, of course. But how many of us are there, really?"

15   "I'll prove it to you," cried Phaethon, stamping his foot. "I'll go to the palace of the sun right now and hold my father to his promise. I'll show you."

16   "What promise?"

17   "He said I was getting to be so good a charioteer that next time he would let me drive the sun chariot *alone*. All by myself. From dawn to night. Right across the sky. And this time is next time."

18   "Proof—words are cheap," said Epaphus. "How will I know it's you driving the sun? I won't be able to see you from down here."

19   "You'll know me," said Phaethon. "When I pass the village I will come down close and drive in circles around your roof. You'll see me all right. Farewell."

20   "Are you starting now?"

21   "Now. At once. Just watch the sky tomorrow, son of Zeus."

My Notes

KEY IDEAS AND DETAILS
Why do you think Phaethon lies about his relationship with his father?

KEY IDEAS AND DETAILS
What choices does Phaethon have at this point?

KEY IDEAS AND DETAILS
What might be the consequences of each choice you stated above?

---

[3] **Epaphus** [ə pā´ fəs]
[4] **Olympus** [ō lim´ pəs]: A mountain in Greece where ancient gods were said to live

Poor Choices: "Phaethon"

pic

My Notes

_____
_____
_____
_____
_____
_____

KEY IDEAS AND DETAILS
How does the argument
between the friends set the
plot in motion? What do
Phaethon's words and actions
reveal about his character?

KEY IDEAS AND DETAILS
How does Apollo feel about
his son, Phaethon? What
dialogue shows his attitude
toward his son?

Chunk 3

23 And he went off. He was so stung by the words of his friend, and the boasting and lying he had been forced to do, that he traveled night and day, not stopping for food or rest, guiding himself by the morning star and the evening star, heading always east. Nor did he know the way. For, indeed, he had never once seen his father Apollo. He knew him only through his mother's stories. But he did know that the palace must lie in the east, because that is where he saw the sun start each morning. He walked on and on until finally he lost his way completely, and weakened by hunger and exhaustion, fell swooning in a great meadow by the edge of a wood.

24 Now, while Phaethon was making his journey, Apollo sat in his great throne room on a huge throne made of gold and rubies. This was the quiet hour before dawn when night left its last coolness upon the Earth. And it was then, at this hour, that Apollo sat on his throne, wearing a purple cloak embroidered with the golden sign of the zodiac.[5] On his head was a crown given him by the dawn goddess, made of silver and pearls. A bird flew in the window and perched on his shoulder and spoke to him. This bird had sky-blue feathers, golden beak, golden claws, and golden eyes. It was one of Apollo's sun hawks. It was this bird's job to fly here and there gathering gossip. Sometimes she was called the spy bird.

25 Now she said, "Apollo, I have seen your son!"

26 "Which son?"

27 "Phaethon. He's coming to see you. But he has lost his way and lies exhausted at the edge of the wood. The wolves will surely eat him. Do you care?"

28 "I will have to see him before I know whether I care. You had better get back to him before the wolves do. Bring him here in comfort. Round up some of your companions and bring him here as befits the son of a god."

---

[5] **zodiac** [zōˊ dē ak]: An imaginary belt of the heavens, divided into 12 parts, called signs, and named after 12 constellations

29 The sun hawk seized the softly glowing rug at the foot of the throne and flew away with it. She summoned three of her companions, and they each took a corner of the rug. They flew over a desert and a mountain and a wood and came to the field where Phaethon lay. They flew down among the howling of wolves, among burning eyes set in a circle about the unconscious[6] boy. They pushed him onto the rug, and each took a corner in her beak, and flew away.

30 Phaethon felt himself being lifted into the air. The cold wind of his going revived him, and he sat up. People below saw a boy sitting with folded arms on a carpet rushing through the cold, bright moonlight far above their heads. It was too dark, though, to see the birds, and that is why we hear tales of flying carpets even to this day.

31 Phaethon was not particularly surprised to find himself in the air. The last thing he remembered was lying down on the grass. Now he knew he was dreaming. A good dream—floating and flying—his favorite kind. And when he saw the great cloud castle on top of the mountain, all made of snow, rise in the early light, he was more sure than ever that he was dreaming. He saw sentries in flashing golden armor, carrying golden spears. In the courtyard he saw enormous woolly dogs with fleece like clouddrift guarding the gate. These were Apollo's great sun hounds.

32 Over the wall flew the carpet, over the courtyard, through the tall portals. And it wasn't until the sun hawks gently let down the carpet in front of the throne that he began to think that this dream might be very real. He raised his eyes shyly and saw a tall figure sitting on the throne. Taller than any man, and appallingly beautiful to the boy—with his golden hair and stormy blue eyes and strong laughing face. Phaethon fell on his knees.

Chunk 4

33 "Father," he cried. "I am Phaethon, your son!"

34 "Rise, Phaethon. Let me look at you."

35 He stood up, his legs trembling.

36 "Yes, you may well be my son. I seem to see a resemblance. Which one did you say?"

37 "Phaethon."

38 "Oh, Clymene's[7] boy. I remember your mother well. How is she?"

39 "In health, sire."

40 "And did I not leave some daughters with her as well? Yellow-haired girls— quite pretty?"

41 My sisters, sire. The Heliads."

42 "Yes, of course. Must get over that way and visit them all one of these seasons. And you, lad—what brings you to me? Do you not know that it is courteous to await an invitation before visiting a god—even if he is in the family?"

43 "I know, Father. But I had no choice. I was taunted by a son of Zeus, Epaphus. And I would have flung him over the cliff and myself after him if I had not resolved to make my lies come true."

My Notes

KEY IDEAS AND DETAILS
Make a prediction about what Phaethon will ask Apollo.

[6] **unconscious** [un kon′ shəs]: Not awake
[7] **Clymene** [klī men ē′]

Poor Choices: "Phaethon"

Chunk 5

44 "Well, you're my son, all right. Proud, rash, accepting no affront,[8] refusing no adventure. I know the breed. Speak up, then. What is it you wish? I will do anything in my power to help you."

45 "Anything, Father?"

46 "Anything I can. I swear by the river Styx,[9] an oath sacred to the gods."

47 "I wish to drive the sun across the sky. All by myself. From dawn till night."

48 Apollo's roar of anger shattered every crystal goblet in the great castle.

49 "Impossible!" he cried. "No one drives those horses but me. They are tall as mountains. Their breath is fire. They are stronger than the tides, stronger than the wind. It is all that *I* can do to hold them in check. How can your puny grip restrain them? They will race away with the chariot, scorching the poor Earth to a cinder."

50 "You promised, Father."

51 "Yes, I promised, foolish lad. And that promise is the death warrant. A poor charred cinder floating in space—well, that is what the oracle predicted for the earth—but I did not know it would be so soon … so soon."

KEY IDEAS AND DETAILS
Predict what might happen if Phaethon drives the horses

KEY IDEAS AND DETAILS
Why does Apollo want Phaethon to change his request?

Chunk 6

52 "It is almost dawn, Father. Should we not saddle the horses?"

53 "Will you not withdraw your request—allow me to preserve my honor without destroying the earth? Ask me anything else and I will grant it. Do not ask me this."

54 "I have asked, sire, and you have promised. And the hour for dawn comes, and the horses are unharnessed. The sun will rise late today, confusing the wise."

55 "They will be more than confused when this day is done," said Apollo. "Come."

56 Apollo took Phaethon to the stable of the sun, and there the boy saw the giant fire-white horses being harnessed to the golden chariot. Huge they were. Fire-white with golden manes and golden hooves and hot yellow eyes. When they neighed, the trumpet call of it rolled across the sky—and their breath was flame. They were being harnessed by a Titan, a cousin of the gods, tall as the tree, dressed in asbestos[10] armor with a helmet of tinted crystal against the glare. The sun chariot was an open shell of gold. Each wheel was the flat round disk of the sun as it is seen in the sky. And Phaethon looked very tiny as he stood in the chariot. The reins were thick as bridge cables, much too large for him to hold, so Apollo tied them around his waist. Then Apollo stood at the head of the team gentling the horses speaking softly to them, calling them by name—Pyrocis,[11] Eous,[12] Aethon,[13] Phlegon.[14]

57 "Good lads, good horses, go easy today, my swift ones. Go at a slow trot and do not leave the path. You have a new driver today."

---

[8] **affront** [ə frunt']: Insult
[9] **Styx** [stiks]: In Greek myths, a river that led to Hades or Hell
[10] **asbestos** [as bes' təs]: A mineral that does not burn or conduct heat
[11] **Pyrocis** [pī rō´ chis]
[12] **Eous** [e' us]
[13] **Aethon** [a' thon]
[14] **Phlegon** [fle´ gon]

58 The great horses dropped their heads to his shoulder and whinnied softly, for they loved him. Phaethon saw the flame of their breath play about his head, saw Apollo's face shining out of the flame. But he was not harmed, for he was a god and could not be hurt by physical things.

Chunk 7

59 He came to Phaethon and said, "Listen to me, son. You are about to start a terrible journey. Now, by the obedience you owe me as a son, by the faith you owe a god, by my oath that cannot be broken, and your pride that will not bend, I put this rule upon you: Keep the middle way. Too high and the earth will freeze, too low and it will burn. Keep the middle way. Give the horses their heads; they know the path, the blue middle course of day. Drive them not too high nor too low, but above all, do not stop. Or you will fire the air about you where you stand, charring the earth and blistering the sky. Do you heed me?"

60 "I do, I do!" cried Phaethon. "Stand away, sire! The dawn grows old and day must begin! Go, horses, go!"

61 And Apollo stood watching as the horses of the sun went into a swinging trot, pulling behind them the golden chariot, climbing the first eastern steep of the sky.

62 At first things went well. The great steeds trotted easily along their path across the high blue meadow of the sky. And Phaethon thought to himself, "I can't understand why my father was making such a fuss. This is easy. For me, anyway. Perhaps I'm a natural-born coachman though … "

63 He looked over the edge of the chariot. He saw tiny houses down below and specks of trees. And the dark blue puddle of the sea. The coach was trundling across the sky. The great sun wheels were turning, casting light, warming and brightening the earth, chasing all the shadows of night.

64 "Just imagine," Phaethon thought, "how many people now are looking up at the sky, praising the sun, hoping the weather stays fair. How many people are watching me, me, me …?" Then he thought, "But I'm too small to see. They can't even see the coach or the horses—only the great wheel. We are too far and the light is too bright. For all they know, it is Apollo making his usual run. How can they know it's me, me, me? How will my mother know, and my sisters? They would be so proud. And Epaphus—above all, Epaphus—how will he know? I'll come home tomorrow after this glorious journey and tell him what I did and he will laugh at me and tell me I'm lying, as he did before. And how shall I prove it to him? No, this must not be. I must show him that it is I driving the chariot of the sun—I alone. Apollo said not to come too close to earth, but how will he know? And I won't stay too long—just dip down toward our own village and circle his roof three times—which is the signal we agreed upon. After he recognizes me, I'll whip up the horses and resume the path of the day.

Chunk 8

65 He jerked on the reins, pulled the horses' heads down. They whinnied angrily and tossed their heads. He jerked the reins again.

66 "Down," he cried. "Down! Down!"

67 The horses plunged through the bright air, golden hooves twinkling, golden manes flying, dragging the great glittering chariot after them in a long flaming swoop. When they reached his village, he was horrified to see the roofs bursting into fire. The trees burned. People rushed about screaming. Their loose clothing caught fire, and they burned like torches as they ran.

KEY IDEAS AND DETAILS
What will happen if Phaethon chooses not to obey Apollo's instructions? Predict whether or not Phaethon will follow the directions. Give a reason for your prediction.

KEY IDEAS AND DETAILS
Mark the portions of the text that reveal Phaethon's character through his thoughts.

My Notes

_____

_____

_____

_____

KEY IDEAS AND DETAILS
Why do you think Phaethon chooses to do exactly what Apollo warned him not to do?

KEY IDEAS AND DETAILS
How does this section set up the climax of the story?

_____

_____

_____

_____

_____

_____

_____

Poor Choices: "Phaethon"

My Notes

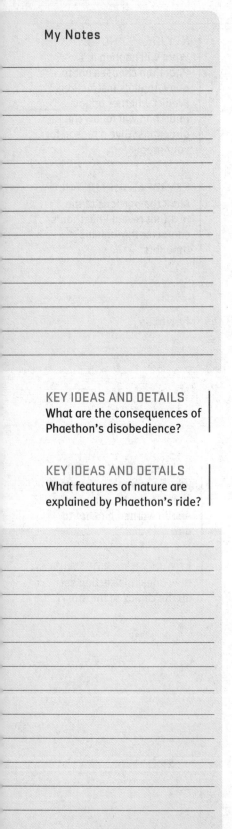

KEY IDEAS AND DETAILS
What are the consequences of
Phaethon's disobedience?

KEY IDEAS AND DETAILS
What features of nature are
explained by Phaethon's ride?

68 Was it his village? He could not tell because of the smoke. Had he destroyed his own home? Burned his mother and his sisters?

69 He threw himself backward in the chariot, pulling at the reins with all his might, shouting, "Up! Up!"

70 And the horses, made furious by the smoke, reared on their hind legs in the air. They leaped upward, galloping through the smoke, pulling the chariot up, up.

71 Swiftly the earth fell away beneath them. The village was just a smudge of smoke. Again he saw the pencil-stroke of mountains, the inkblot of seas. "Whoa!" he cried. "Turn now! Forward on your path!" But he could no longer handle them. They were galloping, not trotting. They had taken the bit in their teeth. They did not turn toward the path of the day across the meadow of the sky, but galloped up, up. And the people on earth saw the sun shooting away until it was no larger than a star.

72 Darkness came. And cold. The earth froze hard. Rivers froze, and oceans. Boats were caught fast in the ice in every sea. It snowed in the jungle. Marble buildings cracked. It was impossible for anyone to speak; breath froze on the speakers' lips. And in village and city, in the field and in the wood, people died of the cold. And the bodies piled up where they fell, like firewood.

73 Still Phaethon could not hold his horses, and still they galloped upward dragging light and warmth away from the earth. Finally they went so high that the air was too thin to breathe. Phaethon saw the flame of their breath, which had been red and yellow, burn blue in the thin air. He himself was gasping for breath; he felt the marrow of his bones freezing.

74 Now the horses, wild with change, maddened by the feeble hand on the reins, swung around and dived toward earth again. Now all the ice melted, making great floods. Villages were swept away by a solid wall of water. Trees were uprooted and whole forests were torn away. The fields were covered by water. Lower swooped the horses, and lower yet. Now the water began to steam—great billowing clouds of steam as the water boiled. Dead fish floated on the surface. Naiads moaned in dry riverbeds.

75 Phaethon could not see; the steam was too thick. He had unbound the reins from his waist, or they would have cut him in two. He had no control over the horses at all. They galloped upward again—out of the steam—taking at last the middle road, but racing wildly, using all their tremendous speed. Circling the earth in a matter of minutes, smashing across the sky from horizon to horizon, making the day flash on and off like a child playing with a lamp. And the people who were left alive were bewildered by the light and darkness following each other so swiftly.

Chunk 9

76 Up high on Olympus, the gods in their cool garden heard a clamor of grief from below. Zeus looked upon earth. He saw the runaway horses of the sun and the hurtling chariot. He saw the dead and the dying, the burning forests, the floods, the weird frost. Then he looked again at the chariot and saw that it was not Apollo driving, but someone he did not know. He stood up, drew back his arm, and hurled a thunderbolt.

77 It stabbed through the air, striking Phaethon, killing him instantly, knocking him out of the chariot. His body, flaming, fell like a star. And the horses of the sun, knowing themselves driverless, galloped homeward toward their stables at the eastern edge of the sky.

78 Phaethon's yellow-haired sisters grieved for the beautiful boy. They could not stop weeping. They stood on the bank of the river where he had fallen until Apollo, unable to comfort them, changed them into poplar trees. Here they still stand on the shore of the river, weeping tears of amber sap.

79 And since that day no one has been allowed to drive the chariot of the sun except the sun god himself. But there are still traces of Phaethon's ride. The ends of the earth are still covered with icecaps. Mountains still rumble, trying to spit out the fire started in their bellies by the diving sun.

My Notes

Poor Choices: "Phaethon"

After Reading

3. Using the plot diagram from Activity 1.11, determine the major conflict of the story and where the climax and falling action of the story occur.

4. Indicate whether you agree or disagree with the following statements about Phaethon and Apollo. Then write the textual evidence that supports your position. Go back to the text and highlight your textual evidence; look for vivid details as textual evidence.

Agree	Disagree	
		Phaethon is a thoughtless, headstrong boy. Textual Evidence:
		Phaethon is an adventurous, courageous boy. Textual Evidence:
		Phaethon is _____. (Insert your description.) Textual Evidence:
		Apollo is a disinterested, ineffective parent. Textual Evidence:
		Apollo is deeply concerned for his son's well-being. Textual Evidence:
		Apollo is _____. (Insert your description.) Textual Evidence:

Check Your Understanding

Writing Prompt: How do the character traits of Apollo or Phaethon drive the story to its tragic conclusion? Choose either Phaethon or Apollo to write about. Be sure to:

- Create a topic sentence that states the character's qualities and how those qualities drive the plot of the story.
- Use precise language to express your ideas clearly; avoid wordiness and unnecessary repetition.
- Include at least one piece of textual evidence as support.

My Notes

Flight to Freedom

LEARNING STRATEGIES:
Discussion Groups, Visual
Prompt, Drafting

Learning Targets

- Analyze how theme is conveyed in a story based on a myth.
- Apply the conventions of dialogue paragraphing in a story.

Before Reading

1. **Freewrite:** Do you think you learn best from other people's advice or from your own experience? Explain with an example from your own life and/or your reading. Be sure to include your analysis of the consequences of taking or not taking the advice.

During Reading

2. Look for and mark the text for elements of characterization:

- What the characters do
- What the characters say
- How the characters appear or look
- What others say about the characters

Also use the strategy of diffusing to help you find meaning. For example, the word *labyrinth* appears in the opening paragraphs of "Daedalus and Icarus." From the context, what is its meaning? What word might you use as a synonym? For example, you might circle the word *labyrinth* (on page 59). Based on context, you might realize that *maze* is a synonym for *labyrinth*. Find the word *delectable* on page 60. What word might be a synonym?

Introducing the Strategy: Diffusing

With this strategy, you use context clues to help find the meaning of unknown words. When **diffusing**, underline words that are unfamiliar. Think of two possible substitutions (synonyms), and confirm your definition. You can confirm your definition by checking reference sources such as a dictionary or a thesaurus.

My Notes

ABOUT THE AUTHOR

Geraldine McCaughrean was born in England, where she studied theater and began writing her versions of traditional texts such as *The Canterbury Tales* and Shakespeare's plays. Her goal was to retell these challenging texts in language that young readers could enjoy and understand. She has received numerous awards for her books, and her writing is noted for its strong use of imagery and narrative structure that bring her stories alive for young readers.

My Notes

Myth

Daedalus and Icarus

from *Greek Myths* by Geraldine McCaughrean

The island of Crete was ruled by King Minos, whose reputation for wickedness had spread to every shore. One day he summoned to his country a famous inventor named Daedalus. "Come, Daedalus, and bring your son, Icarus, too. I have a job for you, and I pay well."

King Minos wanted Daedalus to build him a palace, with soaring towers and a high, curving roof. In the cellars there was to be a maze of many corridors—so twisting and dark that any man who once ventured in there would never find his way out again.

"What is it for?" asked Daedalus. "Is it a treasure vault? Is it a prison to hold criminals?"

But Minos only replied, "Build my labyrinth as I told you. I pay you to build, not to ask questions."

So Daedalus held his tongue and set to work. When the palace was finished, he looked at it with pride, for there was nowhere in the world so fine. But when he found out the purpose of the maze in the cellar, he shuddered with horror.

For at the heart of that maze, King Minos put a creature that was half man, half beast—a thing almost too horrible to describe. He called it the Minotaur, and he fed it on men and women!

Then Daedalus wanted to leave Crete at once, and forget both maze and Minotaur. So he went to King Minos to ask for his money.

"I regret," said King Minos, "I cannot let you leave Crete, Daedalus. You are the only man who knows the secret of the maze and how to escape from it. The secret must never leave this island. So I'm afraid I must keep you and Icarus here a while longer."

"How much longer?" gasped Daedalus.

My Notes

Wings and flying are often a metaphor for what?

"Oh—just until you die," replied Minos cheerfully. "But never mind. I have plenty of work for a man as clever as you."

Daedalus and Icarus lived in great comfort in King Minos's palace. But they lived the life of prisoners. Their rooms were in the tallest palace tower, with beautiful views across the island. They ate delectable food and wore expensive clothes. But at night the door of their fine apartment was locked, and a guard stood outside. It was a comfortable prison, but it was a prison, even so. Daedalus was deeply unhappy.

Every day he put seed out on the windowsill, for the birds. He liked to study their brilliant colors, the clever overlapping of their feathers, the way they soared on the sea wind. It comforted him to think that they at least were free to come and go. The birds had only to spread their wings and they could leave Crete behind them, whereas Daedalus and Icarus must stay forever in their luxurious cage.

Young Icarus could not understand his father's unhappiness. "But I like it here," he said. "The king gives us gold and this tall tower to live in."

Daedalus groaned. "But to work for such a wicked man, Icarus! And to be prisoners all our days! … We shan't stay. We shan't!"

"But we can't get away, can we?" said Icarus. "How can anybody escape from an island? Fly?" He snorted with laughter.

Daedalus did not answer. He scratched his head and stared out of the window at the birds pecking seed on the sill.

From that day onward, he got up early each morning and stood at the open window. When a bird came for the seed, Daedalus begged it to spare him one feather. Then each night, when everyone else had gone to bed, Daedalus worked by candlelight on his greatest invention of all.

Early mornings. Late nights. A whole year went by. Then one morning Icarus was awakened by his father shaking his shoulder. "Get up, Icarus, and don't make a sound. We are leaving Crete."

"But how? It's impossible!"

Daedalus pulled out a bundle from under his bed. "I've been making something, Icarus." Inside were four great folded fans of feathers. He stretched them out on the bed. They were wings! "I sewed the feathers together with strands of wool from my blanket. Now hold still."

Daedalus melted down a candle and daubed his son's shoulders with sticky wax. "Yes, I know it's hot, but it will soon cool." While the wax was still soft, he stuck two of the wings to Icarus's shoulder blades.

"Now you must help me put on my wings, Son. When the wax sets hard, you and I will fly away from here, as free as birds!"

"I'm scared!" whispered Icarus as he stood on the narrow window ledge, his knees knocking and his huge wings drooping down behind. The lawns and courtyards of the palace lay far below. The royal guards looked as small as ants. "This won't work!"

"Courage, Son!" said Daedalus. "Keep your arms out wide and fly close to me. Above all—are you listening, Icarus?"

"Y-y-yes, Father."

"Above all, don't fly too high! Don't fly too close to the sun!"

"Don't fly too close to the sun," Icarus repeated, with his eyes tight shut. Then he gave a cry as his father nudged him off the windowsill. He plunged downward. With a crack, the feathers behind him filled with wind, and Icarus found himself flying. Flying!

"I'm flying!" he crowed.

The guards looked up in astonishment, and wagged their swords, and pointed and shouted, "Tell the king! Daedalus and Icarus are … are … flying away!"

By dipping first one wing, then the other, Icarus found that he could turn to the left and the right. The wind tugged at his hair. His legs trailed out behind him. He saw the fields and streams as he had never seen them before!

Then they were out over the sea. The sea gulls pecked at him angrily, so Icarus flew higher, where they could not reach him.

He copied their shrill cry and taunted them: "You can't catch me!"

"Now remember, don't fly too high!" called Daedalus, but his words were drowned by the screaming of the gulls.

I'm the first boy ever to fly! I'm making history! I shall be famous! thought Icarus, as he flew up and up, higher and higher.

At last Icarus was looking the sun itself in the face. "Think you're the highest thing in the sky, do you?" he jeered. "I can fly just as high as you! Higher, even!" He did not notice the drops of sweat on his forehead: He was so determined to outfly the sun.

KEY IDEAS AND DETAILS
Can you find the similes used in this selection? What is their effect? Remember that similes are comparisons using "like" or "as."

KEY IDEAS AND DETAILS
From what point of view is this myth written? How do you know?

My Notes

_____

_____

_____

_____

_____

_____

Flight to Freedom

KEY IDEAS AND DETAILS
Using the context of this passage, what do you think a "plume" is?

My Notes

_____
_____
_____
_____
_____
_____
_____
_____

ACADEMIC VOCABULARY
A **theme** is the central idea, message, or purpose of a literary work.
A **metaphor** is a comparison between two unlike things in which one thing is spoken of as if it were another.

_____
_____
_____
_____
_____

WORD
CONNECTIONS

Analogies

Think about the relationship (analogy) between feather and wing. Then write a word that has the same relationship with the word *alphabet*.

Feather : wing :: _____ : alphabet.

Soon its vast heat beat on his face and on his back and on the great wings stuck on with wax. The wax softened. The wax trickled. The wax dripped. One feather came unstuck. Then a <u>plume</u> of feathers fluttered slowly down.

Icarus stopped flapping his wings. His father's words came back to him clearly now: *"Don't fly too close to the sun!"*

With a great sucking noise, the wax on his shoulders came unstuck. Icarus tried to catch hold of the wings, but they just folded up in his hands. He plunged down, his two fists full of feathers — down and down and down.

The clouds did not stop his fall.

The sea gulls did not catch him in their beaks.

His own father could only watch as Icarus hurtled head first into the glittering sea and sank deep down among the sharks and eels and squid. And all that was left of proud Icarus was a litter of waxy feathers floating on the sea.

After Reading

"Daedalus and Icarus," like most myths, teaches us a lesson. Daedalus tells his son, "Don't fly too close to the sun." Since it is not likely that any of us will wear wings made of feathers and wax, the main idea, or **theme**, of this story is not a literal lesson about how high to fly. The story of Icarus can be read as a **metaphor** for other, more realistic situations we might face.

3. Discuss the following ideas in a collaborative group:
   - In the story, Icarus thinks to himself, "I'm the first boy ever to fly! I'm making history!" Icarus also says to the sun, "I can fly just as high as you! Higher, even!" What does this dialogue illustrate about the character of Icarus? How could this relate to the story's theme?
   - Daedalus repeatedly warns Icarus not too fly too high, advice that Icarus thoughtlessly ignores. What might this story be saying about relationships between parents and children? What might it be saying about how we learn?
   - The expression "flying too close to the sun" has taken on other meanings, namely about the consequences of risk taking. What is this story saying about the benefits and dangers of taking risks?
   - Sometimes critics of scientific development and rapid technological change bring up the story of Daedalus and Icarus as a warning about the dangers of reckless science taking humans into areas where they might not belong. Explain how this story might illustrate the idea of the dangers of technology and scientific progress.

4. How are the characters' choices related to the lessons of this myth?

Character	Choices	Lesson
Daedalus		
Icarus		

GRAMMAR & USAGE
Dialogue
When writing dialogue, remember to start a new paragraph each time the speaker changes.

Check Your Understanding

Explain a major theme that you think this story presents. Use specific examples from the text as evidence.

5. Revisit the definition of a myth: **Myths** are traditional stories that explain beliefs, customs, or natural phenomenon through the actions of gods or heroes. Does this story meet the criteria to be considered a myth?

- How does the story of Daedalus and Icarus explain beliefs, customs, or natural phenomenon?

- How is the story of Daedalus and Icarus explained through the actions of gods or heroes?

Writing Prompt: Imagine and write an "unseen scene" that might be in the "Daedalus and Icarus" myth. Use your sketches from your plot diagram to generate ideas. Be sure to:

- Use techniques of characterization to maintain characters' personalities.
- Incorporate correctly punctuated dialogue.
- Use vivid details to enhance elements of character and plot.

My Notes

A Matter of Pride

LEARNING STRATEGIES:
Graphic Organizer, Visual Prompt, Discussion Groups, Drafting

My Notes

Learning Targets

- Compare and contrast character traits that lead to self-destruction as presented in Greek myths.
- Analyze the relationship between character and plot and between conflict and resolution.

Before Reading

1. Athena (or Athene) is one of the daughters of Zeus who figures prominently in Greek mythology. Who is Athena? What are her special talents and attributes?

ABOUT THE AUTHOR
Olivia Coolidge grew up in England in the early 1900s. She became a teacher of Latin, Greek, and mythology, while also developing her skills as a writer. She wrote numerous histories and biographies for children and young adults. Her work is noted for high interest and vivid descriptions. Coolidge won the 1963 Newbery Award for contributions to children's literature.

Myth

ARACHNE

by Olivia E. Coolidge

Arachne was a maiden who became famous throughout Greece, though she was neither wellborn nor beautiful and came from no great city. She lived in an obscure little village, and her father was a humble dyer of wool. In this he was very skillful, producing many varied shades, while above all he was famous for the clear, bright scarlet which is made from shellfish, and which was the most glorious of all the colors used in ancient Greece. Even more skillful than her father was Arachne. It was her task to spin the fleecy wool into a fine, soft thread and to weave it into cloth on the high, standing loom within the cottage. Arachne was small and pale from much working. Her eyes were light and her hair was a dusty brown, yet she was quick and graceful, and her fingers, roughened as they were, went so fast that it was hard to follow their flickering movements. So soft and even was her thread, so fine her cloth, so gorgeous her embroidery, that soon her products were known all over Greece. No one had ever seen the like of them before.

At last Arachne's fame became so great that people used to come from far and wide to watch her working. Even the graceful nymphs would steal in from stream or forest and peep shyly through the dark doorway, watching in wonder the white arms of Arachne as she stood at the loom and threw the shuttle from hand to hand between the hanging threads, or drew out the long wool, fine as a hair, from the distaff as she sat spinning. "Surely Athene herself must have taught her," people would murmur to one another. "Who else could know the secret of such marvelous skill?"

KEY IDEAS AND DETAILS
What inference could you make about Arachne's personality? Arachne is ...

Arachne was used to being wondered at, and she was immensely proud of the skill that had brought so many to look on her. Praise was all she lived for, and it displeased her greatly that people should think anyone, even a goddess, could teach her anything. Therefore when she heard them murmur, she would stop her work and turn round indignantly to say, "With my own ten fingers I gained this skill, and by hard practice from early morning till night. I never had time to stand looking as you people do while another maiden worked. Nor if I had, would I give Athene credit because the girl was more skillful than I. As for Athene's weaving, how could there be finer cloth or more beautiful embroidery than mine? If Athene herself were to come down and compete with me, she could do no better than I."

One day when Arachne turned round with such words, an old woman answered her, a grey old woman, bent and very poor, who stood leaning on a staff and peering at Arachne amid the crowd of onlookers.

"Reckless girl," she said, "how dare you claim to be equal to the immortal gods themselves? I am an old woman and have seen much. Take my advice and ask pardon of Athene for your words. Rest content with your fame of being the best spinner and weaver that mortal eyes have ever beheld."

"Stupid old woman," said Arachne indignantly, "who gave you the right to speak in this way to me? It is easy to see that you were never good for anything in your day, or you would not come here in poverty and rags to gaze at my skill. If Athene resents my words, let her answer them herself. I have challenged her to a contest, but she, of course, will not come. It is easy for the gods to avoid matching their skill with that of men."

At these words the old woman threw down her staff and stood erect. The wondering onlookers saw her grow tall and fair and stand clad in long robes of dazzling white. They were terribly afraid as they realized that they stood in the presence of Athene. Arachne herself flushed red for a moment, for she had never really believed that the goddess would hear her. Before the group that was gathered there she would not give in; so pressing her pale lips together in obstinacy and pride, she led the goddess to one of the great looms and set herself before the other. Without a word both began to thread the long woolen strands that hang from the rollers, and between which the shuttle moves back and forth. Many skeins lay heaped beside them to use, bleached white, and gold, and scarlet, and other shades, varied as the rainbow. Arachne had never thought of giving credit for her success to her father's skill in dyeing, though in actual truth the colors were as remarkable as the cloth itself.

Soon there was no sound in the room but the breathing of the onlookers, the whirring of the shuttles, and the creaking of the wooden frames as each pressed the thread up into place or tightened the pegs by which the whole was held straight. The excited crowd in the doorway began to see that the skill of both in truth was very nearly equal, but that, however the cloth might turn out, the goddess was the quicker of the two. A pattern of many pictures was growing on her loom. There was a border of twined branches of the olive, Athene's favorite tree, while in the middle, figures began to appear. As they looked at the glowing colors, the spectators realized that Athene was weaving into her pattern a last warning to Arachne. The central figure was the goddess herself competing with Poseidon for

KEY IDEAS AND DETAILS
Quote one line of dialogue that sets this story in motion.

KEY IDEAS AND DETAILS
How are Arachne's attitude and response to advice similar to those of Phaethon and Icarus? After reading, decide who was the most at fault for his/her fate.

My Notes

_____

A Matter of Pride

My Notes

_____

_____

_____

_____

_____

KEY IDEAS AND DETAILS
How do Arachne's character traits determine how the conflict will resolve itself?

_____

_____

_____

_____

_____

_____

_____

_____

_____

_____

_____

_____

_____

possession of the city of Athens; but in the four corners were mortals who had tried to strive with gods and pictures of the awful fate that had overtaken them. The goddess ended a little before Arachne and stood back from her marvelous work to see what the maiden was doing.

Never before had Arachne been matched against anyone whose skill was equal, or even nearly equal to her own. As she stole glances from time to time at Athene and saw the goddess working swiftly, calmly, and always a little faster than herself, she became angry instead of frightened, and an evil thought came into her head. Thus as Athene stepped back a pace to watch Arachne finishing her work, she saw that the maiden had taken for her design a pattern of scenes which showed evil or unworthy actions of the gods, how they had deceived fair maidens, resorted to trickery, and appeared on earth from time to time in the form of poor and humble people. When the goddess saw this insult glowing in bright colors on Arachne's loom, she did not wait while the cloth was judged, but stepped forward, her grey eyes blazing with anger, and tore Arachne's work across. Then she struck Arachne across the face. Arachne stood there a moment, struggling with anger, fear, and pride. "I will not live under this insult," she cried, and seizing a rope from the wall, she made a noose and would have hanged herself. The goddess touched the rope and touched the maiden. "Live on, wicked girl," she said. "Live on and spin, both you and your descendants. When men look at you they may remember that it is not wise to strive with Athene." At that the body of Arachne shriveled up, and her legs grew tiny, spindly, and distorted. There before the eyes of the spectators hung a little dusty brown spider on a slender thread.

All spiders descend from Arachne, and as the Greeks watched them spinning their thread wonderfully fine, they remembered the contest with Athene and thought that it was not right for even the best of men to claim equality with the gods.

After Reading

2. Myths have been used for generations to explain natural phenomena like lightning, tsunamis, and volcanic eruptions. Identify the element of nature this myth explains, the character's choices, and the lesson this myth teaches (theme)

Phenomenon	Character	Choices	Lesson

3. Work in a collaborative group to brainstorm other natural phenomena you could explain in an original myth.

Language and Writer's Craft: Pronouns and Antecedents

Skilled readers and writers should think about pronouns and their antecedents while reading and crafting texts.

To show that you are able to properly interpret pronoun-antecedent agreement, reread this passage, inserting a proper noun (*Athene* or *Arachne*) in the place of the pronoun. Possessive pronouns like "her" should be replaced with possessive proper nouns like "Athene's" or "Arachne's."

"Never before had Arachne been matched against anyone whose skill was equal, or even nearly equal to her (_____) own. As she (_____) stole glances from time to time at Athene and saw the goddess working swiftly, calmly, and always a little faster than herself (_____), she (_____) became angry instead of frightened, and an evil thought came into her (_____) head. Thus as Athene stepped back a pace to watch Arachne finishing her work, she (_____) saw that the maiden had taken for her (_____) design a pattern of scenes which showed evil or unworthy actions of the gods, how they [the gods] had deceived fair maidens, resorted to trickery, and appeared on earth from time to time in the form of poor and humble people. When the goddess saw this insult glowing in bright colors on Arachne's loom, she (_____) did not wait while the cloth was judged, but stepped forward, her (_____) grey eyes blazing with anger, and tore Arachne's work across."

GRAMMAR & USAGE
Pronouns and Antecedents

Pronouns, such as *he*, *she*, and *it*, take the place of nouns.

An antecedent is the object or person to which the pronoun refers.

My Notes

Symbolic Thinking

LEARNING STRATEGIES:
Graphic Organizer, Visual
Prompt, Discussion Groups,
Brainstorming

Literary Terms
A **symbol** is an object, a
person, or a place that stands
for something else. Symbolism
is the use of symbols in a
literary work.

My Notes

Learning Target
• Analyze and apply symbols used in mythology.

The Meanings of Words
The *literal* meaning of a word or phrase is expected to be understood exactly as it
is stated, while a *figurative* meaning is one that suggests some idea beyond the
literal level.

Writers commonly use words and images in a figurative way in literary works to
add depth of meaning. A *symbol* is a figurative use of an object or image so that
it represents something beyond itself. You might think of a symbol as having two
meanings: one meaning is literal, and the other is figurative. A flag is **literally** a
piece of cloth with a design; it is **symbolic** of a nation or clan or state.

1. Think about objects listed below that appear in well-known fairy tales or in
   stories you have read. In the graphic organizer, identify how each object is used
   literally in the story, and explain its figurative, or symbolic, meaning as well.

Story/Object	Literal Use	Figurative (symbolic) Meaning
"The Three Little Pigs:" straw house	House made of straw; flimsy	Living for the moment; carelessness
"The Three Little Pigs:" brick house	House made of brick; strong	Preparing for the future; carefulness; safety; practicality
"Daedalus and Icarus:" wings		
"Arachne:"weaving		
One of Your Choice:		
One of Your Choice:		

2. Colors can also be used symbolically in both print and nonprint texts. Think about what these colors represent and brainstorm each color's symbolic meaning.

Color	Symbolic representation
Blue	
Green	
Gold	
Red	

3. You may already be familiar with some of the Greek and Roman gods. Complete the chart on the next page. Conduct research to identify the roles, responsibilities, and symbols of Greek gods as well as corresponding gods and goddesses of other cultures.

4. Working with a partner, select one of the gods or goddess from the graphic organizer. Conduct further research in order to create a "Missing" or "Wanted" poster for him or her. Be sure to:

- Include all the relevant information identified from your research.
- Include symbolism, either through your use of colors or images.
- Include a visual (you can sketch or use another visual) of the god or goddess.
- Be prepared to present this poster to a group and display it in the classroom.

Name: _____ Age: _____ Also Known As: _____

Role:

Last known location:

Physical description:

Significant actions/crimes:

Presumed dangerous? Why?

Known associates:

Additional information/distinguishing features:

My Notes

Symbolic Thinking

My Notes

Greek God (Roman name)	Responsibility or Role (similar to culture)	Symbolism Representing God (object/action/color)
Zeus (Jupiter or Jove)		
Poseidon (Neptune)		
Hades (Pluto)		
Hera (Juno)		
Ares (Mars)		
Artemis (Diana)		
Athena/ Athene (Minerva)		
Demeter (Ceres)		
Aphrodite (Venus)		

Animals as Symbols: Aesop's Fables

Learning Targets
- Analyze the symbolic use of animals in a fable.
- Apply the use of symbolism in an original way.

Before Reading
1. Folklore stories commonly use symbolism to add depth of meaning. Remember that a *symbol* represents something beyond itself. Think about animals listed below that appear in well-known fairy tales or stories you have read. Use the graphic organizer to explore their symbolic meanings.

Animal	Figurative (symbolic) Meaning
Snake	
Bear	
Rat	
Ant	
One of Your Choice:	
One of Your Choice:	

My Notes

2. Mark the titles of the Aesop's Fables with which you are familiar.

_____	The Hare and the Tortoise	_____	The Moon and Her Mother
_____	The Wolf in Sheep's Clothing	_____	The Boys and the Frogs
_____	The North Wind and the Sun	_____	The Ant and the Grasshopper
_____	The Fox and the Grapes	_____	The Lion and the Mouse

pic

WORD CONNECTIONS

Roots and Affixes

Mortified comes from the Latin root *-mort-*, meaning "death." When someone is mortified, he or she is humiliated or embarrassed "to death." You can also find the root *-mort-* in other words dealing with death, such as *mortuary*, *mortician*, and *mortal*.

During Reading

3. This fable uses animals as characters. These animals could serve as symbols for certain types of personalities. Mark the text for evidence of symbolic characteristics.

ABOUT THE AUTHOR

Aesop was an ancient story teller whose collection of tales is now known as *Aesop's Fables*. Very little is known about Aesop's early life. In the book *World's Great Men of Color, Volume I,* J. A. Rogers quotes from a fourteenth century monk, who wrote about Aesop as " ... a native of Phrygia, in Asia Minor," and described him as "flat-nosed ... with lips, thick and pendulous and a black skin from which he contracted his name (Esop being the same with Ethiop)."

My Notes

_____

_____

_____

_____

_____

_____

_____

_____

_____

_____

_____

_____

_____

Fable

The Lion, the Fox, and the Stag

from *Aesop's Fables*

A Lion lay sick in his den, unable to provide himself with food. So he said to his friend the Fox, who came to ask how he did, "My good friend, I wish you would go to yonder wood and beguile the big Stag, who lives there, to come to my den: I have a fancy to make my dinner off a stag's heart and brains." The Fox went to the wood and found the Stag and said to him, "My dear sir, you're in luck. You know the Lion, our King: well, he's at the point of death, and has appointed you his successor to rule over the beasts. I hope you won't forget that I was the first to bring you the good news. And now I must be going back to him; and, if you take my advice, you'll come too and be with him at the last." The Stag was highly flattered, and followed the Fox to the Lion's den, suspecting nothing. No sooner had he got inside than the Lion sprang upon him, but he misjudged his spring, and the Stag got away with only his ears torn, and returned as fast as he could to the shelter of the wood. The Fox was much mortified, and the Lion, too, was dreadfully disappointed, for he was getting very hungry in spite of his illness. So he begged the Fox to have another try at coaxing the Stag to his den. "It'll be almost impossible this time," said the Fox, "but I'll try"; and off he went to the wood a second time,

and found the Stag resting and trying to recover from his fright. As soon as he saw the Fox he cried, "You scoundrel, what do you mean by trying to lure me to my death like that? Take yourself off, or I'll do you to death with my horns." But the Fox was entirely shameless. "What a coward you were," said he; "surely you didn't think the Lion meant any harm? Why, he was only going to whisper some royal secrets into your ear when you went off like a scared rabbit. You have rather disgusted him, and I'm not sure he won't make the wolf King instead, unless you come back at once and show you've got some spirit. I promise you he won't hurt you, and I will be your faithful servant." The Stag was foolish enough to be persuaded to return, and this time the Lion made no mistake, but overpowered him, and feasted right royally upon his carcass. The Fox, meanwhile, watched his chance and, when the Lion wasn't looking, filched away the brains to reward himself for his trouble. Presently the Lion began searching for them, of course without success: and the Fox, who was watching him, said, "I don't think it's much use you're looking for the brains: a creature who twice walked into a Lion's den can't have got any."

After Reading

4. Identify a choice one of the characters has to make in the story. What lesson do you think could be taught by this choice?

Character	Choice	Lesson

5. Animals are often used symbolically. Earlier, you found that the Greek gods and goddesses have animals associated with them. How are the animals in "The Lion, the Fox, and the Stag" portrayed? What could these animals symbolize?

Lion	Fox	Stag (adult male deer)

Check Your Understanding

Think back to your wanted poster. What animal(s) could you incorporate to symbolize certain characteristics? Justify your choice by explaining each animal's symbolic meaning in connection to the story or character.

Analyzing Visual Techniques

LEARNING STRATEGIES:
Sketching, Shared Reading,
Graphic Organizer,
Think-Pair-Share

Learning Target

- Identify and apply knowledge of visual film techniques to an illustration.

Visual Techniques

Along with graphic novelists and creators of other nonprint texts, film directors make choices about the visual techniques they use. Choosing to use certain visual techniques for effect is similar to the choices writers make when using language for effect. Thinking like a director can help you practice the skills necessary to create effective illustrations that enhance the ideas of your own original myth.

Camera Point of View

The most common camera point of view, the **objective angle,** takes a neutral point of view, not representing the viewpoint of any one character. Any character may appear in scenes with objective camera angles. In the **subjective camera angle,** the camera takes on the character's point of view, as though the camera lens is the character's eyes.

1. Sketch an object in a scene using an **objective** point of view and then a **subjective** point of view.

Objective Point of View	Subjective Point of View

ACADEMIC VOCABULARY
To say that someone is being **objective** is to mean that the person is trying not to be influenced by personal opinion or beliefs in making judgments. This is the opposite of being **subjective,** which is to be influenced by personal opinions and beliefs. Notice how these meanings are applied to camera techniques.

My Notes

CAMERA ANGLE

While wanted posters feature a photograph at **eye-level,** directors, photographers and illustrators may choose to use different camera angles for different effects. **High angle** is a shot taken from above the subject; **low angle** is a shot taken from below the subject.

2. Sketch a person or object using different angles.

High Angle	Eye-Level	Low Angle

Literary Terms
The **objective camera angle** in film is equivalent to the third-person point of view in written text.

The **subjective camera angle** in film is equivalent to the first-person point of view.

Framing

Long shots, medium shots, close-up, and **extreme close-ups** are commonly used framing techniques. A **shot** is a single piece of film, uninterrupted by cuts. A long shot is framing a shot from far away, while the extreme close-up is zoomed in and close to the subject. You can frame your shots differently and can use a combination of framing techniques in your shots.

3. Sketch the same scene using all four framing techniques.

Long Shot	**Medium Shot**
Close-Up	**Extreme Close-Up**

Identifying Visual Techniques

4. In a film, the director uses a variety of visual techniques. Use the graphic organizer on the next page to record the techniques you observe.

Check Your Understanding

After completing the graphic organizer, respond to the following:

- Create a sketch for a text you have read or created so far in this unit. Consider framing, angle, point of view, color, and symbolic meaning.
- In a collaborative group, describe the changes you made to framing, angle, point of view, color use, or symbolism, and explain why you made each change. Use sharing and responding to react to your peers' explanations.

My Notes

Analyzing Visual Techniques

Clip Point of View (subjective/ objective)	Camera Angle and Evidence (high angle, eye level, low angle)	Framing and Evidence (long shot, medium shot, close-up, extreme close-up)	Symbolic Associations or Meaning of Visual Techniques

Learning Targets

- Compare the genre of informational text to fictional narratives.
- Analyze and compare creation myths.
- Create an original myth explaining a phenomenon of nature.

Before Reading

1. You will be reading an informational text about creation myths. What do you know about the genre of informational texts in comparison to fictional narratives?
   - Informational:
   - Fictional narrative:

During Reading

2. As you read the excerpt by Virginia Hamilton, mark the text to highlight words that provide information.

My Notes

Informational Text

A Note from the Author

Excerpted from Virginia Hamilton's 1988 Newbery Honor Book *In the Beginning: Creation Stories from Around the World.*

1 Myth stories about creation are different. In a prophetic[1] voice, they relate events that seem outside of time and even beyond time itself. Creation myths … go *back beyond anything that ever was* and begin *before* anything has happened.

2 The classic opening, although not the only opening, of a creation myth is "In the beginning … " The most striking purpose of a creation myth is to explain something. Yet it also asks questions and gives reasons why groups of people perform certain rituals and live in a particular way. Creation myths describe a place and time impossible for us to see for ourselves. People everywhere have creation myths, revealing how they view themselves *to themselves* in ways that are movingly personal.

3 Creation, then, means the act of bringing into existence—something. These myths from around the world were created by people who sensed the wonder and glory of the universe. Lonely as they were, by themselves, early people looked inside themselves and expressed a longing to discover, to explain who they were, why they were, and from what and where they came.

---

[1] **prophetic:** relating to a divinely inspired instruction or prediction

Creation Myths from Around the Globe

My Notes

After Reading

3. Summarize the brief informational text you just read.

Before Reading

4. Look over the following elements of nature. Describe how people in the distant past might have explained the origins of these natural phenomena.

Element	Explanation
The Sun	
The Stars	
The Earth	
The Moon	
Rainbows	
Thunder	
Snow	

During Reading

5. In the preceding text, Hamilton explains the purpose of creation myths and identifies several characteristics of these myths. Look for examples of these characteristics in the creation myths you read in the next several texts.

6. Find and mark one key incident in each story that helps explain aspects of the natural world. In the My Notes section, sketch an illustration for one of the incidents to accompany the action of the story.

7. Continue practicing diffusing any words whose meaning you are unsure of.

Two African Creation Myths

From **Voices of the Ancestors:**
African Myth

by Tony Allan, Fergus Fleming, and Charles Phillips

"Huveane and Clay People"

The Bapedi and Bavenda, Bantu tribes from Transvaal in South Africa, recount that the first human, Huveane the shepherd, was a lawless trickster who loved to make mischief.

Huveane cared for his father's goats and sheep—for although he was the first man, he had parents. One day he set about making a being of his own: he took some clay, formed a baby with it and then breathed life into it. Then he hid the baby near his parents' house. He cared for it lovingly, creeping out each dawn to feed it, but his parents noticed the dwindling supply of milk. Curious, Huveane's father followed him one day and saw the child. Taking it in his arms, he hid it beneath the house with the firewood. That evening Huveane discovered that his precious creation was missing; distraught, he slumped glumly with his parents at the fire. Distressed by his low spirits, his mother asked him to fetch some logs, whereupon he discovered the unharmed baby and capered with joy. His parents were so pleased to see him happy again that they allowed him to keep it.

"Mbombo"

The Kuba, who live in the abundant rainforest of Central Africa, call their creator god Mbombo and picture creation as a sudden eruption from his mouth. Once, according to their account, nothing existed but restless water lost in darkness—and Mbombo, a spirit who moved over the water. Then in the deep, dark hours of the first day, Mbombo was stricken by a sharp stomach pain and vomited, producing the sun, moon, and a stream of bright stars. Light fell all around him. As the sun shone, the ocean became clouds and the water level fell, revealing hills and plains. Again Mbombo's stomach convulsed, this time sending forth a wonderful and various stream of life: the tall sky, the sharp-forked lightning, deep-rooted trees, animals in all their lithe power and the first man and woman.

My Notes

_____

_____

_____

_____

_____

_____

KEY IDEAS AND DETAILS
What qualities are important to the Bapedi and Bavenda? How can you tell? Provide textual evidence to support your thinking.

_____

_____

_____

_____

_____

_____

_____

_____

_____

_____

My Notes

ABOUT THE AUTHOR
Donna Rosenberg has written several books on world mythology. She specializes in retelling myths and other stories in vivid prose that appeals to readers. Her writing is known for excellent translations that preserve the character and style of the original.

Myth

Raven and the Sources of Light

by Donna Rosenberg

1   Long ago when the world was young, the earth and all living creatures were shrouded in the darkness of an eternal night, for neither the sun nor the moon shone in the sky. It was said that a great chief who lived at the headwaters of the Nass River was keeping all this light for himself, but no one was certain, for the light was so carefully hidden that no one had ever actually seen it. The chief knew that his people were suffering, but he was a selfish man and did not care.

2   Raven was sad for his people, for he knew that without the sun the earth would not bring forth the food the Haida[1] needed to survive, and without the moon his people could not see to catch fish at night. Raven decided to rescue the light. He knew that the way from the Queen Charlotte Islands to the source of the Nass River was very long, so he collected a group of pebbles. As he flew, whenever he became tired he dropped a pebble into the sea. It immediately formed an island where Raven could alight on solid land and rest for a while.

KEY IDEAS AND DETAILS
What evidence points to Raven's great power and influence in the Haida mythology?

3   When Raven arrived at the chief's village, he said to himself, "I must find a way to live in the chief's house and capture the light." Raven thought and thought. Finally he exclaimed, "I know just the way! I will change myself into something very small and wait in the stream to be caught."

4   So Raven transformed himself into a seed and floated on the surface of the nearby stream. When the chief's daughter came to draw water, Raven was ready. No matter how she tried to drink some of the water, the seed was always in her way. Finally she tired of trying to remove it, and she drank it along with the water.

5   The woman became pregnant, and in time she gave birth to a son, who was Raven in disguise. The chief loved his grandson, and whatever the child wanted, his grandfather gave him.

6   As the boy crawled, he noticed many bags hanging on the walls of the lodge. One by one he pointed to them, and one by one his grandfather gave them to him. Finally his grandfather gave him the bag that was filled with stars. The child rolled the bag around on the floor of the lodge, then suddenly let go of it. The bag immediately rose to the ceiling, drifted through the smoke hole, and flew up into the heavens. There it burst open, spilling the stars into the sky.

---

[1] **Haida:** a Northwest/Alaskan Indian tribe

7　As the days passed, the boy still wanted to play with toys. He pointed to this bag and that box, stored here and there in grandfather's lodge. His grandfather gave him whatever he chose.

8　Finally the child cried, "Mae! Mae!" His grandfather took down a bag containing the moon and gave it to his grandson as a toy. The boy chuckled with delight as he rolled it around and around upon the floor of the lodge. Suddenly he let go of that bag just as he had let go of the bag of stars. The bag immediately rose to the ceiling, drifted through the smoke hole, and flew up into the heavens. There it burst open, spilling the moon into the sky.

9　The boy continued to play with bag after bag and box after box until one day he pointed to the last box left in the lodge. His grandfather took him upon his lap and said, "When I open this box, I am giving you the last and dearest of my possessions, the sun. Please take care of it!"

10　Then the chief closed the smoke hole and picked up the large wooden box he had kept hidden among other boxes in the shadows of one corner of the lodge. Inside the large box a second wooden box nestled in the wrappings of a spider's web, and inside that box, a third wooden box nestled. The chief opened box after box until he came to the eighth and smallest of the wooden boxes. As soon as the chief removed the sun from this box, his lodging was flooded with a brilliant light.

11　The child laughed with delight as his grandfather gave him the fiery ball to play with. He rolled the sun around the floor of the lodge until he tired of the game and pushed it aside. His grandfather then replaced the sun in its box and replaced the box inside the other seven boxes.

12　Day after day Raven and his grandfather repeated this process. Raven would point to the sun's box, play with it until he tired of it, and then watch as his grandfather put the fiery ball away into its series of boxes.

13　Finally the day came when the chief was not as careful as usual. He forgot to close the smoke hole, and he no longer watched Raven play with the fiery ball. The child resumed his Raven shape, grasped the ball of light in his claws, and flew up through the smoke hole into the sky, traveling in the direction of the river.

14　When he spied people fishing in the dark, he alighted on a tree and said to them, "If you will give me some fish, I will give you some light."

15　At first they did not believe him. They knew that the light was well hidden and that Raven was often a lazy trickster. However, when Raven raised his wing and showed enough light for them to fish with ease, they gave him part of their catch. Day after day they repeated this procedure, until Raven tired of eating fish.

16　Finally he lifted his wing, grabbed the sun with both claws and tossed it high into the sky. "Now my people will have light both day and night!" he exclaimed. And from that day until this, the sun, moon, and stars have remained in the sky.

My Notes

KEY IDEAS AND DETAILS
What is the author's purpose in writing this text?

KEY IDEAS AND DETAILS
How is it indicated in this story that the sun is the most valuable of all human possessions?

KEY IDEAS AND DETAILS
Based on the context of the two myths that identify a trickster, what do you think is a "trickster?" Find a dictionary definition and explain how it applies to these two creation myths.

Creation Myths from Around the Globe

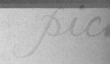

My Notes

After Reading

8. What do these last three myths have in common?

9. How are these creation myths?

Check Your Understanding

Work in a collaborative group to generate ideas for an original myth to explain a natural phenomenon. Create a poster that demonstrates those ideas. You may choose one of the natural phenomenon you explained in the "Before Reading" section of this activity or a natural phenomenon of your choice.

Be creative. Try to fill up as much of the poster (sample format below) as possible, using individual words, phrases, symbols, and visuals. Be sure to incorporate the following elements into your poster:

- The name of your natural phenomenon
- The characters (animals/gods/heroes)
- Setting of the myth
- Main conflict and character choices
- The lesson or theme of the myth

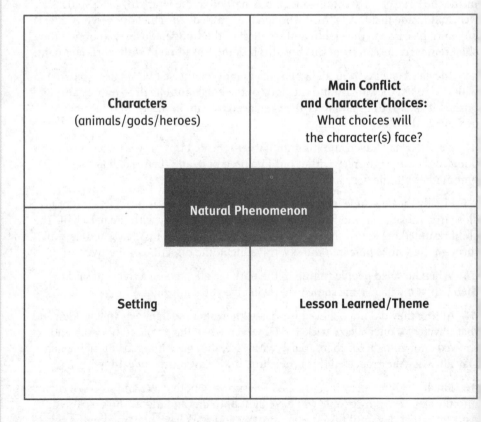

Characters (animals/gods/heroes)	**Main Conflict and Character Choices:** What choices will the character(s) face?
Natural Phenomenon	
Setting	**Lesson Learned/Theme**

Creating an Illustrated Myth

Assignment

Your assignment is to work with a partner to create an original myth that explains a belief, custom, or natural phenomenon through the actions of gods or heroes. Be sure that your myth teaches a lesson or a moral and includes illustrations that complement the myth as it unfolds.

Planning and Prewriting: Take time to make a plan for your illustrated myth.

- How can you use the stories from the unit as models for your own myth?

- How will you choose possible natural phenomena that you could explain in your myth?

- Which prewriting strategy (such as the plot diagram or outline) will you use to plan the organization?

Drafting: Create a draft that includes the elements of an effective narrative.

- How will you hook the reader with an engaging opening or lead?

- How will you apply your knowledge of sensory and figurative language and purposeful dialogue to vividly tell a story?

- How will you show the characters' responses to the event, including their thoughts and feelings?

- How will you express the lesson learned or the significance of the experience?

- How will you find or create illustrations to capture key parts of your myth?

Evaluating and Revising the Draft: Create opportunities to review and revise your work.

- During the process of writing, when will you share your work with your writing group?

- What is your plan to include suggestions and revision ideas into your draft?

- How can the Scoring Guide help you self-evaluate how well your draft meets the requirements of the assignment?

Checking and Editing: Confirm that your final draft is ready for publication.

- How will you proofread and edit your draft to demonstrate command of the conventions of standard English capitalization, punctuation, spelling, grammar, and usage?

- How will you create a title and assemble your illustrations in an appealing manner?

- What technology tools could you use to prepare a final draft for publication?

Reflection

After completing this Embedded Assessment, think about how you went about accomplishing this task, and respond to the following:

- Reflect on the process you used to come up with an original myth. How did reading and studying the myths in this unit help prepare you to write your own myth?

My Notes

Technology TIP:

Avoid using images in a way that would violate copyright law. You may download or copy an image for personal use and provide the source, but you may not broadcast the image without the owner's permission.

Creating an Illustrated Myth

SCORING GUIDE

Scoring Criteria	Exemplary	Proficient	Emerging	Incomplete
Ideas	The myth • describes a natural phenomenon and includes the idea of choice while cleverly teaching a lesson • skillfully uses story elements to engage the reader and lead to a satisfying resolution • includes vivid visuals that use effective symbolism for the ideas in the myth.	The myth • explains a natural phenomenon and teaches a lesson • uses story elements to hook the reader and create a satisfying resolution • includes visuals that connect the ideas in the myth.	The myth • does not explain a natural phenomenon or teach a lesson • is hard to follow and does not include sufficient narrative elements to aid the reader • includes few if any visuals to demonstrate the ideas in the myth.	The myth • does not tell about a natural phenomenon or teach a lesson • does not use narrative elements • has no visuals to support the myth or demonstrate ideas.
Structure	The myth • is well organized and clearly follows the plot structure of a story • uses transitions to skillfully guide the reader.	The myth • uses essential story elements and follows a plot structure • uses some transitions to move between ideas.	The myth • is not well organized and includes only some elements of plot structure • includes few, if any, transitions.	The myth • is disorganized and difficult to follow • does not follow plot structure • includes no transitions.
Use of Language	The myth • effectively uses figurative language and sensory details to vividly "show" the incident • has few or no errors in grammar, spelling, punctuation, or capitalization.	The myth • includes details to enhance the descriptions of characters and setting • contains few errors in grammar, spelling, punctuation, or capitalization, and they do not detract from meaning.	The myth • includes details that do not fit the story or descriptions that are not complete • contains mistakes in grammar, spelling, punctuation, and capitalization that detract from meaning.	The myth • describes details in confusing language • contains errors in grammar, spelling, punctuation, and capitalization that interfere with meaning.

What Influences My Choices?

Visual Prompt: How do you use different sources of information to help you make decisions about what to buy or to do?

Unit Overview

People choose to do something, buy something, or think a certain way for many reasons. Often, it's because they have seen something in the media promoting it. In this unit, you will analyze print, visual, and film texts that are common in the media and advertising. You will also investigate how advertising influences the lives of youth by critically reading and viewing informational text and film. You will analyze the components of argumentation by reading argumentative essays, news articles, and speeches. By the end of the unit, you will become a skilled reader and writer of a variety of nonfiction texts, an engaged collaborator in discussion groups, and an effective argumentative writer.

What Influences My Choices?

GOALS:

- To understand how our lives are affected by media and advertising
- To engage in collaborative discussions
- To write an expository essay
- To identify and analyze the use of appeals, language, and rhetorical devices in informational and argumentative texts
- To write an argumentative essay

ACADEMIC VOCABULARY
text features
hypothesize
credibility
inference
primary source
secondary source
search term
valid
norm
consensus
claim
counterclaim

Literary Terms
expository writing
documentary film
rhetoric

Contents

Texts not included in these materials.

Previewing the Unit

LEARNING STRATEGIES:
Think-Pair-Share, Close
Reading, Marking the Text,
Paraphrasing, Brainstorming,
Quickwrite, Freewriting

My Notes

Learning Targets

- Preview the big ideas and vocabulary for the unit.
- Identify and analyze the skills and knowledge needed to complete Embedded Assessment 1 successfully.

Making Connections

You see some form of advertising around you every day. What catches your attention? Is it television? Internet ads? Print ads? Radio? Advertising influences the choices that you make. You might also be influenced by other things, such as what people are saying on social media or what people are wearing or doing on television. In this unit, you will examine various types of media and the techniques they use to convince you to buy their products.

Essential Questions

Based on your current knowledge, how would you answer these questions?

1. What role does advertising play in the lives of youth?

2. What makes an effective argument?

Developing Vocabulary

Mark the Academic Vocabulary and Literary Terms on the Contents page using the **QHT** strategy.

Unpacking Embedded Assessment 1

Read the assignment below for Embedded Assessment 1: Writing an Expository Essay and Engaging in a Collaborative Discussion found on page 126.

> Your assignment is to write an expository essay that explains the role of advertising in the lives of youth and then to exchange ideas in a collaborative discussion. For your essay, you may use as sources the articles in this unit and at least one additional informational text that you have researched.

With your classmates, identify what you will need to do for the assessment. Create a graphic organizer to list the skills and knowledge you will need to accomplish these tasks. To help you complete the graphic organizer, be sure to review the criteria in the Scoring Guide for Embedded Assessment 1.

INDEPENDENT READING LINK

In the first part of this unit, you will be reading informational texts about marketing to kids. outside reading, choose es about advertising or line advertising. You choose one of your nds and read about s well as how it ucts.

What Is the Issue?

Learning Targets
- Identify text features in informational texts as a strategy to better comprehend ideas and information.
- Closely read an informational text to identify issues and questions.

Before Reading

1. In this part of the unit, you will be reading informational texts. Based on prior knowledge, how do you think informational texts are different from fictional text?

Informational texts usually follow a different structure than short stories or other fiction. For example, you might find the following **text features** in an informational text:

- **Organizing features** such as a table of contents, glossary, index, and references.
- **Text divisions** such as introductions, summaries, sections with headings, footnotes or endnotes, and author information.
- **Graphics** that present information in a visual format, such as diagrams, charts, tables, graphs, maps, timelines, and so on. Graphics support the information and ideas presented in the text.
- **Special formatting** such as boldface, italics, numbered or bulleted text, or the use of different typefaces and sizes. For example, in this list, the types of text features are placed in boldface to draw attention to them.

When you read the informational texts in this part of the unit, notice the features of each text.

2. **Quickwrite:** To begin exploring the topic of the role of advertising in the lives of young people, respond to the following question on a separate sheet of paper: How is advertising to young people different from other advertising?

3. Skim and scan the article that follows to note the text features. To *skim* means to read quickly to form an overall impression; to *scan* means to read with a focus on key words, phrases, or specific details in order to find information.

    a. What impression did you get from the text after quickly skimming and scanning? What did you notice?

    b. What can you predict the article will be about?

LEARNING STRATEGIES:
Skimming and Scanning, Marking the Text, Paraphrasing, Brainstorming, Quickwrite

---

ACADEMIC VOCABULARY
Text features are aspects of a text designed to help you locate, understand, and organize information.

My Notes

What Is the Issue?

During Reading

4. Mark the text to note interesting or surprising statistics or information. Use the My Notes section to write any questions you might have or comments in response to the text.

Informational Text

$211 Billion
and So Much to Buy
American Youths, the New Big Spenders

Youths are extremely engaged in all aspects of technology and media and influence family purchases. Plus they have huge spending power of their own.

New York, N.Y. – October 26, 2011 – Eight to 24 year olds are ready to spend money in 2012. Two-hundred eleven billion dollars, to be more precise. According to the 2012 Harris Poll Youth Pulse^{SM} study, the purchasing power of today's youth is something that should not be overshadowed by the spending power of adults. Over half of eight to 12 year olds will spend their own money on candy (61%) and toys (55%) while a quarter will buy books (28%) and one-in-five will purchase clothing (19%). Teens, those 13–17, still crave candy, and half (51%) will make a point of treating themselves to sweets. However, clothing (42%) and entertainment, like movie tickets (33%) have become bigger priorities for this older group.

The 2012 Harris Poll Youth Pulse study was conducted online among 5,077 U.S youth ages 8–24 in August 2011.

While the purchasing power of today's youth is strong, it is made even stronger when coupled with the influence these kids have on what parents buy. For example, seven-in-ten teens have cell phones (69%) and three-in-ten have smartphones (30%). When it comes to smartphone or cell phones, one-third of teens (34%) say they influenced that purchase decision. With over 23 million teens in the United States, that's a lot of influence.

"When we look at what youth today personally own, it's definitely more than the generation before them and immensely more than what kids owned two generations ago. What is also important to remember is that youths are not passive receivers of things," said Regina A. Corso, Senior Vice President for Youth and Education Research at Harris Interactive. "Today's youth actively have input into what they have and what their families have."

Youth and media

Tweens, teens, and young adults have not only more things than previous generations, they also have more consistent, available access to vast amounts of information than their parent or grandparent could have imagined in their youths. Accessibility is made easy by the click of a mouse or the tap of a screen. In fact, over three-quarters of 8–9 year olds (76%) and up to nine-in-ten 16–17 year olds (91%) are on the Internet an hour or more a day, excluding email.

GRAMMAR&USAGE
Prepositional Phrases

A **preposition** links the noun or pronoun following it (its object) to another word in a sentence. Prepositional phrases add specific or necessary detail in sentences. They function as adjectives or adverbs.

Adjective phrase modifying the noun *power*: ". . . purchasing power *of today's youth* . . ."

Adverb phrase modifying the verb *overshadowed* ". . . should not be overshadowed *by the spending power of adults*."

Use prepositional phrases to add specific details to your writing. Take care to use correct subject-verb agreement. When ... ositional phrase ...es the subject and ... verb agrees with the ... with the object of ... nal phrase.

When looking at all types of media, on average, tweens spend 8.4 hours engaged versus teens, who spend 12.6 hours engaged with media per day. On average, teens spend 3.6 hours per day online, 2.9 hours watching television, and 1.6 hours each playing video games and listening to an MP3 player.

These visuals also show how tweens and teens spend money.

Percent that will personally buy or influence the purchase by others in the next few months

	8-12 year olds	13-17 year olds	18-24 year olds
Tickets to entertainment/sporting	40%	43%	45%
Hand held video games	35%	20%	17%
Video game system	31%	27%	24%
Cell phone/smart phone	22%	30%	29%
Digital media player	21%	24%	20%
Computer	17%	24%	28%
TV	12%	17%	20%
Camera	10%	20%	18%
Camcorder or video camera	7%	14%	13%
New car/truck/SUV	Not asked	18%	19%

Source: *Trends & Tudes,* Harris Interactive Youth & Education Research, 2010.

After Reading

5. Revisit your response to the Quickwrite question in Item 2. Add to your response by summarizing at least two relevant details from the text you just read. Can you begin to predict possible issues relating to advertising and youth?

Collaborative Discussion: For the next questions, you will participate in a collaborative discussion of the text "$211 Billon and So Much to Buy—American Youths, the New Big Spenders." As you and a partner discuss the text, remember the guidelines for effective collaborative discussions. Practice effective communication as you and your partner discuss the article and your responses to the ideas in the text. Remember to add to and adjust your own ideas as you hear and discuss your partner's thoughts. To review the elements of collaborative discussion, read the table on the next page.

My Notes

KEY IDEAS AND DETAILS
How does the chart at the left support the introductory points made in the article's first two paragraphs?

KEY IDEAS AND DETAILS
How does the information in the chart at left relate to the importance of a relationship between youth and advertising?

What Is the Issue?

Collaborative Discussions

All group members should do the following:

- Be prepared for the discussion by reading or writing ahead of time.
- Be polite; discuss the topic, not a person in the group.
- Be alert; use appropriate eye contact and engage with other group members.
- Take turns speaking and listening; everyone should have an opportunity to share ideas.
- Keep the goals of the discussion in mind; stay on topic and watch the time to make sure you meet deadlines.
- Ask questions to help guide the discussion.
- Paraphrase others' comments to ensure understanding; adjust your own ideas based on evidence provided by group members.

Paraphrase the points above by writing the actions you will take in group discussions, as both a speaker and a listener.

As a speaker, I will ...	As a listener, I will ...

6. How does the structure of the text and presentation of information contribute to your understanding of this writer's ideas?

7. What do you think is the writer's purpose in writing this text? What is the point of view?

8. Brainstorm a list of questions you have about the issue of advertising, media, and youth.

Check Your Understanding

Explain how text features help you understand a text. Include information from at least one specific text feature in your answer.

Analyzing Informational Text

Learning Targets
- Identify factors that affect consumer choices and discuss relevant facts with a partner.
- Draft and evaluate an original research question.

Before Reading

1. **Anticipation Guide:** Before you read the article on the next page, read the statements below and mark each statement as either true or false in the "Before Reading" column.

My Notes

Before Reading	After Reading	
		1. The average American child is exposed to almost 22,000 television commercials a year.
		2. American youth typically spend more time with various media (TV, iPods, cell phones, and instant messaging) than they do in the classroom.
		3. Twenty-five percent of kids say that buying a certain product makes them feel better about themselves.
		4. American children aged 12 to 17 will ask their parents for products they have seen advertised an average of three times until the parents finally give in.
		5. Over half of American kids say that nagging their parents for products almost always works.
		6. Advertising aimed at children is estimated at $5 billion.

2. Preview the text "Facts About Marketing to Children" by skimming and scanning for text features. What features do you notice? How is this text arranged? What is the purpose of this text arrangement?

During Reading

3. Mark the text with textual evidence you find that connects to each Anticipation Guide statement. Write the number of the statement in the margin of the article.

WORD CONNECTIONS

Multiple Meaning Words

Market (noun) refers not only to a place to buy goods, but also generally to the world of business and commerce.

Market (verb) means "to offer for sale." *Marketers* plan how products will be sold and advertised to customers.

My Notes

Informational Text

Facts About Marketing to Children

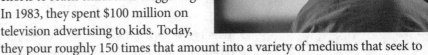

from The Center for a New American Dream

Children as Targets

- Advertising directed at children is estimated at over $15 billion annually—about 2.5 times more than what it was in 1992.

- Over the past two decades, the degree to which marketers have scaled up efforts to reach children is staggering. In 1983, they spent $100 million on television advertising to kids. Today, they pour roughly 150 times that amount into a variety of mediums that seek to infiltrate every corner of children's worlds.[1]

- According to a leading expert on branding, 80 percent of all global brands now deploy a "tween strategy."[2]

Commercial Television

- The average American child today is exposed to an estimated 40,000 television commercials a year—over 100 a day.[3]

- A task force of the American Psychological Association (APA) has recommended restrictions on advertising that targets children under the age of eight, based on research showing that children under this age are unable to critically comprehend televised advertising messages and are prone to accept advertiser messages as truthful, accurate and unbiased.[4]

[1] Juliet Schor, *Born to Buy: The Commercialized Child and the New Consumer Culture* (New York: Scribner, 2004), 21.

[2] Ann Hulbert, "Tweens 'R' Us," *The New York Times*, November 28, 2004, www.nytimes.com/2004/11/28/magazine/28WWLN.html?ex=1259384400&%2338;en=056ae35fb63f65eb&%2338;ei=5088& (accessed March 8, 2006).

[3] American Psychological Association, "Television Advertising Leads to Unhealthy Habits in Children; Says APA Task Force," February 23, 2004, (accessed March 8, 2006).

[4] Ibid.

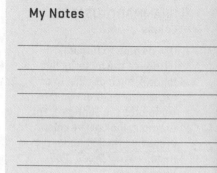

Beyond the Tube

- According to the Kaiser Family Foundation, youth are multitasking their way through a wide variety of electronic media daily, juggling iPods and instant messaging with TV and cell phones. In fact, they pack 8.5 hours of media exposure into 6.5 hours each day, seven days a week—which means that they spend more time plugged in than they do in the classroom.[5]

- By the mid 1990s, direct marketing, promotions, and sponsorships actually accounted for 80 percent of marketing dollars.[6]

New Dream Poll, "Nag Factor"

According to a national survey commissioned by the Center for a New American Dream:

- American children aged 12 to 17 will ask their parents for products they have seen advertised an average of nine times until the parents finally give in.

- More than 10 percent of 12- to 13-year-olds admitted to asking their parents more than 50 times for products they have seen advertised.

- More than half of the children surveyed (53%) said that buying certain products makes them feel better about themselves. The number is even higher among 12- to 13-year-olds: 62% say that buying certain products makes them feel better about themselves.

- Nearly a third of those surveyed (32%) admitted to feeling pressure to buy certain products such as clothes and CDs because their friends have them. Over half of 12- to 13-year-olds (54%) admitted to feeling such pressure.

- The nagging strategy is paying dividends for kids and marketers alike: 55% of kids surveyed said they are usually successful in getting their parents to give in.[7]

What Kids Really Want

- According to a 2003 New American Dream poll, 57 percent of children age 9–14 would rather do something fun with their mom or dad than go to the mall to go shopping.[8]

In Schools

- The American Beverage Association (formerly National Soft Drink Association) at one point estimated that nearly two thirds of schools nationwide had exclusive "pouring rights" contracts with soda companies.[9]

---

[5] Donald F. Roberts, Ulla G. Foehr, Victoria Rideout, *Generation M: Media in the Lives of 8–18 Year-Olds*, The Henry J. Kaiser Family Foundation, March 9, 2005, www.kff.org/entmedia/7251.cfm (accessed March 9, 2006).

[6] Schor, 85.

[7] "Thanks to Ads, Kids Won't Take No, No, No, No, No, No, No, No, No for an Answer," Center for a New American Dream, 2002, www.newdream.org/kids/poll.php (accessed March 5, 2006).

[8] "What Do Kids Really Want That Money Can't Buy?" Center for a New American Dream, 2003, www.newdream.org/publications/bookrelease.php (accessed March 8, 2006).

[9] Katherine Battle Horgen, "Big Food, Big Money, Big Children," in *Childhood Lost: How American Culture is Failing Our Kids,* Sharna Olfman, ed, 128. (Westport, Connecticut: Praeger Publishers, 2005).

[10] American Psychological Association, 2004.

My Notes

KEY IDEAS AND DETAILS
According to the text, how much of a youth's day is spent using technology? What might be the advantages and disadvantages for youth to be "plugged in" this much?

KEY IDEAS AND DETAILS
What is the function of footnotes in an informational article such as this one?

WORD CONNECTIONS

Foreign Words

Footnotes and endnotes sometimes contain foreign words such as *ibid* and *et al.* (short for *et alia*). *Ibid* means "in the same place" and refers to a previous reference. *Et al.* means "and others" and is used to refer to a list of people.

Analyzing Informational Text

pic

GRAMMAR & USAGE
Colons

Use a **colon** to formally introduce the material that follows, such as a list or an explanatory statement that completes the sentence. For example, look at the colon preceding the list under the heading *New Dream Poll, "Nag Factor."*

On this page, notice the colon after the short headings that introduce the topic of the sentences that follow.

Do not use a colon between a preposition or a verb and the rest of the sentence.

Harming Children's Well-Being

- Obesity: Rising levels of childhood obesity track an explosion of junk food ads in recent years.[10]

- Emotional well-being: Author and Boston College sociology professor Juliet Schor finds links between immersion in consumer culture and depression, anxiety, low self-esteem, and conflicts with parents.[11]

- Financial self-control: National surveys reveal that kids are leaving high school without a basic understanding of issues relating to savings and credit card debt. No surprise, then, that over the past decade, credit card debt among 18–24 year olds more than doubled.[12]

After Reading

4. Advertising like that described in the article is directed at your age group. How might information such as this help you make different choices in your buying decisions?

5. Summarize the central ideas in this text (just the main ideas, not the statistics).

6. Based on this text, how do you think advertising directed at children influences what they buy or ask their parents to buy?

My Notes

Check Your Understanding

What text features did you notice in this text? How do they contribute to the development of the ideas in the text and to the text as a whole?

[10] American Psychological Association, 2004.

[11] Schor, 167–172.

[12] "Young People Taking on More Debt," www.pbs.org/newshour/extra/features/jan-june05/debt_5-25.html (accessed March 8, 2006).

Preparing for Research

If you were using the previous article to research the topic of marketing to young people, what additional information would you want to know? Identifying what you need to know is a part of the research process.

7. How familiar are you with the research process? For each step in the anticipation guide below, circle the word that best describes what you know about that step.

Research Process		
1. Identify the topic, issue, or problem to be researched.	Familiar	Somewhat Familiar	Not Familiar
2. Write questions that can be answered through research.	Familiar	Somewhat Familiar	Not Familiar
3. Gather evidence; write additional questions to narrow or broaden research.	Familiar	Somewhat Familiar	Not Familiar
4. Evaluate sources for reliability and relevance.	Familiar	Somewhat Familiar	Not Familiar
5. Draw conclusions about findings.	Familiar	Somewhat Familiar	Not Familiar
6. Communicate findings.	Familiar	Somewhat Familiar	Not Familiar

Choosing a Research Topic

In this unit, you will be researching the influence of advertising on young people. When choosing your own topic for research, you might consider several approaches:

- Brainstorm ideas with a partner.
- Write down any ideas that come to mind about topics that interest you.
- Choose an interesting general topic about which you would like to know more. An example of a general topic might be "The Toy Industry in America" or "Films of the 1950s."
- Do some preliminary research on your general topic to see what's already been done and to help you narrow your focus. What questions does this early research raise?

Analyzing Informational Text

My Notes

_____

_____

_____

_____

_____

_____

_____

_____

_____

_____

_____

_____

_____

_____

Writing a Research Question

A research question is a clear, focused, concise, and complex question around which you center your research. Research questions help you focus your research by providing a path through the research process. Creating research questions will help you work toward supporting a clear thesis.

To write a research question:

- **Think about your general topic.** What do you want to know?
- **Consider the purpose of your research.** Will you be writing a paper, making a presentation, holding a discussion?
- **Consider your audience.** For most school research, your audience will be academic, but always keep your audience in mind when narrowing your topic and developing your question. Would that particular audience be interested in this question?
- **Start asking questions.** Ask open-ended "how" and "why" questions about your general topic to help you think of different areas of your topic.
- **Evaluate your possible questions.** Research questions should not be answerable with a simple "yes" or "no" or by easily found facts. They should, instead, require both research and analysis on the part of the researcher. Which of these questions can be considered effective research questions?
  1. How did Abraham Lincoln get the 13th Amendment to the Constitution passed?
  2. When was slavery abolished in the United States?
  3. What book did Fredrick Douglass write during the abolitionist movement?
  4. Why were slave narratives effective tools in working to abolish slavery?
- **Hypothesize possible answers.** After you have written your research question, think about the path you think the answer will take and how that path will help guide your research.

8. Practice writing research questions about the influence of advertising on young people. Write at least five possible questions.

> **Research Topic:** The influence of advertising in the lives of youth

Research Questions:

ACADEMIC VOCABULARY

To **hypothesize** means to propose an explanation for something or make an assumption or guess. Your guess or assumption is a **hypothesis**. Notice the relationship between *hypothesis*, which is a guess or proposed explanation, and the word *thesis*, which is the purpose statement of an essay.

_____

_____

_____

_____

_____

_____

_____

_____

How Do They Do It? Analyzing Ads

Learning Targets
- Identify advertising techniques used in advertisements.
- Write an expository response describing the effectiveness of advertising techniques in an advertisement.

Advertising Techniques

1. To understand how advertisers market to teens, it is important to understand the many persuasive advertising techniques they use to make people want to purchase their products. Read the descriptions of advertising techniques that follow. Then, paraphrase and create a visual representation of each technique. Your visualization may include both words and symbols.

2. As you read about the techniques, think about the **cause and effect** relationship in advertising. For example, with bandwagon the persuasion may be that "Everyone is buying this product (cause), so you should buy this product, too (effect)." With the avant-garde appeal, it might be "This product is the newest on the market (cause), and you should be one of the first to have it (effect)."

LEARNING STRATEGIES:
Paraphrasing, Visualizing, Graphic Organizer

WORD CONNECTIONS

Roots & Affixes

Persuade comes from a Latin word meaning "to advise or urge." The root *-suad-* is also related to "sweet." To persuade, then, is to present an argument in a pleasing manner.

Technique	Paraphrase	Visualize
Bandwagon: Advertisers make it seem that everyone is buying this product, so you feel you should buy it, too. For example, an ad for a new video game may claim: "The ultimate online game is sweeping the nation! Everyone is playing! Join the fun!" This statement is intended to make you feel left out if you are not playing.		
Avant-Garde: This technique is the opposite of bandwagon. Advertisers make it seem that the product is so new that you will be the first on the block to have it. The idea is that only supercool people like you will even know about this product.		
Testimonials: Advertisers use both celebrities and regular people to endorse products. For example, a famous actor might urge consumers to buy a certain car. Pay close attention: Sometimes the celebrity does not actually say that he or she uses the product.		

How Do They Do It? Analyzing Ads

Technique	Paraphrase	Visualize
Facts and Figures: Statistics, percentages, and numbers are used to convince you that this product is better or more effective than another product. However, be aware of what the numbers are actually saying. What does "30 percent more effective than the leading brand" really mean?		
Transfer: To recognize this technique, pay attention to the background of the ad or to the story of the commercial. The transfer technique wants you to associate the good feelings created in the ad with the product. For example, a commercial showing a happy family eating soup may want you to associate a feeling of comfort and security with their soup products.		

3. What advertising techniques might you see together in one ad? Why would they work well together to influence an audience?

4. As you look at print, online, or television advertisements, analyze the use of advertising techniques. Circle the technique(s) used in the ads, and provide evidence for each technique used.

Advertisement	Persuasive Techniques + Evidence from Ad
Source:	Bandwagon:
Product:	Avant-Garde:
Target Audience:	Testimonials:
	Facts and Figures:
	Transfer:

Advertisement	Persuasive Techniques + Evidence from Ad
Source:	Bandwagon:
Product:	Avant-Garde:
Target Audience:	Testimonials:
	Facts and Figures:
	Transfer:
Source:	Bandwagon:
Product:	Avant-Garde:
Target Audience:	Testimonials:
	Facts and Figures:
	Transfer:

5. Think about an advertisement that you consider interesting and effective. You might consider if you or someone you know would buy this product based on the advertisement. Which persuasive technique does the advertiser use successfully? What is the cause/effect relationship being suggested?

Expository Writing

In contrast to narrative, whose purpose is to tell a story, the primary purpose of **expository writing** is to provide information. Expository paragraphs follow a specific structure:

- **Topic sentence:** A sentence that presents a topic and the writer's claim about or position on the topic.
- **Transitions:** Words and phrases used to connect ideas (*for example, however, on the other hand*).
- **Supporting information:** Specific and relevant facts and details that are appropriate for the topic.
- **Commentary:** Sentences that explain how the detail is relevant to the topic sentence.
- **Concluding Statement:** A final piece of commentary (*as a result, overall, in conclusion*) that supports the explanation. The concluding sentence brings a sense of closure to the paragraph.

> **Literary Terms**
> **Expository writing** is a form of writing whose purpose is to explain or inform.

> **WORD CONNECTIONS**
>
> Analogies
>
> An analogy may show a part-to-whole relationship in which the first word is part of the second word. In a whole-to-part relationship, the opposite occurs. Which of the following has a part-to-whole relationship like that in *topic sentence : paragraph*?
> a. exclamation point : period
> b. chapter : book
> c. book : movie

My Notes

Expository Writing Prompt: Write a response explaining how an advertisement you identified in question 4 tries to influence its target audience. Be sure to:

- Introduce and develop your topic with relevant details/examples from the advertisement.
- Use transitions, the precise language of advertising techniques, and formal style.
- Include a concluding statement that supports your explanation.

Language and Writer's Craft: Revising for Cohesion and Clarity

Cohesion and **clarity** in writing refer to how ideas flow together. A way to write with cohesion and clarity is to use the **TLQ** format when writing a detail sentence. The **TLQ** format includes:

T—Transition word or phrase such as:

For example,

According to

To illustrate,

In this case,

In addition,

Most important,

Likewise,

Finally,

L—Lead-in: The lead-in is usually a phrase that sets the context for the specific information that follows; it often answers the question "Where?" or "When?"

Q—Quote: A quote may be used to support the topic. The "quote" portion of the detail sentence does not always need to be a direct quote in quotation marks; it can be paraphrased material explaining the fact, detail, or example.

EXAMPLE: For instance [**transition**], in the magazine advertisement for Gatorade sports drink [**lead in**], the ad uses the technique of testimonial by showing a picture of Major League Baseball player Derek Jeter holding up his fist to the fans and by including text under the picture stating "Gatorade has always been a part of Derek Jeter's team." [**quote**]

Check Your Understanding

Use TLQ to evaluate the writing you did for the Expository Writing Prompt above. Revise to improve the lead-in, add quotations, or change or add transitions.

Advertising for All

Learning Targets

- Analyze advertising for commonly used products and identify their target buyers.
- Evaluate the impact of brands and celebrity endorsements on product purchases.

The Effect of Advertising on Consumers

Just about every type of media is supported by advertising. Advertising refers to any form of communication—print, video, sound—that businesses and organizations use to try to convince people to buy their products. Commercials appear throughout TV shows, and ads fill many pages of a magazine. Both commercials and ads are common online.

When you go to your favorite website, you will likely see pop-up ads for several products. Advertising dollars support companies using the Internet, making many of their services free to users. Advertisers hope that their advertising dollars will draw Internet users to buy their products.

1. Respond to the questions that follow:
   - Where else do you see ads?

   - Do you ever see ads in your school? If so, where and when?

2. Now, with your discussion group, talk about your impressions, feelings, and reactions to advertisements. Are they necessary, annoying, interesting, or funny? Are they effective? Be sure to practice the skills necessary to engage in a collaborative discussion.

Collaborative discussion sentence starters
Are you saying that ...
Can you please clarify?
To share an idea, ...
Another idea is to ...
What if we tried ...
I have an idea, ...
I see your point, but what about ...
Another way of looking at it is ...
I'm still not convinced that ...
How did you reach your conc lusion?
What makes you think that?

LEARNING STRATEGIES:
Webbing, Discussion Groups, Brainstorming

My Notes

Advertising for All

Consumer Choices

3. Think about some of the things you recently bought. Next to each category in the chart below, list at least one specific item that you spent money on or had someone else buy for you within the past year. You may leave some categories blank. In the last column, note whether or not you saw an advertisement for the product before you made the purchase.

Category	Brand, Name, or Title of Product	Saw Ad?
Personal Item (e.g., clothing, shoes, sports equipment, makeup, hobby supplies)		
Entertainment (e.g., music, movies, video games)		
Technology (e.g., computer, phone, mobile devices, accessories, apps)		
Food/Beverage (e.g., fast food, snacks, sports drinks, bottled water)		
Other:		

4. Choose one of your purchases for which you saw an ad. Who was the target consumer for this ad? How do you know? What techniques were used?

5. Are you influenced by advertisements? Explain.

Celebrities and Marketing

6. With a partner or a small group, identify famous singers, musicians, actors, or sports figures who have influenced how people dress or behave.

Celebrity	Influence

7. Many celebrities earn millions of dollars promoting products to consumers. Working again in pairs or groups, identify two celebrities who regularly promote particular products.

Celebrity	Product	Have you bought this product, or do you know someone who has?
Class example:		

My Notes

Advertising for All

Expository Writing Prompt: Respond to the following question in a well-developed paragraph: Why can celebrities have a significant influence on consumer choices? Be sure to:

- Introduce your topic clearly.
- Develop your topic with relevant details and examples.
- Express your ideas with precise, clear language, and avoid wordiness.

(Topic Sentence) Celebrities can have significant influence on consumer choices because ...

(Example/Detail) For example, ...

(Commentary) This examples shows ...

(Example/Detail) Another example, ...

(Commentary) This example shows ...

(Example/Detail) One last example, or Finally ...

(Commentary) This example shows ...

Writing Research Questions

Keeping the topic of marketing to children and young people in mind, write at least two more research questions.

Evaluating Sources: How Credible Are They?

Learning Targets

- Evaluate research sources for authority, accuracy, credibility, timeliness, and purpose/audience.
- Distinguish between primary and secondary sources.
- Evaluate an Internet website's content and identity to determine appropriate Internet sources for research.

Research Sources

After choosing a topic and writing research questions, the next step is to find sources of information. Sources might be books, magazines, documentary films, or online information. Not all sources are equal, however. Some are better than others. Learning how to tell the difference is a skill you need both for your academic success and your life.

Evaluating Sources

1. You can evaluate both print and online resources using five separate criteria. Predict the definition of each criterion and write your prediction. Take notes from your peers and teacher to complete each definition.

Source Criteria	Definition
1. Authority	
2. Accuracy	
3. Credibility	
4. Timeliness	
5. Purpose/Audience	

LEARNING STRATEGIES:
Predicting, Note-taking, Graphic Organizer

My Notes

ACADEMIC VOCABULARY
Credibility comes from the word *credible*, which means "believable or trustworthy."

Evaluating Sources: How Credible Are They?

My Notes

2. Look back at the two informational texts in this unit. For each text, write the title in the graphic organizer below. Then analyze how well the texts meet each of the criteria. Check that you have correct definitions for each term.

Text 1:	Text 2:
Authority:	Authority:
Accuracy:	Accuracy:
Credibility:	Credibility:
Timeliness:	Timeliness:
Purpose/Audience:	Purpose/Audience:

3. Do you think one of these sources is more credible or worthy of your trust than the other? Explain why.

During Reading

4. Read the following excerpt from the Mars website. Mark the text to highlight words or phrases that connect to the topic of marketing to young people.

Online Text "Not Marketing to Children"
from Mars webpage

One important aspect of the Mars Marketing Code is our commitment not to direct advertisements to children under 12 years of age. In 2007, we were the first food company to announce a global commitment to stop advertising food, snack and confectionery products to children under 12.

Specifically, we do not buy advertising time or space if more than a quarter of the audience is likely to be under 12 and we do not advertise on websites aimed at those under 13. Visitors to most of our web pages have to enter their birth date before downloading branded wallpapers or screensavers or participating in activities. Our advertisements and promotions never **depict** unaccompanied children under 12 eating snack foods, nor do we use them as spokespeople for our brands.

We continue to use established brand characters such as the M&M'S® Characters, but will **refrain from** creating new characters with child appeal for chocolate, gum and confections. The actions and speech of the M&M'S® Characters are intended for an audience over 12 years of age, and we continue to emphasize their mature personalities and adult characteristics.

Our Marketing Code also states that Mars does not place vending machines offering our snack food products in primary schools and does not offer

KEY IDEAS AND DETAILS
The first paragraph states that Mars is committed to not marketing to children. How does it support this statement? Why might the company want readers to know about its commitment?

Mars-branded educational materials or sponsor sporting events at primary schools, except in connection with established educational or public service messaging programs on responsible gum disposal and oral health care, or upon the request of schools.

We are a member of the International Food and Beverage Alliance (IFBA) industry coalition, which commits member companies to upholding shared marketing standards. The IFBA monitors its members' performance, and a third party audits a sample of ten countries with a global spread.

In addition to our global Marketing Code, we have signed country-specific marketing pledges around the world.

After Reading

5. Use the graphic organizer below to further analyze the text. Make inferences—conclusions based on details in the text—and cite specific evidence to support your inferences.

	Mars
Role Who is the author? Where is this text published?	Inference: Evidence:
Audience Who is the intended audience?	Inference: Evidence:
Format How does the format match the intended audience?	Inference: Evidence:
Topic What is the purpose of this text? What is the point of view of the company regarding marketing to youth?	Inference: Evidence:

6. How would you rate this website and text for the five criteria for evaluating sources? Explain your reasoning.

KEY IDEAS AND DETAILS
How does the phrase "or upon the request of schools" affect the claim that the company does not sponsor sporting events at primary schools?

KEY IDEAS AND DETAILS
Choose one of the claims in the text. How accurate is this claim? How credible is this source?

My Notes

Evaluating Sources: How Credible Are They?

pi

ACADEMIC VOCABULARY

A **primary source** is an original account or record created at the time of an event by someone who witnessed or was involved in it. Autobiographies, letters, and government records are types of primary sources. **Secondary sources** analyze, interpret, or critique primary sources. Textbooks, books about historical events, and works of criticism, such as movie and book reviews, are secondary sources.

WORD CONNECTIONS

Idioms

You may have heard the phrase "going to the source." It means going to the original document or person who knows about an event first hand. The closer to the source, the more credible the research information is likely to be.

My Notes

_____

_____

_____

_____

_____

_____

_____

_____

_____

_____

_____

_____

_____

_____

_____

Primary and Secondary Sources

When choosing credible research sources, you will find **primary and secondary sources**. Primary sources are original documents; they are often used in historical research. For example, if you are researching the era of the Civil War, you might use the primary resource of Lincoln's *Gettysburg Address*. You might find that speech in a secondary source written about the Civil War or on the Internet.

7. Look at the two texts you have read. Are they primary or secondary sources? How do you know?

Evaluating Online Resources

Anyone can publish on the World Wide Web. This openness is both one of the strengths and weaknesses of the Internet. In order to be an effective researcher, you must be aware of the differences in quality that exist among websites.

A good place to start evaluating a website's authority is by looking at its domain suffix. The domain name is the Web address, or Internet identity. The domain suffix, the three letters that follow the dot, is the category in which that website falls. The most commonly used domain suffixes are described below.

Domain Suffix	Definition/Description
.com	Stands for "commercial." Usually, websites with this suffix intend to make some sort of profit from their Internet services. Typically these are the websites that sell goods or services.
.org	Stands for "organization." Primarily used by not-for-profit groups such as charities and professional organizations.
.net	Stands for "network." Used by Internet service providers or Web-hosting companies.
.edu	Stands for "education." Used by major universities or educational organizations or other institutions.
.gov	Stands for "government." Used by U.S., state, and local government sites.

8. Which of the domain suffixes would lead you to expect that the information was more geared to selling something than giving information?

9. Visit the list of the sites provided by your teacher. Choose two that you want to investigate further in order to practice evaluating online sources. As you surf through the site, use the graphic organizer on the next page to help you decide whether the website provides reliable information without **bias**.

- Circle "yes" or "no" for each question. You want to be able to answer "yes" to as many of the questions as possible to consider the source reliable and credible.

- If you are able to answer "yes" to the question, answer the question by taking notes about the site.

Site 1 _____

Site 2 _____

10. Is one of the sites you explored more credible (trustworthy) than the other? Why?

Searching for Sources

When using the Internet for research, your first step might be to use a search engine to find likely sources. Search engines work from a type of index. When you enter a **search term** that is in the index, the search engine finds websites that also use that word or phrase.

Depending on your search term, a search might return hundreds (or even thousands) of possible sites. For example, if you enter the search term "Civil War," you will get pages and pages of sites because the term is so broad. If you are just looking for the battle at Antietam, narrowing your search to that word would give you better results.

11. How might you choose good sites from your search?

12. To research the effect of marketing and advertising to young people, what search terms might you use?

13. Using your search term(s), find information on the topic of marketing and advertising aimed at young people. Choose one or two sites to explore further. Record information about the sites (URL, type of information provided, and your comments on the site or the information).

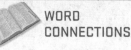

WORD CONNECTIONS

Roots and Affixes

The word *bias* comes from the Old French word *biais* and means "slant or slope." The noun *bias* refers to a preference, especially one that prevents impartial judgment.

My Notes

ACADEMIC VOCABULARY
A **search term** is a single word or short phrase used in a database search.

Evaluating Sources: How Credible Are They?

Criteria	Question	Yes/No	Site 1	Site 2
Authority	1. Is it clear who is sponsoring the creation and maintenance of the page?	Yes No	Notes:	Notes:
	2. Is there information available describing the purpose of the sponsoring organization?	Yes No		
	3. Is there a way to verify the authority of the page's sponsor? For instance, is a phone number or address available to contact for more information?	Yes No		
	4. Is it clear who developed and wrote the material? Are his/her qualifications for writing on this topic clearly stated? Is there contact information for the author of the material?	Yes No		
Accuracy	1. Are the sources for factual information given so they can be verified?	Yes No		
	2. If information is presented in graphs or charts, is it labeled clearly?	Yes No		
	3. Does the information appear to have errors?	Yes No		
Credibility	1. Is the page and the information from a reliable source?	Yes No		
	2. Is it free of advertising?	Yes No		
	3. If there is advertising on the page, is it clearly separated from the informational content?	Yes No		
	4. Are there any signs of bias?	Yes No		
Timeliness	1. Do dates on the page indicate when the page was written or last revised?	Yes No		
	2. Are there any other indications that the material is updated frequently to ensure timely information?	Yes No		
	3. If the information is published in print in different editions, is it clear what edition the page is from?	Yes No		
Purpose/ Audience	1. Does the site indicate who the intended audience is?	Yes No		
	2. Is there any evidence of why the information is provided?	Yes No		

Language and Writer's Craft: Revising for Precise Language and Formal Style

Most of your expository writing will be for an academic audience. For this audience, you should use precise language and a formal writing style.

Precise language. Your choice of words (diction) should include the academic vocabulary and literary terms that you are learning, as they apply to the topic. For example:

Original: The advertisement used a celebrity to help sell its product.

Revised: The advertisement used the advertising technique of a testimonial to sell its product by using the professional athlete Derek Jeter.

Another way to be precise is to provide detailed information about a text or resource you are citing.

Original: In the news story it says that . . .

Revised: In the news story from the *New York Times* on Sunday, March 18, the author claims that . . .

Formal language. Formal language avoids slang, and it generally does not use contractions. Most slang that you might use in everyday language is too casual for academic writing. Words or phrases you use with your peers may not be understood by different audiences or appropriate for an academic topic.

Original: I'm a teenager, and, like, most of us look at famous people as cool and in the know.

Revised: Teenagers generally believe that famous people are models for their own thoughts and behavior.

Check Your Understanding

Expository Writing Prompt: Using information from one of your searches, write a paragraph summarizing the information you found about marketing to young people. Be sure to:

* Introduce your topic clearly.
* Use details and examples that relate to the topic.
* Use formal language and transitions that create coherence.

My Notes

Gathering Evidence from a Film: Part One

LEARNING STRATEGIES:
Graphic Organizer,
Note-taking, Double-Entry
Journal, Discussion Groups

Learning Targets
- Identify and record relevant research information from a documentary film.
- Participate in a collaborative discussion about research findings.

Documentary Film

1. To help you understand the genre and purpose of the film *The Myth of Choice: How Junk-Food Marketers Target Our Kids*, record details using the following graphic organizer as you listen to information about the film.

My Notes

Role Who created this film?	Inference: Evidence:
Audience Who do you think it was created for?	Inference: Evidence:
Format What type of film is it? How will the information be presented? Is the film a primary or secondary source?	Inference: Evidence:
Topic What will this be about? What is its purpose?	Inference: Evidence:

Literary Terms
A **documentary** film is a nonfiction motion picture intended to document, or record, some aspect of real life, primarily for the purposes of instruction or maintaining a historical record.

2. Use the graphic organizer on the next page or some other form to take notes about the film that might help you answer the research question you will develop. Write your research question(s) below.

Research question(s) I hope to answer:

Evidence from the Film	Personal Response	What evidence answers your research questions? What new questions do you have?
Food companies tell us they're just doing their job.	I have experienced ... I have read about ... I have heard about ... This reminds me of ... I think ... I feel ...	
"Still, I can just say no, right?"	_____ _____	_____ _____
"The food industry has spent millions."	_____ _____	_____ _____

Check Your Understanding

In preparation for a group discussion, answer the following questions:

1. How did this resource help you answer your research question? Provide specific details from the film as support.

2. What additional information did you find interesting?

3. What is one other question the film prompted you to think about?

4. Respond to the Essential Question: How do advertisers attempt to influence consumers?

5. From what you can tell, how reliable is this source?

In **collaborative discussion groups,** share your responses. Remember to:

• Explicitly refer to facts and examples from note-taking.

• Ask open-ended questions that bring about further discussion.

• Paraphrase others' comments and respond to others' questions.

• Revise your own ideas as you gain information from others.

My Notes

Gathering Evidence from a News Article

LEARNING STRATEGIES:
Skimming/Scanning, Marking
the Text, Close Reading

Learning Targets

• Compare and contrast how similar information is presented in different texts.

Before Reading

1. Skim and scan the text features and discuss with a partner what you already know about information in the bold headings. If you are unclear, make a prediction.

During Reading

2. Mark the text by stopping, thinking, and writing a response for each chunk of the text in the margin. Your annotations (written responses) may include:
   • Connecting (text to self/text/world)
   • Questioning ("I wonder ... " "Why did ... ")
   • Visualizing (draw a picture or symbol)
   • Paying attention to new learning ("Wow," "Cool," "No way," etc.)
   • Summarizing each section in a sentence or two
3. Underline or draw arrows to any portion of text that specifically supports your personal response.

My Notes

KEY IDEAS AND DETAILS
Explain how technology is helping advertisers reach more kids.

News Article

Marketing to kids gets more savvy[1] with new technologies

Isabella Sweet doesn't wear a target on her chest. But kid marketers covet[2] this 9-year old as if she does. Perhaps it's because she's a techie.

The fourth-grader from Davis, Calif., spends almost an hour a day on the Webkinz website. The site charms kids by linking Webkinz plush animals—of which she owns 18—with online games that encourage kids to earn and spend virtual money so they can create elaborate rooms for virtual versions of their Webkinz pets.

The site does one more thing: It posts ads that reward kids with virtual currency when they click. Every time a kid clicks on an ad, there's a virtual ka-ching at the other end for Ganz, which owns Webkinz.

At issue: With the use of new, kid-enchanting technologies, are savvy marketers gaining the upper hand on parents? Are toy marketers such as Ganz, food marketers such as McDonald's and kid-coddling apparel retailers such as 77kids by American Eagle too eager to target kids?

---

[1] **savvy:** shrewd, knowledgeable
[2] **covet:** to desire or yearn for something

At stake: $1.12 trillion. That's the amount that kids influenced last year in overall family spending, says James McNeal, a kid marketing consultant and author of "Kids as Consumers: A Handbook of Marketing to Children." "Up to age 16, kids are determining most expenditures in the household," he says. "This is very attractive to marketers."

It used to be so simple. A well-placed TV spot on a Saturday-morning cartoon show or a kid-friendly image on a cereal box was all it took. No longer. The world of marketing to kids has grown extremely complex and tech-heavy. Marketers that seek new ways to target kids are aware of new calls for federal action—including voluntary marketing guidelines that would affect food marketers. Kids, who are spending less time watching TV and more time on computers or smartphones, are becoming targets online.

"Marketers are getting more and more devious," says Susan Linn, director of Campaign for a Commercial-Free Childhood, a watchdog group. With the growing use of smartphones and social media, she says, "They have new avenues for targeting children that parents might miss."

Even ad-savvy parents are sometimes unaware how marketers are reaching out to their children, getting around ad blockers. While on the Webkinz site, Sweet recently clicked once a day for seven days on an ad for a film trailer that was posted for *Judy Moody and the NOT Bummer Summer*. She says that she wasn't really interested in the movie. But each day that she clicked it and answered three questions, she earned a virtual lime-green dresser and bulletin board for the rooms she created online for her Webkinz.

"I've got five dressers and seven bulletin boards," says the girl. "I don't have enough rooms to fit them all in."

This kind of marketing to kids drives Isabella's mother crazy. "They're doing this right under the noses of parents," says Elizabeth Sweet, a doctoral student at University of California-Davis doing her dissertation on the marketing of kids' toys. Even so, she says, she had no idea about the video ads on Webkinz until her daughter told her.

"This whole planting of movie videos in the online game experience is new to me," Sweet says. "What bothers me most is that when she first signed up for the site, I thought it was OK."

Sweet has an ad-blocker app on her browser. These movie ads are woven into the site content in such a way that her daughter sees—and responds to them—anyway, she says.

"We occasionally introduce limited-time promotions so that our Webkinz World members can enjoy fun, unique activities and events," says Susan McVeigh, a Ganz spokeswoman, in an e-mail.

But Elizabeth Sweet isn't the only parent who's unhappy with how and what Webkinz markets to kids.

My Notes

KEY IDEAS AND DETAILS
How do the opinions of kids and parents differ about the influence of ads within a website?

Gathering Evidence from a News Article

Last month, Christina Cunningham, a fulltime mother from Port St. Lucie, Fla. happened to look over as two of her daughters — ages 9 and 7—were signing onto the Webkinz website. On the log-in screen, an ad flashed for BabyPictureMaker.com, which nudges consumers to download pictures of two people—promising to send back a picture of what a baby they might have together would look like.

"This is not acceptable," says Cunningham, who shooed her kids away from the site and fired off an e-mail to Webkinz. When she didn't hear back, she sent another. Again, she says, she received no response. But McVeigh says Webkinz e-mailed Cunningham responses, twice. A frustrated Cunningham contacted Campaign for a Commercial-Free Childhood. The group contacted Webkinz, which removed the ad. "We will make sure to open an investigation into the matter and take the appropriate steps," spokeswoman McVeigh assured the group in a letter.

The fast-food connection

Webkinz declined to share the outcome of this investigation with USA TODAY—nor would it explain how the ad got on the site. "We're fully committed to a responsible approach regarding advertising and the advertisers we allow on the site," says McVeigh, in an e-mail.

KEY IDEAS AND DETAILS
This article presents a cause-and-effect relationship between what two things?

But in the eyes of some parents, no one goes more over the top in marketing to kids than the big food sellers—particularly sellers of high-sugar cereals and high-fat, high-calorie fast food.

That's one reason the Obama administration is proposing that food makers adopt voluntary limits on the way they market to kids. These proposed voluntary guidelines, to be written by a team from four federal agencies, have set the food and ad industries howling—even before they've been completed.

"I can't imagine any mom in America who thinks stripping tigers and toucans off cereal boxes will do anything to address obesity," said Scott Faber, a spokesman for the Grocery Manufacturers Association, at a May hearing.

But Wayne Altman thinks the voluntary guidelines are critical. He's a family physician in the Boston area who has three sons ages 13, 5 and 4. He's particularly concerned about Ronald McDonald. "We know that children under 8 have no ability to [distinguish] between truth and advertising," he says. "So, to have this clown get a new generation hooked on a bad product just isn't right."

Because of the obesity, heart disease and food-related illnesses fed partly by savvy food marketers such as McDonald's, Altman says, "We have a generation of children that is the first to have a life expectancy less than its parents."

Plenty of others think as Altman does, even though Ronald is regularly used to promote Ronald McDonald House Charities. Ronald also shows up in schools. He's got his own website, Ronald.com, where the clown promises that kids can "learn, play and create while having fun." And he's the focal point of a new social-media campaign that nudges kids to download their own photos with images of Ronald and share them with friends.

More than 1,000 doctors, including Altman, recently signed a petition that asked McDonald's to stop using Ronald to market to kids. "People have a right to sell and advertise," he says. "But where do we draw the line?"

McDonald's—which recently announced it will modify its Happy Meals in September by reducing the number of fries and adding apple slices—has no plans to dump Ronald. "Ronald McDonald is an ambassador for McDonald's and an ambassador for good," CEO Jim Skinner told shareholders in May at the company's annual meeting. "Ronald McDonald is going nowhere."

77 kids entertains shoppers

But American Eagle is going somewhere. And if any retailer[3] exemplifies the techie new world of marketing to kids, it may be 77kids by American Eagle.

The outside-the-box store that it just opened at New York's Times Square sells midpriced clothing targeting boys and girls from toddler to 12. But the heart of the target is the 10-year-old. Getting a 10-year-old's attention is all about whiz-bang technology—like the chain's virtual ticket to rock stardom.

In the center of the Times Square store sits a "Be a Rock Star" photo booth. It's all about music and tech. The booth has a big-screen TV that shows a video of a rock band composed of 10- to 12-year-old kids singing "I Wanna Rock" by Twisted Sister. Any tween, with parental permission, can download his or her photo and substitute it on the screen for one of the rock stars.

"Our brand ideology is: Think like a mom, see like a kid," explains Betsy Schumacher chief merchandising officer at 77kids. "It made sense to us to have technology in the store that speaks to a kid's experience—and how they play."

Each 77kids store also has two iPad-like touch-screens that allow kids to virtually try on most of the clothing in the store. Who needs a dressing room when you can download your own photo and have it instantly matched online with that cool motorcycle vest or hip pair of distressed jeans? The same touch-screen also allows kids to play instant DJ, where they can mess online with the very same music that's being played in the store—slowing it down, speeding it up or even voting it off the playlist.

Nearly nine in 10 kids who shop at 77kids try one of these technologies while visiting the store, Schumacher estimates. The company makes no bones about laser targeting 10-year-olds. "The point is to keep a kid engaged so that shopping is enjoyable, Schumacher says." Kids are looking for entertainment when they come to the mall."

Ex-adman wants change

Marketers, in turn, are looking for kids. And profits.

It isn't just advertising watchdogs who think it's time for a change. So does the guy who two years ago was arguably the ad world's top creative executive, Alex Bogusky. The agency that he has since left, Crispin Porter + Bogusky, has created campaigns for such kid-craving companies as Burger King and Domino's. Now, with the ad biz in his rearview mirror, Bogusky suggests it may be time for marketers to rethink.

---

[3] **retailer:** a person or business that sells goods directly to the consumer

My Notes

KEY IDEAS AND DETAILS
What is meant by the phrase "think like a mom, see like a kid"?

WORD CONNECTIONS

Idioms

A "watchdog group" is one that investigates companies and organizations to publicize their actions or policies. The goal is to protect the public health and welfare.

Gathering Evidence from a News Article

GRAMMAR & USAGE
Compound Sentences

Compound sentences are formed by combining two sentences with a coordinating conjunction such as *but, and, for, yet, or,* or *so*.

Example: Advertisers market to children, and children in turn pressure their parents to buy.

Complex sentences contain dependent clauses that begin with markers such as *after, since, because, although, even though,* or *when*.

Example: When I turn on the television, I always see advertisements with kids my age in them.

My Notes

"So what if we stopped it?" he recently posed on his personal blog. "What if we decided that advertising to children was something none of us would engage in anymore? What would happen? A lot of things would happen, and almost all seem to be for the good of society."

Babies as young as 6 months old can form mental images of logos and mascots—and brand loyalties can be established as early as 2, says the watchdog group Center for a New American Dream. McNeal, the kids marketing guru, says he consults with companies that are constantly trying to figure out how to get inside day care centers and bore their images inside the minds of preschoolers. Back at Isabella Sweet's Webkinz-filled home, she's still saving her weekly $1 allowance to buy yet more. She can't help it, she says, even though each one costs $5 to $13. Even the family cats drag out her Webkinz to play." I wish I had a favorite Webkinz, but I don't," says Isabella. "I love them all."

After Reading

4. Join another pair or small group and share your understandings and summaries. Then discuss by making connections to your own or others' ideas. To ensure active listening, you may be asked to share an interesting point made by a peer. As a listener, remember to make eye contact with the speaker, take notes, and actively respond with questions or comments.

Check Your Understanding

Respond to the following compare-and-contrast questions.

- What is one way information from *The Myth of Choice: How Junk-Food Marketers Target Our Kids* is **like** information from "Marketing to kids gets more savvy with new technologies?" Be sure to give at least one detail from both texts in your answer.

- What is one way information from *The Myth of Choice: How Junk-Food Marketers Target Our Kids* is **different** information from "Marketing to kids gets more savvy with new technologies"? Be sure to give at least one detail from both texts in your answer.

Language and Writer's Craft: Sentence Variety

Using a variety of sentence structures is important to emphasize and connect ideas and as a way to create reader interest. Writing that contains many sentences of the same pattern bores both the writer and the reader.

Add variety and clarity by experimenting with different sentence structures.

Simple sentences: Note that these two simple sentences do not show a connection between ideas.

Advertisers are concerned about kids. Advertisers want kids to buy their products.

Compound sentence: Note the relationship that is now established between advertisers and kids.

> Advertisers care about kids, but they are more concerned that kids buy their products.

Complex sentence:

> Even though advertisers say they care about kids, they are more concerned about selling their products to kids.

Practice

Combine the following simple sentences into compound and complex sentences to show more connections between the ideas.

- Advertisers know that children influence what parents buy. Children are the targets of advertisers.

- Marketers are very smart and persistent. Children are influenced to buy without thinking about it.

- Parents try to protect their children from marketers. Watchdog agencies also try to keep advertisers honest.

Writing to Compare and Contrast

To make comparisons between two things, you would mention both in your topic sentence(s).

Sample Topic Sentence: Both *The Myth of Choice: How Junk-Food Marketers Target Our Kids* and "Marketing to kids ... " emphasize the importance of children as targets for advertisers, but "Marketing to kids gets more savvy" includes more personal examples.

Transitions: To compare and contrast the texts, use words or phrases as transitions between the ideas from each text.

For comparison and contrast:

similarly, on the other hand, in contrast, although, like, unlike, same as, in the same way, nevertheless, likewise, by contrast, conversely, however

For conclusion:

as a result, therefore, finally, last, in conclusion, in summary, all in all

Examples:

On the other hand, some parents have started to limit the amount of television their toddlers watch each day.

All in all, most parents of toddlers agree that they will start regulating the number of hours their children spend in front of a screen.

Expository Writing Prompt: Write a paragraph in which you compare information from the film to information from the article you read. What information is similar? What is different? Be sure to:

- Introduce your topic clearly.

- Use transitional words and phrases to show comparison and contrast.

- Use formal style and precise language.

- Provide a concluding statement that follows and supports the explanation.

My Notes

Gathering Evidence from a Film: Part Two

LEARNING STRATEGIES:
Note-taking, Webbing

Learning Targets

- Identify and record information relevant to a research question from a documentary film.
- Participate in a collaborative discussion about research findings.

1. Use the graphic organizer below to take notes as you view another short documentary film. You will use your notes to help answer the research question you have selected or refined. Write your question below as a reminder.

   Research Question(s):

Viewing Two: *Ads in Schools*

Evidence from the Text	Personal Response	Peer Response	What evidence answers your research questions? What new questions do you have?
Introduction: (0:00–0.56) Selling to Schools			
Coles–Sports for Schools (0.57–2.43)			

Viewing Three:

Evidence from the Text	Personal Response	Peer Response	What evidence answers your research questions? What new questions do you have?
America (2.43–3.40)			
"Flipside" (3.40–end)			

Expository Writing Prompt: Think about how the two short documentaries you have viewed are alike. Write a brief comparison in which you use evidence to show how the two films treat topics in a similar way. Be sure to:

- Introduce your topic clearly and develop it with relevant details and examples.
- Use transitions to create cohesion and clarify ideas.
- Use precise language and formal style.

Check Your Understanding

Reread your notes from the viewings of this film. Summarize the main points made by the documentary makers.

My Notes

_____
_____
_____
_____
_____
_____
_____
_____
_____
_____
_____
_____
_____
_____
_____
_____

Gathering Evidence: Bringing It All Together

LEARNING STRATEGIES:
Outlining, Brainstorming

ACADEMIC VOCABULARY
Facts and details in a text are
valid when they support the
claim a writer is making.

My Notes

Learning Targets
- Organize research, notes, and ideas to prepare for writing.
- Write a conclusion for an expository essay.

Characteristics of Expository Writing

You learned about the structure of an expository paragraph in Activities 2.4 and 2.5. The characteristics of this writing mode must be expanded to create an expository essay so that each paragraph contains the following:

- **Topic sentence** that presents a topic and the writer's claim or position about the topic in relation to the thesis.
- **Transitions** to connect ideas (*for example, however, on the other hand*).
- **Supporting information** that includes specific and relevant facts and details that are **valid** for the topic.
- **Commentary** that explains how the detail is relevant to the topic sentence.
- **Concluding Statement**, a final piece of commentary (*as a result, overall, in conclusion*), that supports the explanation. The concluding sentence brings a sense of closure to the paragraph and essay.

Outlining Ideas

Many writers find it helpful to create an outline of their ideas prior to drafting an essay. You might use the following format to outline your ideas to share the information from your research question(s).

Marketing to Youth

I. Introduction/Thesis Statement That Answers the Prompt

II. Body Paragraphs (with examples and information to support the main ideas of the thesis) that include the following:

  A. Evidence and Commentary in Each Paragraph

III. Concluding Statement

1. In this part of the unit, you have read several texts on marketing to young people, viewed a documentary film, and had numerous group discussions about the topic. In addition, you have collected information from websites. Using the information from these sources, create an outline for an expository essay about this topic.

Drawing Conclusions

2. Based on your reading about this topic and the notes you have taken, what are the top 10 opinions or conclusions you have come to as a result of your reading and research?

Expository Writing Prompt: Write a conclusion for an essay on the topic of advertising to young people. Be sure to:

- Write a final statement that supports the thesis topic sentences.
- Bring a sense of closure by using transitions and explanations that follow from the essay's main points.
- Use a formal writing style.

Writing an Expository Essay and Participating in a Collaborative Discuss

Assignment

Your assignment is to write an expository essay that explains the role of advertising in the lives of youth and then to exchange ideas in a collaborative discussion. For your essay, you may use as sources the articles in this unit and at least one additional informational text that you have researched.

Planning and Prewriting: Take time to make a plan for your essay.

- How will you review the ideas you have generated to select the most relevant examples and information?

- How can you work with a peer to revise your plan to be sure you have a clear topic?

Drafting: Create an organized draft to identify and explain your topic.

- How will you use what you have learned about beginning an essay as you write your draft?

- Have you reviewed and evaluated your sources and examples to be sure they are clear and relevant?

- How will you finish your draft with a conclusion that supports the information in your essay?

Revising and Editing: Strengthen your writing with attention to task, purpose, and audience.

- How can you use strategies such a adding and replacing to revise your draft for cohesion, clarity, diction, and language?

- How can the Scoring Guide help you evaluate how well your draft meets the requirements of the assignment?

- How will you proofread and edit your draft to demonstrate formal style and a command of the conventions of standard English capitalization, punctuation, spelling, grammar, and usage?

Preparing for Discussion: Take time to make a plan for your collaborative discussion.

- What personal speaking and listening goals will you set for participation in the collaborative discussion?

- How can you use an outline or a copy of your essay to plan your talking points?

- How will you take notes in order to actively engage as an audience participant as you listen to your peers?

Reflection

After completing this Embedded Assessment, think about how you went about accomplishing this task, and respond to the following:

- How did writing, speaking, and listening help you engage with your topic on a deeper level?

- Did you meet the speaking and listening goals that you set for yourself? How could you improve for next time?

SCORING GUIDE

Scoring Criteria	Exemplary	Proficient	Emerging	Incomplete
Ideas	The essay • presents a topic with a clearly stated and insightful controlling idea • supports the topic with specific and relevant facts, evidence, details, and examples to guide understanding of main ideas • skillfully combines ideas from several sources.	The essay • presents a topic with a controlling idea • supports the topic with facts, evidence, details, and examples that guide the reader's understanding of the main ideas • combines ideas accurately from several sources.	The essay • presents a topic with an unfocused, controlling idea • contains insufficient or vague facts, evidence, details, and examples that confuse the reader's understanding of the main ideas • uses ideas from limited sources.	The essay • presents an unclear or vague topic with no controlling idea • contains few facts, evidence, details, or examples • cites few or no sources or misstates ideas from sources.
Structure	The essay • leads with an effective, engaging introduction • effectively sequences ideas and uses meaningful transitions to create cohesion and clarify relationships • provides an insightful conclusion that follows from and supports the explanation presented.	The essay • presents a clear and focused introduction • sequences ideas and uses transitions to create coherence • provides a conclusion that connects the larger ideas presented in the essay.	The essay • contains an underdeveloped and/or unfocused introduction • presents disconnected ideas and limited use of transitions • contains an underdeveloped or unfocused conclusion.	The essay • contains a vague, unfocused introduction • presents little, if any, commentary and no use of transitions • contains a vague and/or no conclusion.
Use of Language	The essay • uses precise diction deliberately chosen to inform or explain the topic • uses a variety of sentence structures to enhance the explanation • demonstrates technical command of the conventions of standard English.	The essay • uses appropriate diction to inform or explain • uses a variety of sentence structures • demonstrates general command of conventions; minor errors do not interfere with meaning.	The essay • uses informal diction that is not appropriate to inform or explain • shows little or no variety in sentence structure • demonstrates limited command of conventions; errors interfere with meaning.	The essay • uses informal diction that is inappropriate for the purpose • shows no variety in sentence structure • demonstrates limited command of conventions; errors interfere with meaning.

Unpacking Embedded Assessment 2: Preparing for Argumentative Writing

LEARNING STRATEGIES:
QHT, Graphic Organizer,
Summarizing, Marking the Text,
Note-taking, Drafting

INDEPENDENT READING

In this part of the unit, you will be reading informational texts as well as some well-known speeches. Speeches are often made to persuade an audience on a topic. You might consider reading famous speeches or informational texts about issues on which you have a definite position.

Learning Targets

- Identify the knowledge and skills needed to complete Embedded Assessment 2 successfully and reflect on prior learning that supports the knowledge and skills needed.
- Examine the essential components and organizational structure of a successful essay of argumentation.

Making Connections

In the first part of this unit, you learned how to conduct research and to write an expository essay explaining a topic. In this part of the unit, you will expand on your writing skills by writing an argumentative essay to persuade an audience to agree with your position on an issue.

Essential Questions

Now that you have analyzed how advertising affects young people, would you change your answer to the first Essential Question on the role that advertising plays in young people's lives? If so, how would you change it?

My Notes

Developing Vocabulary

Look at your **Reader/Writer Notebook** and review the new vocabulary you learned as you studied the research process and expository writing. Which words do you know in depth, and which words do you need to learn more about?

Unpacking Embedded Assessment 1

Read the assignment below for Embedded Assessment 2: Writing an Argumentative Essay on page 161.

Your assignment is to write an argumentative essay that states and supports a claim about an issue of importance to you.

In your own words, summarize what you will need to know to complete this assessment successfully. With your class, create a graphic organizer to represent the skills and knowledge you will need to complete the tasks identified in the Embedded Assessment.

Writing to Persuade

Writers and speakers use persuasive arguments to convince others to support their positions on a topic.

1. Brainstorm a list of times you tried to convince someone of something. What did you say to achieve the result you wanted?

2. **Quickwrite:** Choose an argument in which you were successful. On a separate sheet of paper, write about the situation and how you convinced your audience. Share your ideas in a small group.

Writing Process: Generating a Topic for an Argument

In this part of the unit, your class will write a model argumentative text to learn about the elements of an argument. Following are 20 issues you might consider. Feel free to add your own. As a class, choose a topic on which to write your class-constructed essay and write it below:

Class topic:_____

Possible argumentative essay topics:

1. People should go to jail when they abandon their pets.

2. Kids should get paid for good grades.

3. Kids should have less homework.

4. Magazine advertisements send unhealthy signals to young women.

5. Penmanship is important.

6. We should teach etiquette in schools.

7. I'm old enough to babysit.

8. Recycling should be mandatory for everyone.

9. Children should be required to read more.

10. We shouldn't have to pay for Internet access.

11. Cell phones should be allowed in school.

12. All schools should implement bullying awareness programs.

13. Bullies should be kicked out of school.

14. Parents of bullies should have to pay a fine.

15. The school year should be longer.

16. School days should start later.

17. All students should wear uniforms.

18. Teens should be able to choose their bedtimes.

19. Pets should be allowed in school.

20. Skateboard helmets should be mandatory.

Unpacking Embedded Assessment 2: Preparing for Argumentative Writing

ACADEMIC VOCABULARY
A **norm** refers to something that is usual or expected. Group norms refer to the social behavior that is typical or expected of a group.

Writing with a Group

You have worked a lot in collaborative groups. Now, as you begin writing a model argumentative text, it is important to think specifically about the actions that will help your group successfully write together. Consider the following writing group **norms**.

Writing Group Norms

1. A writing group is a safe place to try out new ideas and present work very much "in progress." Use it to take intellectual risks.

   Paraphrase:

2. As a thinker and contributor, don't apologize for your ideas or work. Don't be embarrassed to share your thoughts or work.

   Paraphrase:

3. As a peer, be thoughtful and specific in your feedback.

   Paraphrase:

4. As a group, celebrate together.

   Paraphrase:

My Notes

Which Claims to Believe

Learning Targets
- Identify elements of argument in a sample text.
- Analyze the thesis (or claim), audience, purpose, and occasion in a sample text.

LEARNING STRATEGIES:
Metacognitive Markers,
Predicting, Rereading,
Think-Pair-Share

Before Reading

1. Review the statements below, and decide whether you agree or disagree with them. Circle *Agree* or *Disagree*. Provide an explanation for your opinion.

Statement	Explanation
America is a wasteful society. Agree or Disagree	
Everyone should be forced to recycle his or her used goods. Agree or Disagree	
Excessive trash is destroying our planet. Agree or Disagree	
There should be a law that mandates the number of items people can buy and throw away annually. Agree or Disagree	
People should be allowed to create as much trash as they want as long as they dispose of it properly. Agree or Disagree	

Share your responses with a partner. Remember the norms of a collaborative discussion (use appropriate speaking and listening skills) to gain understanding of your partner's positions. As you listen to your partner's ideas, adjust and add to your own ideas as appropriate.

My Notes

_____

_____

_____

_____

My Notes

During Reading

2. As you read the text "American the Not-So-Beautiful," use metacognitive markers to question the text (?), to make a comment (*), and to signal an interesting idea (!).

ABOUT THE AUTHOR

From 1978 to 2011, Andrew (Andy) Rooney was a television commentator on the program *60 Minutes*. He wrote more than 800 essays, which he presented on television or in a national newspaper column. His essays, which are sometimes humorous and sometimes controversial, earned him three Emmy awards.

AMERICA
the Not-So-Beautiful

by Andrew A. Rooney

Next to saving stuff I don't need, the thing I like to do best is throw it away. My idea of a good time is to load up the back of the car with junk on a Saturday morning and take it to the dump. There's something satisfying about discarding almost anything.

Throwing things out is the American way. We don't know how to fix anything, and anyone who does know how is too busy to come, so we throw it away and buy a new one. Our economy depends on us doing that. The trouble with throwing things away is, there is no "away" left.

Sometime around the year 500 B.C., the Greeks in Athens passed a law prohibiting people from throwing their garbage in the street. This Greek law was the first recognition by civilized people that throwing things away was a problem. Now, as the population explodes and people take up more room on Earth, there's less room for everything else.

The more civilized a country is, the worse the trash problem is. Poor countries don't have the same problem because they don't have much to discard. Prosperity in the United States is based on using things up as fast as we can, throwing away what's left, and buying new ones.

We've been doing that for so many years that (1) we've run out of places to throw things because houses have been built where the dump was and (2) some of the things we're throwing away are poisoning the Earth and will eventually poison all of us and all living things.

WORD CONNECTIONS

Roots and Affixes

Prosperity comes from the Latin word meaning "to cause to succeed" or "fortunate." The root *-sper-*, meaning "hope," is also found in *desperate*. The suffix *-ity* forms a noun.

Ten years ago most people thought nothing of dumping an old bottle of weed or insect killer in a pile of dirt in the back yard or down the drain in the street, just to get rid of it. The big companies in America had the same feeling, on a bigger scale. For years the chemical companies dumped their poisonous wastes in the rivers behind the mills, or they put it in fifty-gallon drums in the vacant lots, with all the old, rusting machinery in it, up behind the plants. The drums rusted out in ten years and dumped their poison into the ground. It rained, the poisons seeped into the underground streams and poisoned everything for miles around. Some of the manufacturers who did this weren't even evil. They were dumb and irresponsible. Others were evil because they knew how dangerous it was but didn't want to spend the money to do it right.

The problem is staggering. I often think of it when I go in the hardware store or a Sears Roebuck and see shelves full of poison. You know that, one way or another, it's all going to end up in the Earth or in our rivers and lakes.

I have two pint bottles of insecticide with 3 percent DDT in them in my own garage that I don't know what to do with. I bought them years ago when I didn't realize how bad they were. Now I'm stuck with them.

The people of the city of New York throw away nine times their weight in garbage and junk every year. Assuming other cities come close to that, how long will it be before we trash the whole Earth?

Of all household waste, 30 percent of the weight and 50 percent of the volume is the packaging that stuff comes in.

Not only that, but Americans spend more for the packaging of food than all our farmers together make in income growing it. That's some statistic.

Trash collectors are a lot more independent than they used to be because we've got more trash than they've got places to put it. They have their own schedules and their own holidays. Some cities try to get in good with their trash collectors or garbage men by calling them "sanitation engineers." Anything just so long as they pick it up and take it away.

We often call the dump "the landfill" now, too. I never understood why land has to be filled, but that's what it's called. If you're a little valley just outside town, you have to be careful or first thing you know you'll be getting "filled."

If 5 billion people had been living on Earth for the past thousand years as they have been in the past year, the planet would be nothing but one giant landfill, and we'd have turned America the beautiful into one huge landfill.

The best solution may be for all of us to pack up, board a spaceship, and move out. If Mars is habitable, everyone on Earth can abandon this planet we've trashed, move to Mars, and start trashing that. It'll buy us some time.

GRAMMAR & USAGE
Parallel Structure

Notice that when Rooney uses a series in the final paragraph, he puts all of the elements in the same grammatical form:

... for all of us to *pack* up, *board* a spaceship, and *move* out.

The words *pack, board,* and *move* are all verbs that are parallel in structure. Remember to check your writing and make sure that nouns, verbs, and phrases are parallel.

My Notes
_____
_____
_____
_____

KEY IDEAS AND DETAILS
Why does Rooney use humor in the last paragraph of his essay? What is the effect?

Which Claims to Believe

Introducing the Strategy: SOAPSTone

The letters in SOAPSTone stand for Speaker, Occasion, Audience, Purpose, Subject, and Tone. This acronym gives you a helpful tool for analyzing text by breaking it down into separate parts.

After Reading

3. Use the **SOAPSTone** strategy to analyze this argumentative text. It works particularly well when analyzing nonfiction texts.

SOAPSTone: "America the Not-So-Beautiful"

SOAPSTone	Analysis	Textual Support
Subject: What is the topic?		
Occasion: What are the circumstances surrounding this text?		
Audience: Who is the target audience?		
Purpose: Why did the author write this text?		

SOAPSTone	Analysis	Textual Support
Speaker: What does the reader know about the writer?		
Tone: What is the writer's attitude toward the subject?		

4. While a thesis in an expository text most often explains the writer's main idea, a thesis or **claim** in an argumentative text is the writer's position or point of view on an issue. Read the example of a claim below. Mark the claim by underlining its subject (usually nouns) and circling its opinion (words with strong connotations) and by highlighting the reasons to be developed.

Claim: There are numerous downsides to year-round schooling: It has no positive effects on education, it adds to the cost, and it disturbs the long-awaited summer vacation.

ACADEMIC VOCABULARY
A **claim** in this usage is a statement that can be argued, such as whether a fact is true or not, a situation is good or bad, or one action is better than another.

My Notes

_____

_____

_____

_____

_____

_____

_____

Which Claims to Believe

5. Write a clear and concise claim for Andrew Rooney's essay. Use information from your SOAPSTone analysis. Reread the text as needed to write the claim.

Writing Process: Writing a Claim for an Argumentative Essay

6. **Quickwrite:** Write your ideas about both sides of the issue your class chose to write about. Share your position with your writing group. As a group, come to a **consensus** about your position and make a claim. Present your writing group's position and claim to the class.

> **ACADEMIC VOCABULARY**
> When a group reaches **consensus**, it has come to an agreement that satisfies everyone in the group.

7. As a class, select a position and claim.
   Class position/claim about the issue:

8. Use the SOAPSTone graphic organizer on the next page to generate your initial ideas about the class position/claim.

9. Draft your claim.

Check Your Understanding

Review the draft of your claim. Does it clearly state the issue and your position? If not, revise your draft to achieve a clear and concise claim.

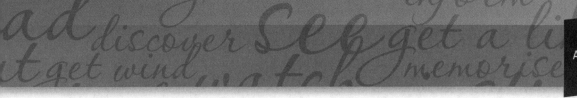

This graphic organizer uses the SOAPSTone strategy to help you prewrite by identifying major elements of your argument. Respond to the questions about your topic.

Subject:

What is the issue?

Occasion:

What circumstances surrounding the issue make it important or relevant?

Audience:

Who would care about or be affected by this issue?

Purpose:

What do you want the audience to do?

Speaker/writer:

How do you show authority in presenting this issue?

Tone:

What attitude do you want to show about this issue (serious, humorous, passionate, indignant)?

Exploring and Evaluating Reasons and Evidence

LEARNING STRATEGIES:
Brainstorming, Skimming/
Scanning, Graphic Organizer,
Marking the Text, Discussion
Groups

Learning Targets

- Analyze claim, reasoning, and evidence in an argument.
- Identify and evaluate an author's claims and use of reasons and evidence to support a position.
- Identify reasons and evidence to develop a topic and support a claim.

Supporting a Claim

My Notes

1. In a successful argument, the claim must be backed up with support. A writer can support his or her viewpoint with both **reasons** and **evidence**. Brainstorm what you already know about these concepts.

   Reasons are:

   Evidence is:

   Types of evidence are:

2. In the space below, write the claim you wrote for Andrew Rooney's essay "America the Not-So-Beautiful." Scan the essay for examples of reasons and evidence to support the claim.

Claim: Americans must be less wasteful before it is too late to save the planet.

Reasons	Evidence

Before Reading

3. Your teacher will assign you a text to read about vending machines in schools. What can you predict the arguments *for* and *against* might be?

Topic	My Predictions
Vending machines in schools	For: Against:

During Reading

4. As you read the text, identify and mark the writer's claim. Highlight the reasons and evidence the writer uses to support that claim.

Informational Text

Another study highlights the insanity of selling junk food in school vending machines

by Karen Kaplan/*Los Angeles Times*

For many students, "back to school" means back to a vending machine diet. As you might guess, this isn't necessarily a good thing for student health.

Vending machines are found in 16% of U.S. elementary schools, 52% of middle schools and 88% of high schools. About 22% of students in grades 1 through 12 buy food in vending machines each day—and those purchases added an average of 253 calories to their diets, according to a new study in the September issue of the *Journal of School Health*.

Just to be clear, those were not 253 calories' worth of tofu, yogurt or carrot sticks. The most popular vending machine items included soft drinks, candy, chips, crackers, cookies, cakes and ice cream. On the plus side, kids also bought low-fat milk, fruit juice and even fruit, the study found.

But the net effect on kids' diets was not good. Those who bought from vending machines ate an average of 156 grams of sugar per day, compared with 146 grams for those who abstained. They also consumed less dietary fiber, iron and B vitamins like thiamine, riboflavin, niacin and folate.

GRAMMAR & USAGE
Easily Confused Words

Learn to use *affect* and *effect* correctly. *Affect* is generally used as a verb and means "to influence." *Effect* is generally used as a noun and means "a result." Notice in the sentence "But the net effect on kids' diets was not good" that *effect* is a noun.

My Notes

_____

_____

_____

_____

_____

_____

_____

_____

_____

_____

_____

KEY IDEAS AND DETAILS
What evidence supports the "insanity" of selling junk food in school vending machines?

_____

_____

_____

_____

_____

Exploring and Evaluating Reasons and Evidence

KEY IDEAS AND DETAILS
Notice the emphasis on facts
and statistics. What does
this indicate about how the
writer is trying to convince
the audience?

My Notes

One silver lining: Vending machine customers ate 4% less sodium than other students—an average of 3,287 milligrams per day compared with 3,436 mg for those who didn't buy from vending machines. That's probably because the extra snacks made kids too full to eat as much at mealtime, when dishes are especially salty. In any event, kids should eat no more than 1,200 to 1,500 mg of sodium each day, according to the Mayo Clinic. (Even for adults, the government recommends a daily limit of 2,300 mg.)

Overall, vending machines in school appear to be taking a toll on public health. The researchers—from the University of Michigan, Michigan State University and Food & Nutrition Database Research Inc. of Okemos, Mich.—calculated that all that snacking adds up to about 14 extra pounds per child per school year.

"For some students this might be a serious contributor to weight issues," they wrote. Other public health problems include Type 2 diabetes and cavities.

The study was based on data collected from 2,309 children nationwide for the third School Nutrition Dietary Assessment Study, which was conducted by the U.S. Department of Agriculture's Food and Nutrition Service.

After Reading

5. Complete a SOAPSTone analysis of the text.

6. Meet in a collaborative discussion group to share your analysis. In order to come to the discussion prepared, use a graphic organizer similar to the one below to complete your portion of the analysis.

Text	Claim (directly stated or implied)	Most Logical Reason(s) and Relevant Evidence	Credibility of Reasons/ Evidence (explain)
"Another study highlights the insanity of selling junk food in school vending machines"			

Conducting Research for the Class-Constructed Argument

7. Review the class claim and brainstorm a list of questions you have about your position.

8. Use your prior knowledge and list reasons and evidence in support of the claim.

9. You will need to conduct research to gather reasons and evidence to support your claim. What sources should you consider? Make a list of the resources that might be most reliable for helping you learn about the topic and position.

Possible sources:

10. You will need a plan for your research. With the guidance of your teacher, use the graphic organizer on the next page to create a plan to conduct research for your class essay.

11. As you conduct research, record the following information for each source in a graphic organizer like the one below. Be prepared to share your top pieces of evidence and reasoning in your writing group. Be sure to select reasons that are logical and evidence that is relevant and accurate. Both should clearly support your position. If you prefer, you can create a note card for each resource and record information on that card.

Argumentative Essay Research Log

Topic/Issue: _____

Claim (position on the issue): _____

_____

Source Plus Citation	Notes/Examples/ Quotes	Comments

Exploring and Evaluating Reasons and Evidence

My Notes

Research Plan for an Argumentative Essay

Steps of Research Process	Plan
1. Identify the issue or problem.	**K:** What do you already **know** about your topic?
2. Write questions that can be answered through research.	**W:** What do you **want** to know? What are you are curious about?
3. Gather evidence.	**H: How** will you research your topic? What primary and secondary sources will be most helpful to learn about the issue? **L:** Use a research log to record what you have **learned**.
4. Evaluate sources.	
5. Draw conclusions.	
6. Communicate findings.	

12. **Evaluate your reasoning and evidence:** During the class discussion, are you hearing repeated reasons and evidence? Think about how this evidence may signal support that will resonate with your audience.

13. Do you need to conduct further research about your issue or change your research questions? Do you need more evidence from accurate and credible sources? What other sources could you use?

14. As a class, use outlining to begin drafting a body paragraph for the class argumentative essay. You might plan the essay as follows:

   I. Claim: The claim is part of the introductory paragraph.

   II. Supporting Paragraph

      a. Main reason of support for the claim; this reason or evidence will become a topic sentence for a paragraph.

      b. Evidence to support the reasoning

      c. Commentary that includes an explanation of the significance of the evidence or the connection to the claim

Language and Writer's Craft: Sentence Structure and Transitions

When writing about evidence to support a claim, writers use introductory words and transitions that help the reader connect the evidence and its source.

A study by _____ gives evidence that ...

Research from _____ shows that ...

A recent article in _____ indicates that ...

Example: *According to the Environmental Protection Agency*, Americans send over 250 million tons of trash to landfills each year.

"According to the Environmental Protection Agency" is an introductory phrase; it is followed by an independent clause. Together they create a transitional sentence. This sentence cites the facts and makes their source clear. Readers can then determine whether they agree that the source would have accurate and credible information.

My Notes

Exploring and Evaluating Reasons and Evidence

My Notes

15. Draft paragraph(s) with your writing group, following your teacher's directions. Be sure to:
    - Introduce a clear claim.
    - Support your claim with valid reasons and relevant evidence.
    - Use transitional words or phrases that create coherence among the evidence presented.

16. If you need a reminder about transitional words and phrases, return to the texts you have read so far in this part of the unit and use skimming and scanning. Add what you find and others to a transitions word bank. You might also keep a transitions word bank in your Reader/Writer Notebook.

Transitions Word Bank

17. Copy the draft of the class-created body paragraph to your Reader/Writer Notebook.

Just the Right Rhetoric: Logical Appeals

Learning Target
• Identify a writer's use of rhetorical appeals and analyze their effectiveness.

You have learned about claims, reasons, and evidence as important elements of effective arguments.

Rhetoric is the art of using words to persuade in writing or speaking. Writers find interesting ways to use just the right words that appeal to their audience in order to convince them.

Rhetorical Appeals

Rhetorical appeals can strengthen an argument by appealing to logic *(logos)*, emotions *(pathos)*, or a sense of right and wrong *(ethos)*.

Let's look more closely at the appeal of logos, or logic, as a way to build and strengthen an argument with statistics, facts, and examples.

Logos is one of the most important appeals in an effective argument because of its use of facts and logic to build relevant and sufficient reasoning.

Paraphrase the appeal of logos:

Before Reading

1. Activating Prior Knowledge: What do you know about the abolitionist movement or women's suffrage in America?

2. Skim and scan the following two speeches to notice the titles. What can you predict each speech is about?

During Reading

3. Conduct a close reading of the following speeches. Mark the text to identify the elements of argumentation: claim, reasons and evidence, and opposing arguments or **counterclaims**. Then read the text a second time to mark the text with L for logos when you see a statistic, fact, or example.

LEARNING STRATEGIES:
Close Reading, Marking the Text, Paraphrasing, Note-taking

Literary Terms
Rhetoric is the language a writer or speaker uses to persuade an audience.

My Notes

WORD CONNECTIONS
Word Meanings

The word *suffrage* refers to the right to vote in political elections. Abolition refers to the act of abolishing or ending something. The abolitionist movement promoted the ending of slavery in the United States.

ACADEMIC VOCABULARY
A **counterclaim**, also called a counterargument, is a claim made by someone with an opposing opinion on a given issue. When creating an argument, you must be able to argue against counterclaims.

My Notes

ABOUT THE AUTHOR
Born into slavery in New York State, Sojourner Truth (1797–1883) became a well-known anti-slavery speaker sometime after she gained her freedom in 1827. "Ain't I a Woman" is the name given to an extemporaneous speech she delivered at the Women's Convention in Akron, Ohio, on May 29, 1851. The speech received wide publicity in 1863 during the American Civil War when Frances Dana Barker Gage published a new version that became known as "Ain't I a Woman?"

KEY IDEAS AND DETAILS
Why would Sojourner Truth be invited to speak at an anti-slavery convention?

Speech

Ain't I a Woman?

by Sojourner Truth

Well, children, where there is so much racket there must be something out of kilter. I think that 'twixt the negroes of the South and the women at the North, all talking about rights, the white men will be in a fix pretty soon. But what's all this here talking about?

That man over there says that women need to be helped into carriages, and lifted over ditches, and to have the best place everywhere. Nobody ever helps me into carriages, or over mud-puddles, or gives me any best place! And ain't I a woman? Look at me! Look at my arm! I have ploughed and planted, and gathered into barns, and no man could head me! And ain't I a woman? I could work as much and eat as much as a man—when I could get it—and bear the lash as well! And ain't I a woman? I have borne thirteen children, and seen most all sold off to slavery, and when I cried out with my mother's grief, none but Jesus heard me! And ain't I a woman?

Then they talk about this thing in the head; what's this they call it? [member of audience whispers, "intellect"] That's it, honey. What's that got to do with women's rights or negroes' rights? If my cup won't hold but a pint, and yours holds a quart, wouldn't you be mean not to let me have my little half measure full?

Then that little man in black there, he says women can't have as much rights as men, 'cause Christ wasn't a woman! Where did your Christ come from? Where did your Christ come from? From God and a woman! Man had nothing to do with Him.

If the first woman God ever made was strong enough to turn the world upside down all alone, these women together ought to be able to turn it back , and get it right side up again! And now they is asking to do it, the men better let them.

Obliged to you for hearing me, and now old Sojourner ain't got nothing more to say.

ABOUT THE AUTHOR

Hillary Rodham Clinton (1947 –) has served as First Lady of the United States, as well as the Secretary of State. In both roles, she has been an advocate for women's rights. During her years as the First Lady, she traveled to many countries and made speeches calling attention to women's issues and urging improvement in their rights.

Speech

From

Remarks to the U.N. 4th World Conference on Women Plenary Session

by Hillary Rodham Clinton
delivered 5 September 1995, Beijing, China

1 I would like to thank the Secretary General for inviting me to be part of this important United Nations Fourth World Conference on Women. This is truly a celebration, a celebration of the contributions women make in every aspect of life: in the home, on the job, in the community, as mothers, wives, sisters, daughters, earners, workers, citizens, and leaders.

...

2 By gathering in Beijing, we are focusing world attention on issues that matter most in our lives—the lives of women and their families: access to education, health care, jobs and credit, the chance to enjoy basic legal and human rights and to participate fully in the political life of our countries.

...

3 What we are learning around the world is that if women are healthy and educated, their families will flourish. If women are free from violence, their families will flourish. If women have a chance to work and earn as full and equal partners in society, their families will flourish. And when families flourish, communities and nations do as well. That is why every woman, every man, every child, every family, and every nation on this planet does have a stake in the discussion that takes place here.

4 Over the past 25 years, I have worked persistently on issues relating to women, children, and families. Over the past two and a half years, I've had the opportunity to learn more about the challenges facing women in my own country and around the world.

5 I have met new mothers in Indonesia who come together regularly in their village to discuss nutrition, family planning, and baby care. I have met working parents in Denmark who talk about the comfort they feel in knowing that their children can be cared for in safe and nurturing after-school centers. I have met women in South Africa who helped lead the struggle to end apartheid and are now helping to build a new democracy. I have met with the leading women of my own hemisphere who are working every day to promote literacy and better health

KEY IDEAS AND DETAILS
How does the audience and the occasion relate to the purpose as established in the claim of this speech?

My Notes

_____

_____

_____

_____

_____

_____

_____

_____

_____

Just the Right Rhetoric: Logical Appeals

KEY IDEAS AND DETAILS
Explain why this text would
or would not be a credible
source if you were researching
women's rights.

My Notes

care for children in their countries. I have met women in India and Bangladesh who are taking out small loans to buy milk cows, or rickshaws, or thread in order to create a livelihood for themselves and their families. I have met the doctors and nurses in Belarus and Ukraine who are trying to keep children alive in the aftermath of Chernobyl.

6 The great challenge of this conference is to give voice to women everywhere whose experiences go unnoticed, whose words go unheard. Women comprise more than half the world's population, 70% of the world's poor, and two-thirds of those who are not taught to read and write. We are the primary caretakers for most of the world's children and elderly. Yet much of the work we do is not valued—not by economists, not by historians, not by popular culture, not by government leaders.

    ...

7 Those of us who have the opportunity to be here have the responsibility to speak for those who could not. As an American, I want to speak for those women in my own country, women who are raising children on the minimum wage, women who can't afford health care or child care, women whose lives are threatened by violence, including violence in their own homes.

After Reading

4. Revisit your earlier prediction about the topic of the two speeches. What can you now determine about the purpose and audience for each speech?

5. The use of logos is critical in presenting an argument that contains relevant and valid evidence. Scan both speeches to find an example of logos in each. Discuss the effectiveness of each example for the purpose and audience of the speech.

6. Search the Internet for a recording of Sojourner Truth's speech "Ain't I a Woman," and listen carefully for the speaker's argument and claim. Identify the reasoning and evaluate its soundness. Is the evidence sufficient to support the claim?

Language and Writer's Craft: Using Rhetorical Devices

Authors of argumentative texts use rhetorical devices to create their appeals. Three commonly used rhetorical devices used in argumentation are the **rhetorical question**, **parallel structure**, and **repetition**.

- A **rhetorical question** is one for which the writer expects no reply, or the writer clearly directs the reader to one desired reply. Use rhetorical questions to emphasize an idea or to draw a conclusion from the facts. A rhetorical question may help remind your reader of a main point.

  Example: *Is that truly what we want for the environment? How can these facts lie?*

- **Parallel structure** is using the same pattern of words to show that two or more ideas have the same level of importance. This can happen at the word, phrase, or clause level.

  Example: *"He had cooked dinner and eaten, boiled water for the next day's canteen, pulled his packs up in a tree, set up the tent and arranged his sleeping bag and weapons."* (from Brian's Return *by Gary Paulsen)*

- **Repetition** is when key words or phrases are repeated for emphasis or deliberate effect.

  Example: *"I have a dream that one day this nation will rise up and live out the true meaning of its creed . . . I have a dream that one day on the red hills of Georgia . . . I have a dream that one day even the state of Mississippi . . ."* (Martin Luther King, Jr.)

GRAMMAR &USAGE

A **phrase** is a small group of words that functions as a part of speech within a sentence. A phrase may act as a noun, verb, adverb, adjective, or preposition.

A **clause** has both a subject and verb. If the clause can stand alone as a complete sentence, it is an independent clause. If the clause does not form a complete idea, it is a dependent clause.

Coordinating conjunctions connect words, phrases, and clauses. Examples are *and, or, but, yet, nor, for,* and *so.*

My Notes

Just the Right Rhetoric: Logical Appeals

7. Reread Sojourner Truth's speech. What rhetorical question(s) does she use? What is the purpose?

8. Reread Clinton's speech for rhetorical devices, and record your findings in the graphic organizer on the next page. What rhetorical device stands out to you the most? Why?

Argumentative Writing Prompt: Return to the body paragraph you drafted in Activity 2.13. Consider how you can use rhetorical devices and appeals to logic to strengthen your argument. Work collaboratively in your writing group to revise for logical appeals and rhetorical devices by adding or replacing. Be sure to:

• Incorporate logical reasoning to strengthen your argument.

• Make use of at least one rhetorical device.

• Ask for revision suggestions from a peer and incorporate suggested changes into your argument.

After drafting, exchange your text with a peer or a different writing group. Mark the text you receive to identify the use of logos and rhetorical devices. Provide feedback by celebrating successes and by suggesting ideas for improvement.

Hillary Clinton, "Remarks to the UN"	
Rhetorical Devices	Effect

Sojourner Truth, "Ain't I a Woman?"	
Rhetorical Devices	Effect

Differing Opinions: Acknowledging Opposing Claims

LEARNING STRATEGIES:
Quickwrite, Marking the Text, Skimming/Scanning, Metacognitive Markers, Graphic Organizer, Debate

My Notes

Learning Targets

- Analyze the logic in the development of different points of view on the same subject.
- Create a claim and argue a position incorporating counterclaims in a class debate.

Before Reading

1. **Quickwrite:** Should violent video games be banned to minors?

2. Skim and scan both texts, paying attention to text features, to predict the opinions of each author.

During Reading

3. Mark the text by annotating the claim and reasons the writer makes about the topic. Use the My Notes space to add your comments.

KEY IDEAS AND DETAILS
What is this author's claim? Considering the author's role, what reasoning do you see? Explain the effect.

Online Article

Failure to Ban
Violent Video Games
Makes Job Harder for Parents

by Tamika Mallory

As a mother of a teenage son, I can't begin to tell you how many times I've walked into a room and turned off a video game or TV program that I felt was inappropriate for a still developing child. But despite how often I pull the plug or refuse to let him buy certain products, the reality is that our Supreme Court just made my job and the job of other parents that much more difficult. Ruling on Monday that violent and dangerous video games could not be banned to minors, the Supreme Court in essence said to all of us: you're on your own.

Raising a child in today's culture of aggression, accessibility to negative influences and overall instability is a challenge for any mother out there. Once upon a time, there used to be a concept of the community. Regardless of how much our mothers and fathers were working, we knew that a neighbor or elder could and would keep an eye on us. We knew that we couldn't engage in certain behaviors because it would without fail get back to our parents. There was a real sense of looking out for each other, and a profound sense of looking out for future generations. But today, the "unity" in community is lost and the ones to suffer the most are the kids.

As a busy, working mother, how can I physically be everywhere my son is? The reality is, no parent can be with his or her child 24/7. And while we may restrict gruesome video games in our homes, who will protect the kids when they set foot into the outside world? Knowing that my son wasn't running around in the streets, I took comfort in the notion that video games at least provided an alternative, safe form of recreation for young people. But what are we teaching them if these games are inundated with nothing but guns, shooting and graphic violence? How different is that from what's tragically out on the streets? And what kind of subliminal impact are we having on these kids if we flood them with these messages?

The Supreme Court has failed to protect us in the most fundamental manner. Who will prevent our children from the devastating material designed to pollute and tarnish their minds, body and soul? In order to raise a strong, educated and focused generation, it takes a village—including all levels of government. It's unfortunate that ours just let us down.

News Article

It's Perverse,
but It's Also Pretend

by Cheryl K. Olson, Op-Ed Contributor

ON Monday the Supreme Court struck down, on First Amendment grounds, California's law barring the sale or rental of violent video games to people under 18. On a practical level, the law was vague. It was never clear which games might fall under the law, or whose job it would be to decide.

But more important, the state's case was built on assumptions—that violent games cause children psychological or neurological harm and make them more aggressive and likely to harm other people—that are not supported by evidence. In the end, the case serves only to highlight how little we know about this medium and its effects on our children.

In my research on middle schoolers, the most popular game series among boys was Grand Theft Auto, which allows players to commit cartoon violence with chain saws as well as do perfectly benign things like deliver pizza on a scooter.

Teenage boys may be more interested in the chain saws, but there's no evidence that this leads to violent behavior in real life. F.B.I. data shows that youth violence continues to decline; it is now at its lowest rate in years, while bullying appears to be stable or decreasing.

This certainly does not prove that video games are harmless. The violent games most often played by young teens, like most of the Grand Theft Auto series, are rated M, for players 17 and older, for a reason and do merit parental supervision.

My Notes

KEY IDEAS AND DETAILS
What is this author's claim?

KEY IDEAS AND DETAILS
Why does the author compare violent video games to traditional fairy tales? What is the purpose and effect?

Differing Opinions: Acknowledging Opposing Claims

But despite parents' worst fears, violence in video games may be less harmful than violence in movies or on the evening news. It does seem reasonable that virtually acting out a murder is worse than watching one. But there is no research supporting this, and one could just as easily argue that interactivity makes games less harmful: the player controls the action, and can stop playing if he feels overwhelmed or upset. And there is much better evidence to support psychological harm from exposure to violence on TV news.

In fact, such games (in moderation) may actually have some positive effects on developing minds.

As the court opinion notes, traditional fairy tales are chock-full of violence; a child experiences and learns to manage fears from the safety of Mom or Dad's lap. Similarly, a teen can try out different identities—how it feels to be a hero, a trickster or someone of a different age or sex—in the safe fantasy world of a video game.

In the end, the most harmful assumption in the California law is that we know enough about the effects of video games to recommend policy solutions. (I was one of dozens of advisers for a supporting brief filed by those who challenged the law.) Almost no studies of video games and youth have been designed with policy in mind. If we want to mitigate risks of harm to our children (or the risk that our children will harm others), we need research on the specific effects of the most commonly played violent games, and of playing violent games in social groups.

We know virtually nothing, for instance, about how youths who are already prone to violent behavior, such as those exposed to violence at home and in their neighborhoods, use these games. Do they play them differently from the way other children do? Do they react differently? And if so, how might we limit the risks involved?

We need to reframe our view of video games. Chief Justice John G. Roberts Jr. and Justice Samuel A. Alito Jr. concurred with the majority's opinion, but with some reservations: "We should take into account the possibility that developing technology may have important societal implications that will become apparent only with time," Justice Alito wrote. This is excellent advice, but only if we are willing to consider that video games may have potential benefits as well as potential risks.

Cheryl K. Olson, a public health researcher, is a co-author of "Grand Theft Childhood The Surprising Truth About Violent Video Games and What Parents Can Do."

After Reading

4. Reread and **mark the text** for logical reasoning and devices. Annotate by analyzing or commenting on the effect of the reasoning and devices in the My Notes section.

My Notes

5. Complete the graphic organizer to evaluate the arguments.

Reasons + evidence for banning video games to minors	My opinion	Reasons + evidence against banning video games to minors	My opinion

Acknowledging Counterclaims

Part of arguing effectively is to acknowledge opposing claims, also known as counterclaims—the "other side" of the issue. Recognizing counterclaims adds to a writer's credibility (ethos) because it shows that he or she is knowledgeable about the issue. To acknowledge a counterclaim, a writer or speaker recognizes an opposing viewpoint and then argues against it, perhaps by finding weaknesses within the opposing reasons and evidence. In other words, it is the "yes, but" part of the argument. "Yes" is recognizing the counterclaim; "but" is the writer's response to it.

Example:

Issue: A teenager wants parental permission to go to a concert.

Claim: I should be allowed to go to a concert without an adult.

- *Of course you are worried about me going without you;* however, I have a cell phone with me, and we can check in throughout the concert.

- *Certainly I can see why you might be concerned because you don't know all my friends,* but I'll be glad to ask their parents to call and reassure you.

- *Admittedly, it is a good point that I do have homework;* on the other hand, the concert is only a few hours long, and I plan to get most of it completed before I go.

> **GRAMMAR & USAGE**
> Complex sentences
>
> Notice that a **complex sentence** with a dependent marker is a structure that helps the writer to acknowledge and refute a counterclaim.

Differing Opinions: Acknowledging Opposing Claims

My Notes

Practice Scenario

Issue: Mobile devices (e.g., cell phones, tablets)

Claim: Mobile devices should be banned at school.

The Principal's Argument	The Student's Argument

Sentence Starters

While _____ may be the case, it is still true that ...

Even though _____ , the claim that _____ still stands because ...

Prepare for the Debate

Violent video games should be banned to minors.	
Assigned Position (circle one) FOR AGAINST	
Claim:	
Reasons:	**Evidence (Logos):**
Recognizing counterclaim:	
Rhetorical appeals I can use for effect: **Pathos:**	
Ethos:	
Rhetorical devices I can use for effect:	

After the Debate

Reflect: How clear was your claim? In what ways did you incorporate adequate evidence (logos) and address the counterclaim?

Language and Writer's Craft: Phrases and Clauses

A **clause** is a group of words that includes a subject and a verb. An **independent clause** has a subject and a verb and can stand alone as a sentence. A **dependent clause** has a subject and a verb, but it cannot stand alone as a sentence.

Examples:

Independent clause: *Screen addiction is a serious problem.*

Dependent clause: *because children spend too much time in front of screens*

A **phrase** is a group of words that does not include both a subject and a verb.

Examples:

being isolated from others, of a whole society, and difficulties with peers are all types of phrases.

When writing, take care to ensure that you use phrases and clauses correctly. For example, make sure that you place modifying phrases so that they modify (add information to) the proper word in the sentence. Phrases that are incorrectly placed are called **misplaced modifiers** because it is difficult to tell which word is being modified.

Example: *Two students strolled down the street with cell phones.* (Does the street have the cell phones or the students?)

Argumentative Writing Prompt: In your writing group, revise your text to incorporate an acknowledgment of a counterclaim. Use adding or replacing in your draft. Be sure to:

• Clearly describe and acknowledge the counterclaim.
• Use transitions and complex sentences with phrases and clauses to make your point.
• Use correct spelling, grammar, and punctuation.

My Notes

To Introduce and Conclude

LEARNING STRATEGIES:
Note-taking, Chunking the
Text, Close Reading, Marking
the Text

Learning Targets

- Analyze and identify the components of an introductory and a concluding paragraph in an argumentative essay.

Before Reading

1. Access your prior knowledge of writing introductions and conclusions. Then take notes as you view the opening and closing of an argument.

My Notes

Introduction	Conclusion
<u>What do you know?</u> What makes a successful **introduction** to an argument?	<u>What do you know?</u> What makes a successful **conclusion** to an argument?
<u>What do you see and hear?</u> What does the speaker do to introduce the argument?	<u>What do you see and hear?</u> What does the speaker do to conclude the argument?

2. Chunk the text by boxing the first paragraph and the last paragraph. Then, number the sentences of the introductory and concluding paragraph.

During Reading

3. Closely read the introduction and conclusion of the sample student text about the issue of teenagers' use of technology. Mark the text by labeling the function of each sentence in those paragraphs.

Student Essay

Screen Time?

How does screen time really affect you and others you know? Does the new technology make life better? The answer is no, screen time affects youth in a negative way. Imagine a future world without teenagers, instead, as people in the United Kingdom like to call it, screenagers—kids that have a variety of mental and physical illnesses and are no longer capable of doing some of the jobs that are most important to our society. Because spending too many hours in front of any kind of screen, even a phone, can become addicting, spark psychological difficulties, and cause lower grades in school, screen time for youth should be limited to two hours a day or less.

Screen addiction is a serious problem in our society. A study conducted by the "Kaiser Family Foundation" states that nearly every kid in the U.S. uses an electronic device almost every second outside of school. Kids ages eight to eighteen spend an average time of seven and one half hours a day. That's over 53 hours a week which is way too much considering that the recommended time per day is two hours. An experiment on kids who got all their screens withdrawn had positive outcomes. The kids seemed calmer, fought less often, and slept better. A lot of kids feel like the overuse of screens has no effect on them, but it actually does, they just don't notice it at all. In addition, in a survey of youth ages eight to eighteen, nearly one in four kids felt addicted to screens. Preventing the over-use of screens could prevent addiction and the failure of a whole society.

Something else the overuse of screens causes is psychological difficulties such as hyperactivity, emotional and conduct problems, as well as difficulties with peers. A survey by the Chiba University says that 25,000 people that spend most of their time in front of a screen feel depressed. The cause of this is not necessarily looking at the screen, but much rather the addiction, not knowing when to stop, and being isolated from others. Depression is a severe illness which causes lots of deaths. In addition, the hyperactivity caused by the screen addiction causes an unhealthy diet and might lead to other dangerous diseases. All these psychological and physical problems caused by one screen, it's really not worth it.

Finally, using screens too much may cause a decrease in grades at school. It is proven that adolescents who watch three or more hours of television a day are

---

GRAMMAR & USAGE
Dangling Modifiers

A phrase that modifies the wrong word is called a **dangling modifier**. Look at these examples:
Dangling: The two students talked quietly in the *corner with cell phones.* (It sounds like the corner has the cell phones.)
Correct: The two *students with cell phones* talked quietly in the corner. (The students have the cell phones.)

My Notes

To Introduce and Conclude

at especially high risk for poor homework completion, negative attitudes toward school, poor grades, and long-term academic failure. This might result in a bad future with a bad job or no job at all. This mainly happens because of the lack of enthusiasm towards school and the time spent using a screen instead of studying. In addition, the content of some TV shows out there don't necessarily make you smarter, in fact, some of them make you dumber. Considering this, you should think about how every hour you watch TV instead of studying makes it harder to have a promising future.

In conclusion, decreasing screen time below two hours a day could prevent youth from having a bad life. Reduced screen time helps you in school, helps you have a healthier diet, be more physical, and tends to get you more engaged in activities. The end of our world will most likely not be caused by a bunch of earthquakes and tsunamis as shown in the movie "2012"; it is going to be our young generation wasting away in front of screens. So, go home, unplug your screen, and save our future society. The results will be much better than some TV Show.

After Reading

4. Use the same questions as before to collaboratively discuss your observations of the student text.

- What does the speaker do to introduce the argument?

- What does the speaker do to conclude the argument?

Check Your Understanding

Argumentative Writing Prompt: Create an outline and then generate ideas for a potential introduction and conclusion to your class-constructed body paragraph. Be sure to:

- Introduce your claim in an introduction.
- Include a hook, a connection between the hook and the claim, and the claim.
- Provide a conclusion that supports your argument. (Why does the claim that you made matter? What should the audience do based on your claim? What is your call to action?)

Writing an Argumentative Essay

Assignment

Your assignment is to write an argumentative essay that states and supports a claim about an issue of importance to you.

Planning and Prewriting: Take time to make a plan for generating ideas and research questions.

- What prewriting strategies (such as freewriting or webbing) can you use to select and explore a timely and relevant issue that interests you?

- How will you draft a claim that states your position?

- What questions will guide your research?

Researching: Gather information from a variety of credible sources.

- What strategies can you use (such as KWHL or SOAPSTone) to guide your research and evaluate sources?

- How will you take notes by summarizing, paraphrasing, quoting, responding, and recording bibliographic information?

- Will you use a research log (see Activity 2.15) to record your research and sources?

Drafting: Write an argumentative essay that is appropriate for your task, purpose, and audience.

- How will you select the best reasons and evidence from your research?

- What strategies can you use (such as outlining) to organize your draft?

- Who is the audience, and what would be an appropriate tone and style for this audience?

Evaluating and Revising the Draft: Create opportunities to review and revise your work.

- During the process of writing, when can you pause to share and respond with others?

- What is your plan to include suggestions and revision ideas into your draft?

- How can the Scoring Guide help you evaluate how well your draft meets the requirements of the assignment?

Checking and Editing for Publication: Confirm your final draft is ready for publication.

- How will you proofread and edit your draft to demonstrate command of the conventions of standard English capitalization, punctuation, spelling, grammar, and usage?

Reflection

You have used and been introduced to a number of strategies for constructing a well-reasoned and researched argumentative essay. Which strategies were most effective in helping you to write an effective argument, and how did you use them?

My Notes

Writing an Argumentative Essay

SCORING GUIDE

Scoring Criteria	Exemplary	Proficient	Emerging	Incomplete
Ideas	The argument • skillfully presents a claim and provides appropriate background and a clear explanation of the issue • effectively supports claims with logical, convincing reasoning and evidence, as well as skillful use of rhetorical devices • summarizes and refutes counterclaims with relevant reasoning and clear evidence.	The argument • supports a claim that is clearly presented with appropriate background details • develops claims and counterclaims fairly and uses valid reasoning, relevant and sufficient evidence, and a variety of rhetorical devices • concludes by revisiting the main points and reinforcing the claim.	The argument • presents a claim that is vague or unclear and does not adequately explain the issue or provide background details • presents reasons and evidence that may not logically support the claim or come from credible sources • concludes by listing the main points of the thesis.	The argument • states an unclear claim and does not explain the issue or provide background details • presents few if any relevant reasons and evidence to support the claim • includes reasons that are not relevant or sufficient for the evidence • concludes without restating the claim.
Structure	The argument • follows a clear structure with a logical progression of ideas that establish relationships between the essential elements of an argument • links main points with effective transitions that establish coherence.	The argument • establishes clear relationships between the essential elements of an argument • uses transitions to link the major sections of the essay and create coherence.	The argument • demonstrates an awkward progression of ideas, but the reader can understand them • uses some elements of hook, claim, evidence, and conclusion • spends too much time on some irrelevant details and uses few transitions.	The argument • does not follow a logical organization • includes some detail and elements of an argument, but the writing lacks clear direction and uses no transitions to help readers follow the line of thought.
Use of Language	The essay • uses precise diction deliberately chosen to inform or to explain the topic • uses a variety of sentence structures to enhance the explanation • demonstrates technical command of conventions of standard English.	The essay • uses appropriate diction for the information or explanation • uses a variety of sentence structures • demonstrates general command of conventions; minor errors do not interfere with meaning.	The essay • uses informal diction that is inappropriate at times for the information or explanation • shows little or no variety in sentence structure • demonstrates limited command of conventions; errors interfere with meaning.	The essay • uses informal diction that is inappropriate for the purpose • shows no variety in sentence structure • demonstrates limited command of conventions; errors interfere with meaning.

Visual Prompt: Both sports and academics are valued by society, but sports seem to get more attention. Should academic achievement be as important as or more important than athletic achievement? Can sports participation help prepare you for future success?

Choices and Consequences

Unit Overview

How do the choices you make now shape your future self? In this unit, you will explore how decisions can have far-reaching consequences that determine your character, values, and contribution to society. You will read a novel that focuses on one young man's emerging realizations about how his personal history continues to affect his relationships with his friends, teammates, family, and school. You will analyze the choices made by different literary characters and write an essay about the consequences. Also, you will apply your understanding of choices and consequences to a research presentation about a historical figure or world leader who made inspiring choices that helped shape our world.

Choices and Consequences

pic

GOALS:

- To use textual evidence to support analysis and inferences
- To write a literary analysis essay
- To evaluate, analyze, and synthesize a variety of informational texts
- To create and present a biographical research project

ACADEMIC VOCABULARY
subordinate
perspective
interpret
annotated bibliography

Literary Terms
imagery
motif
setting
atmosphere
mood
flashback
foreshadowing
point of view
conflict
subplot
allusion
biography
autobiography

Contents

Activities:

*Texts not included in these materials.

Language and Writer's Craft

- Revising with Subordinate Clauses (3.4)
- Revising with Coordinating Conjunctions (3.7)
- Understanding Phrases (3.8)
- Active versus Passive Voice (3.11)
- Adjectival and Prepositional Phrases (3.17)
- Dangling and Misplaced Modifiers (3.21)

Previewing the Unit

LEARNING STRATEGIES:
QHT, Marking the Text,
Skimming/Scanning

My Notes

Learning Targets
- Preview the big ideas and vocabulary for the unit.
- Identify and analyze the skills and knowledge needed to complete Embedded Assessment 1 successfully.

Making Connections

In prior units, you have read narratives and other fictional stories, as well as articles and informational texts. Learning to write an argument gave you experience in identifying claims and using evidence from texts to support a claim. In this unit, you will read the novel *Tangerine*. After reading the novel, you will write a literary analysis essay in which you will analyze the novel's characters, setting, and actions and cite evidence from the novel to support your analysis.

Essential Questions

Based on your current knowledge, write your answers to these questions.

1. What is the relationship between choices and consequences?

2. What makes a great leader?

Vocabulary Development

Go back to the Contents page and look at the Academic Vocabulary and Literary Terms for the unit. Use a QHT or other vocabulary strategy to determine which terms you know and which you need to learn more about.

Unpacking Embedded Assessment 1

Read the assignment below for Embedded Assessment 1: Writing a Literary Analysis Essay found on page 209.

> Write a multi-paragraph literary analysis essay in response to the following prompt (or another provided by your teacher): In Edward Bloor's novel *Tangerine*, how did one character's choices and the consequences of those choices affect the development of the main character?

In your own words, summarize what you will need to know to complete this assessment successfully. With your class, create a graphic organizer to represent the skills and knowledge you will need to complete the tasks identified in the Embedded Assessment.

INDEPENDENT READING LINK
You will be reading the novel *Tangerine* in this unit. For independent reading, choose informational and other texts about Florida, especially sinkholes, muck fires, the citrus industry, environmental issues, or wildlife.

Peeling a *Tangerine*

Learning Targets
- Use imagery in a written response to a narrative prompt.
- Make inferences and predictions about the author's purpose.

LEARNING STRATEGIES:
Note-taking, Graphic
Organizer, Predicting

1. Examine the tangerine your teacher has given you. Take notes about it using sensory details to create imagery.

   Appearance:

   Smell:

   Feel:

   Taste:

2. **Similes** and **metaphors** are a common type of figurative language that creates imagery. Review your notes above, and then create a simile and a metaphor about a tangerine. Use the following sentence starters.

   Peeling a tangerine is like ...

   Peeling a tangerine is ...

Writing Prompt: Write a narrative paragraph describing the experience of examining a tangerine. Be sure to:
- Start with a topic sentence that uses figurative language.
- Use imagery (description and figurative language) for supporting detail.
- Include personal commentary (your opinions or explanations).

My Notes

Literary Terms
Imagery is the use of descriptive or figurative language to create word pictures.

Peeling a *Tangerine*

3. Examine carefully the design, color, images, and text on the front and back cover of the novel *Tangerine*. Take notes in the graphic organizer.

Front Cover Color and Images	Text and Title on Front Cover
Back Cover Color and Images	**Text and Title on Back Cover**
Questions and Comments	**Inferences and Predictions**

Literary Terms
A **motif** is a recurring element, image, or idea that has symbolic significance in a work of literature. A novel with the title *Tangerine* might make use of tangerine-related imagery many times and in different ways.

4. **Group Discussion:** Which aspect of the book cover helped you make predictions and inferences—the images or the text? Which generated more questions and comments? Which is more important in terms of marketing or selling the book to an audience? Based on the imagery of the cover, predict what some of the **motifs** of the novel might be.

Check Your Understanding
Compare and contrast examining an actual tangerine with examining the book cover of *Tangerine*. How were these experiences similar and different?

Reading the Novel *Tangerine*

Learning Targets
- Record and respond with personal commentary to textual evidence from a novel.
- Write, discuss, and evaluate levels of questions about the text with your peers.

Before Reading
1. **Quickwrite:** Can human beings choose not to remember? When and why might a person make a choice to forget?

As you read *Tangerine*, you will take notes in a double-entry journal. Copy or summarize passages from the book on the left side (textual evidence) and write your response to each passage on the right side (commentary). Draw a horizontal line under each entry. For reference, record the page number of each quote.

Responses could include the following:
- **Questions** about things you don't understand
- **Opinions** about characters or plot events
- **Connections** you make to real life or other texts
- **Predictions** (guesses) about how characters will react to events
- **Inferences** (logical conclusions) about why characters are saying or doing things

Consider this example from the first lines of *Tangerine*.

LEARNING STRATEGIES:
Think-Pair-Share,
Note-taking, Questioning
the Text

GRAMMAR & USAGE
Citing Literature

When analyzing literature, do not use the first-person "I." Instead, use the characters' names or third-person pronouns such as "he" or "she."

In addition, when discussing or writing about literature, use the present tense because the characters and events of a story are described in present tense.

Textual Evidence	Page #	Commentary
"The house looked strange. It was completely empty now …"	1	**Inference:** I think Paul's family is moving out of their house. **Question:** Where is he moving? **Connection:** My classroom looks like this after the last day of school.

My Notes

Reading the Novel *Tangerine*

2. Below, you will find a page of a blank double-entry journal form to use as you read and discuss the prologue together as a class. Try to use a variety of responses (question, opinion, connection, prediction, inference).

Title of Novel:		
Author:		
Textual Evidence	**Page #**	**Commentary**

You will use several double-entry journal pages as you read *Tangerine*. Follow your teacher's directions to create double-entry journal pages in your Reader/Writer Notebook for taking notes on the novel.

Introducing the Strategy: Questioning the Text

A strategy for thinking actively and interpretively about your reading is to ask questions. As you read any text, you can ask questions that aid your understanding with different levels of ideas.

- **Literal questions** (Level 1): You can answer questions on the literal level by looking to the text directly.

  Example: What kind of car does Mrs. Fisher drive?

- **Interpretive questions** (Level 2): You cannot find answers to interpretive questions directly in the text; however, textual evidence points to and supports your answers.

  Example: What emotions does Paul feel as he remembers the incident with the mailbox?

- **Universal questions** (Level 3): These questions go beyond the text. They require you to think about the larger issues or ideas raised by a text.

  Example: Is it possible that people who are visually impaired can see some things more clearly than people who can see perfectly?

3. Write three questions, one of each type, about the prologue to *Tangerine*.

Literal:

Interpretive:

Universal:

4. **Collaborative Discussion:** Remember to follow group norms about discussions, speaking clearly, listenting carefully, and allowing each person a turn to question and respond.

Share your levels of questions with a small group of peers and ask them to respond to each. After all group members have shared and responded to one another's three questions, discuss how the questions and responses helped each of you come to a new understanding. Which questions were the easiest to answer, and which were more difficult? Which questions led to the most interesting and informative discussions?

WORD CONNECTIONS

Roots and Affixes

The word *literal* contains the root *-liter-* from the Latin word *littera*, meaning "letter." This root also appears in *literacy*, *literature*, and *alliteration*.

Interpretive contains the root *interpret*, which means "to come to an understanding."

Universal contains the Latin prefix *uni-*, meaning "one," and the root *-ver-*, meaning "turn." The root *-ver-* appears in *reverse*, *adversary*, *introvert*, *vertigo*, and *conversation*.

The suffix *-al* indicates an adjective.

My Notes

There's a New Kid in Town

LEARNING STRATEGIES:
Skimming/Scanning,
Note-taking, Predicting,
Visualizing

Learning Targets

- Understand how textual details contribute to a novel's mood or atmosphere.
- Analyze textual evidence about choices and consequences and record commentary in a double-entry journal.
- Write and revise a literary analysis paragraph that uses textual evidence.

Understanding Setting and Mood or Atmosphere

1. **Skim** the first few journal entries in Part 1 of *Tangerine* (August 18–19) looking for details about Paul's new neighborhood. List as many as you can.

2. **Visualize and sketch** a map of the neighborhood in Lake Windsor Downs. Give attention to color, structures, and other details that create this setting. The **setting** helps create the **mood** and **atmosphere** of the novel. What specific details about the setting seem most important?

My Notes

Literary Terms

Setting is the time and place in which a narrative occurs. Details of setting often create **atmosphere**, the feeling created by a literary work or passage. Atmosphere contributes to the **mood**, the overall emotional quality of a work, which is created by the author's language and tone and the subject matter.

3. In *Tangerine*, as in real life, people make decisions that carry consequences. Some consequences are obvious right away, while others are not apparent until some time has passed. As you read the novel, use your double-entry journal to keep a record of the choices made by Paul, his parents, and other characters. For some of the choices, you will be able to fill in the consequences and the impact on Paul right away. For other choices, you may not know a consequence or its impact on Paul until you have read more of the novel.

My Notes

Textual evidence of a choice made by a character	Page #	Commentary on the consequences of that choice and the possible impact on Paul
Paul's mother calls the fire department about the smoke	13	Paul's mother and Paul learn about muck fires and Paul begins to see that his new community has problems.

Continue to take notes in your double-entry journal as you read Part 1 of *Tangerine* by recording textual evidence of choices and making predictions and inferences about possible consequences.

There's a New Kid in Town

pi

GRAMMAR & USAGE
Direct Quotations

When using **direct quotations**, place the quoted words inside quotation marks.

In the paragraph, notice the two different ways quotes from the novel are used.

WORD CONNECTIONS

Roots and Affixes

The word *subordinate* is made up of the Latin prefix *sub-*, meaning "under" or "below," and the Latin root *-ord-*, meaning "order "or "rank."

My Notes

4. Mark the text of the following literary analysis paragraph as follows:
   - Underline the topic sentence that states the main idea.
   - Highlight textual evidence.
   - Put an asterisk at the start of any sentence that provides commentary.

Mrs. Fisher's decision to call the fire department affects Paul's initial impression of his new community. Paul notices smoke the first morning he wakes up in the house on Lake Windsor Downs. He writes, "The air had a gray tint to it, and a damp, foul smell like an ashtray. *Smoke*, I thought. *Something around here is on fire.*" When he tells his mother, Mrs. Fisher immediately panics and calls the fire department. After the volunteer fire department representative explains to her that there's nothing she can do to stop the muck fires, she "stares at him in disbelief." Paul realizes that his parents don't know all that much about their new home, and he begins to suspect that everything is not as perfect as they would like him to believe.

Expository Writing Prompt: On a separate page, write a literary analysis paragraph about another choice that a character made. Be sure to:
   - Write a topic sentence that states the main idea.
   - Use textual evidence, with quotation marks around direct quotes.
   - Provide commentary about the consequences of that choice for Paul.

Language and Writer's Craft: Revising with Subordinate Clauses

A **subordinate clause** is a group of words with a subject and a verb. It cannot stand alone as a sentence, though, because it does not contain a complete thought. **Subordinating conjunctions** introduce subordinate (dependent) clauses.

Subordinate clauses and the subordinating conjunctions that introduce them enable you to show a relationship between ideas in a sentence. A subordinate clause is lower in rank than an independent clause and indicates that the idea in the suboridinate clause is of less importance.

Some common subordinating conjunctions are:

after	*although*	*if*	*when*	*though*	*because*
unless	*whenever*	*since*	*before*	*until*	*while*

Writing Sentences with Subordinate Adverbial Clauses

An adverbial clause functions as an adverb to answer questions such as *how*, *when*, *where*, *in what way*, or *how often*.

Examples (subordinate adverbial clauses are in italics):

- *Although Mr. Fisher seems like a concerned father*, he is inattentive to Paul.
- Alternative: Mr. Fisher is inattentive to Paul *although he seems like a concerned father*.
- *Because Paul is serious about soccer*, the Seagulls accept him as a teammate.
- Alternative: The Seagulls accept Paul as a teammate *because he is serious about soccer*.

Notice that when a subordinate clause begins a sentence, it is followed by a comma. When the sentence ends with the subordinate clause, no comma is necessary.

Complex sentences contain an independent clause and at least one dependent clause. In complex sentences using adverbial clauses, the independent clause carries the important information of the sentence while the less important, or subordinate, information is contained in the subordinate clause. Notice the two different structures in the examples above and how the order of the clauses changes the meaning.

Try rearranging the words in the sentences above one more time. Write them below.

How has the meaning changed? What part of the meaning of the sentence becomes important with your revisions?

Check Your Understanding

Find and highlight at least one subordinate clause in the sample paragraph. Then, return to the paragraph you wrote in response to the expository writing prompt on the preceding page and revise it to incorporate a sentence using a subordinate clause. Experiment with different subordinating conjunctions.

> **ACADEMIC VOCABULARY**
> The word **subordinate** has many meanings. A *subordinate* is a person of lower rank. *To subordinate* is to make something less important. Used as an adjective, subordinate describes a relationship in which something is less important than or lower than another thing.

My Notes

Like Mother, Like Son?

LEARNING STRATEGIES:
Close Reading, Graphic
Organizer, Drafting

My Notes

Literary Terms
A **flashback** is an interruption
in the sequence of events to
relate events that occurred in
the past.

Learning Targets

- Analyze an author's use of flashback, foreshadowing, and characterization and provide support of your analysis with textual evidence.
- Compare the use of literary techniques from two different genres.

Flashback Novel Study

In this activity, you will consider the author's use of flashback, foreshadowing, and characterization in *Tangerine*.

1. *Tangerine* is also a text that uses flashbacks. Conduct a close reading of Paul's entry for Monday, August 28. How does the author let you know that what you are about to read is a flashback? Make notes in the graphic organizer below.

Flashbacks in *Tangerine*	
Signal	**Notes**

Foreshadowing

2. Novels often use **foreshadowing** to prepare the audience for action that is to come. Foreshadowing creates an atmosphere of suspense and keeps the audience wondering about what will happen next in the story. Identify examples of foreshadowing in *Tangerine* and use them to make inferences. Write your evidence and inferences in the graphic organizer below.

> **Literary Terms**
> **Foreshadowing** is the use of clues to hint at events that will occur later in the plot.

Evidence of foreshadowing in *Tangerine*	Inference about what is being foreshadowed in *Tangerine*

Check Your Understanding

Both flashback and foreshadowing affect the plot and conflict of a story. With your group, discuss how these techniques help the reader think about the conflict. Then, write a quickwrite to capture your ideas and those of your group about how flashback and foreshadowing affect plot and conflict.

My Notes

Like Mother, Like Son?

Characterization

3. Characterization is the way an author reveals what the characters are like. Many authors prefer to do this indirectly, through the characters' own words, appearance, thoughts, and actions. Take notes about the ways the author reveals details about the characters of Paul and Mrs. Fisher.

Elements of Characterization	Paul Fisher	Mrs. Fisher
Actions		
Appearance		
Thoughts		
What the Character Says		
What Others Say About the Character		

4. The author has given Paul a certain set of character traits. Write a summary statement about Paul's character and how you think he will confront any conflicts that you predict will occur in the novel.

Check Your Understanding

Writing Prompt Write an explanation of how Paul Fisher is similar to and different from his mother, Mrs. Fisher, based on the details you wrote in the chart on the previous page. Tell how the author's characterizations helped create mental images of the characters in your mind as you read.

- Start with a topic sentence of comparison.
- Cite evidence—details, examples, quotations—from the text to support your ideas.
- Include details about the characters' differences and similarities.

Oh, Brother!

LEARNING STRATEGIES:
Quickwrite, Graphic Organizer,
Sharing and Responding

Learning Targets

- Write a literary analysis paragraph about sibling relationships and provide support with textual evidence.
- Identify and apply the organizing elements of a compare/contrast essay.

Before Reading

1. Family relationships are important in *Tangerine*, especially relationships between brothers and the idea of brotherhood. Think about the motif of brothers and brotherhood in this novel.

After Reading

2. After reading or rereading the entries for September 5–6, use the graphic organizer below to record and discuss the ways the Costello and Fisher brothers relate to each other.

My Notes

Joey's Relationship with Mike	Mike's Relationship with Joey
Paul's Relationship with Erik	**Erik's Relationship with Paul**

3. With a small group, share your notes and respond to your group members' opinions about the relationships of the Costello and Fisher brothers. Then, write one sentence describing each relationship.

Relationship of the Costello brothers:

Relationship of the Fisher brothers:

4. Work with your partner or small group to write a **thesis statement** comparing the Costello brothers' relationship to the Fisher brothers' relationship. Use a subordinate adverbial clause to show which of the two relationships you think is better or more important.

Expository Writing Prompt: With your writing group, write a literary analysis paragraph about one of the sibling relationships (Costello or Fisher brothers). Half the group should write about the Costellos and the other half about the Fishers. Be sure to:

- Use one of the sentences from Step 2 as a topic sentence.
- Provide supporting detail from the story as textual evidence and write commentary.
- Use transition words and subordinate clauses.

Before you read the two drafts, get sets of four different colored pencils, one set for each member of your group. Choose a color code and fill in the blanks below:

_____ (1st color): topic sentence
_____ (2nd color): textual evidence
_____ (3rd color): commentary
_____ (4th color): transitions

Mark one another's drafts by underlining according to your color key.

Review the markings made on each draft. What do the text markings tell you about your own writing? Are you missing any key elements of the literary analysis paragraph? Use the information to revise and improve your writing.

My Notes

GRAMMAR & USAGE
Punctuating Transitions

When you use a transition at the beginning of a sentence, follow it with a comma. When you use a transition to connect two complete thoughts, precede the transition with a semicolon and follow it with a comma.

Oh, Brother!

My Notes

With your writing group, you have created a thesis statement and two support paragraphs that you could use for a compare/contrast literary analysis essay. You still need an **introduction** and a **conclusion** to have a complete essay.

5. With your class, brainstorm the key elements of an effective introduction to a literary analysis essay.

6. Next, brainstorm the key elements of an effective conclusion to a literary analysis essay.

7. Write either an introduction or conclusion for your essay while your partner or half of your small group writes the other. Share drafts and respond by marking each other's drafts for the key elements you identified in Step 2.

8. Compare/contrast essays use special transition words. Revise your draft to add precise transition words that will help your reader follow your ideas.

    Transitions to use when comparing: *also, alike, both, in the same way, likewise, similarly*

    Transitions to use when contrasting: *but, different, however, in contrast, instead, on the other hand, unlike, yet*

9. **Final Draft:** Following your teacher's guidelines, use technology to produce and publish a final draft of your co-constructed essay in collaboration with your partner or small group. As you collaborate, eliminate unnecessry wordiness and repetition. With your class, brainstorm ways that you could use technology to share and respond as a class to the other groups' essays.

Learning Targets

- Compare a fictional account of an event with a nonfiction account of an event.
- Evaluate author's purpose in selecting a point of view.

LEARNING STRATEGIES:
Think-Pair-Share,
Note-taking, Summarizing

Before Reading

1. **Quickwrite:** The novel *Tangerine* was first published in 1997. At that time, most people had no special associations with the date of September 11, which is the date of the sinkhole disaster in *Tangerine*. What are some of the connotations Americans have with that date since the events of 9/11 in 2001?

During Reading

News writers often answer questions related to the 5 Ws and an H: Who, What, When, Where, Why, and How. As you read the following news article, mark the text for details that will help you identify the 5 Ws and an H. Take notes in the margin.

My Notes

News Article

A stunning tale of escape traps its hero in replay

by Harry Bruinius, from *The Christian Science Monitor*

KEY IDEAS AND DETAILS
How is this article organized—as an expository explanation of the 9/11 escape or as a narrative retelling of the 9/11 events? Why is this structure effective?

JERSEY CITY, N.J. Sunlight seeps through the translucent curtains on his living room window, making the lacquered *matrioshka* dolls on the wall case gleam. Sitting on the sofa, Jan Demczur leafs through a thick binder of news clippings about his heroic Sept. 11 escape, still in a daze at the story they tell.

He stays home often now, speaking more Ukrainian than English, a language still difficult for him. When he does venture out, he's sometimes overcome with a sense of fear, his head dizzy and heavy, like a big ball of lead. It's been almost a year, but Mr. Demczur has still not returned to his job as one of the workers who wash the endless sheets of glass stacked to the sky in Manhattan.

It's become a safe new routine, sitting here amid pillows adorned with his wife's cross stitchings, telling how he survived. His ordeal was compelling—he was trapped in an elevator with five others after the first plane struck Tower 1, and barely escaped by clawing through the walls with only his squeegee—and media from around the world have since flocked to him, reporting his story of survival, and the tiny tool that saved him.

Before, he'd wake up at 4:45 a.m., five days a week, jump on the train to the city, and do his job. Like the thousands of lunch-pail workers who pass each day through the tunnels to the island, Demczur wasn't part of the Manhattan clichés: the vaunting ambition, the ceaseless pace, the glare of art and commerce. Instead, like the steel frames within a skyscraper's facade, he was one of the people behind the city's glamour, those who built, maintained, and ultimately removed piece-by-piece the twisted wreckage of the World Trade Center.

"Window cleaners have been much like the glass they clean: transparent," says Richard Fabry, publisher of an industry magazine.

But Jan Demczur [pronounced John DEMshur] was never a guy to seek attention. Small and demure, he spoke little, and except for occasional mirth in his pale blue eyes, he revealed few emotions.

Content with a predictable routine, he rarely missed a day at work, was honest and industrious, paid his mortgage, and spent time with his wife and kids. His Jersey City house, which had a view of the Twin Towers, was just minutes from the PATH train that took him straight to the sprawling Trade Center, a place he liked to call his second home.

***

That Tuesday, he punched in at 6 a.m. and spent most of the morning cleaning glass doors and partitions on floors 90 to 95 in the North Tower, the impact zone. He worked through his 8 a.m. break so he could finish those top floors early; otherwise, he'd be there until 9. He finished at 8:20 and took the elevator down to the 43rd-floor cafeteria.

At about 8:45, finishing his coffee and danish, he left the cafeteria, and dashed to make an express elevator about to run up to the 77th floor. At 8:48, as he and five others zipped up the shaft, they felt a jolt and then the building sway. The elevator dropped before the emergency brakes ground it to a halt. Later, when smoke started seeping into the car, they knew they had to try to get out.

Demczur quietly took charge. After they pried open the elevator doors, he saw the surface was drywall. "Does anyone have a knife?" he asked. No, nothing. So Demczur started chopping at the wall with the 18-inch blade of the squeegee. When the blade broke and fell down the shaft, he used the handle. It took over an hour, but the six men took turns scraping and poking, and finally burst through to a men's bathroom on the 50th floor. Startled firefighters guided them in different directions. Demczur went down the stairs.

The other tower collapsed at 9:59, when he was at the 11th floor. Soon engulfed in darkness, dust, and confusion, he put his hand on the shoulder of the stranger ahead, continuing down. Seeing him in a maintenance uniform, firefighters screamed to him, "How do we get out?" Demczur had them pan the smoke and dust-filled hallways on the third floor with their flashlights, and he spotted an exit to another stairwell. He instinctively held it open as others went through first, until a fireman grabbed him by the arm and led him out.

Outside, emergency workers gave him oxygen, and water to rinse his eyes. He made his way to the West Side Highway, just a few blocks away, and was finally able to see the sky. "When I look up, and see the tower burning, I turned like ice," Demczur recalls. "Everything was freezing in me." Then, the antennas of Tower 1 start to teeter.

"I start to run. I kept looking back, saw the building banging down like a pancake." As he ran, his eyes were burning, his head was pounding, the dust was choking him, and then his body felt numb. A few more blocks away, he noticed how beautiful the day was and, sheepishly admits he began to touch himself to see if he was really alive, like a scene from a silly cartoon.

Demczur couldn't have imagined he'd tell this story to so many, or that his squeegee handle and uniform would become a part of the Smithsonian's National Museum of American History. He'll relive a lot of it again this week, when he attends ceremonies in New York and Washington, D.C. But by the end of the year, he hopes to be able to get back to work.

"It is a different kind of life. But I prefer the way it was, when people were alive," Demzcur says.

After Reading

2. Review the description of the sinkhole disaster and rescue in Paul's entry for Monday, September 11. Can you identify the 5 Ws and an H in the description of the event?

Who:

What:

When:

Where:

Why:

How:

GRAMMAR & USAGE
Verbs

A writer's **verbs** determine the intensity and the precision of the content. Intense, strong verbs make a story come alive for the reader. Notice the strong verbs in this sentence:
The kids came *diving* out, *jamming* in the doorways, *pushing* into the backs of other kids, *knocking* each other flat.
Weak, vague verbs can often make what was originally an exciting story seem dull and boring.

My Notes

September 11 Perspectives

Literary Terms
Point of view is the perspective from which a story is told. In **first-person point of view**, the speaker is a character in the story telling what he or she sees or knows. In **third-person point of view**, the narrator is someone outside the story.

ACADEMIC VOCABULARY
The word **perspective** can have different meanings, depending on how it is used. For example, in art *perspective* refers to how objects are painted on a flat surface to show depth and distance. When referring to point of view, *perspective* describes one's opinion or outlook about a topic.

My Notes

3. Think about the different purposes of the two texts you have examined. How is the purpose of the nonfiction newspaper article different from Bloor's purpose for writing a fictional incident about the sinkhole disaster?

4. *Tangerine* is all told in **first-person point of view**, while most news articles are written in **third-person point of view**. Using the T-chart below, record the benefits and limits of each.

Point of View	Benefits	Limits
First Person		
Third Person		

5. **Collaborative Discussion: Socratic Seminar**

Consider the following focus question for the Socratic Seminar:

How did the central character have an effect on the events described?

Write Level 2 (interpretive) questions based on the events of 9/11 as presented in the texts: the sinkhole disaster in *Tangerine* and "A stunning tale of escape traps its hero in replay." Be prepared to ask and respond to questions with your peers about these texts. Be sure that all of your questions are based on the texts and can be answered with evidence from the texts. See Activity 3.3 for a review of questioning the text.

6. What similarities are there between the nonfiction article about the historical events of 9/11 and the fictional event in *Tangerine*?

Language and Writer's Craft: Revising with Coordinating Conjunctions

One way to structure sentences is to create compound sentences. It is easy to combine short sentences (independent clauses) by using a **coordinating conjunction**. This structure is a way of showing specific relationships among ideas. Following is a list of coordinating conjunctions:

> and, but, or, for, so, yet, nor

Here are examples of sentences that could be combined with coordinating conjunctions: What is the relationship created?

Old Charley Burns did not inspect construction sites.

Buildings were constructed in unsafe places.

What would be the best conjuction to use?

Old Charley Burns neglected to inspect construction sites, _____ buildings were constructed in unsafe places.

The sinkhole was extremely dangerous.

Paul and Joey rescued many students.

What would be the best conjunction to use?

The sinkhole was extremely dangerous, _____ Paul and Joey rescued many students.

Try combining the two sentences above by using adverbial clauses from Activity 3.4.

Check Your Understanding

Revise one of the sentences from your Socratic Seminar freewrite by combining sentences using coordinating conjunctions and/or adverbial clauses.

GRAMMAR & USAGE
Conjunctions

Conjunctions join words or groups of words that perform the same function in a sentence. When you join two sentences with a coordinating conjunction, use a comma before the coordinating conjunction. To achieve a formal style, as in academic writing, avoid beginning sentences with coordinating conjunctions.

My Notes

SIFTing Through *Tangerine*

My Notes

Learning Targets

- Analyze how symbol, imagery, and figurative language contribute to tone and theme.
- Revise a literary analysis paragraph to include phrases and appositives.

1. **Quickwrite:** Part 1 of *Tangerine* ends with Paul experiencing what he calls a "miracle." What is your definition of a miracle? What "miracle" does Paul experience?

Introducing the Strategy: SIFT

SIFT is a strategy for analyzing a fictional text by examining stylistic elements, especially symbol, imagery, and figures of speech in order to show how these elements work together to reveal tone and theme.

2. Use your glossary to define each term in the first column. In the second column, take notes as you work with your class to SIFT through "Friday, September 15." Working with your group, apply the SIFT strategy to another chapter as your teacher directs. Record your analysis in the third column.

Symbol		
Imagery		
Figurative Language		
Tone		
Theme		

Expository Writing Prompt: After you have shared examples from different chapters with your class, choose one theme that you have identified from Part 1 of *Tangerine*. Write a literary analysis paragraph analyzing how literary elements such as symbol, imagery, figurative language, and tone contributed to that theme. Be sure to:

- Include a topic sentence that identifies a theme.
- Identify specific literary elements.
- Provide textual evidence in the form of quotes.

Write your paragraph below or on a separate piece of paper or in your Reader/ Writer Notebook.

GRAMMAR & USAGE
Appositives

An **appositive** is a noun or phrase placed near another noun to explain or identify it. For example, in the following sentence, "a sixth-grade teacher" is an appositive identifying Mrs. Harrison.

Mrs. Harrison, *a sixth-grade teacher*, has taught at El Rancho Middle School for ten years.

My Notes

Language and Writer's Craft: Understanding Phrases

You have studied dependent and independent clauses and how to use them to convey complex ideas. Phrases are another important part of every sentence because they add information and detail.

A **phrase** is a small group of words that functions as a part of speech within a sentence. Phrases do not have a subject and verb. Common phrases are noun, verb, adverb, adjective, appositive, and prepositional phrases. Why are all the examples below phrases, not clauses?

smashing into the fence
before the first test
a well-known historian
after the devastation
between ignorance and intelligence
broken into thousands of pieces
her glittering smile

SIFTing Through *Tangerine*

Prepositional phrases all begin with a preposition and end with a noun. You have probably already memorized a list of common prepositions, all of which establish a relationship to a noun. Common prepositions are *in, on, to, under, near, above, by, from, around, beyond*. Use prepositions to create your own sentences like the ones below.

Prepositional Phrase Examples:

I took the casserole *in the refrigerator* to the party.

John took a book *about dinosaurs* from the library.

Using Appositives

An **appositive** is a noun or noun phrase placed near another noun to explain or identify it. It is separated from the noun it renames with commas.

Read the following examples of appositives and appositive phrases:

- *Tangerine, Edward Bloor's first novel*, takes place in Florida.
- Paul, *the main character of the novel*, is a soccer player.
- Erik, *Paul's older brother*, is a senior in high school.
- Edward Bloor's first novel, *Tangerine*, takes place in Florida.
- Eric, *the star athlete*, and Arthur, *his devoted sidekick*, are bullies.

Notice the punctuation of the sentences above. Which sentence does not use a phrase as an appositive?

3. Choose one sentence from your literary analysis paragraph above. Revise it to include a prepositional phrase and/or an appositive. Copy your revised sentence here and share it with a partner.

Check Your Understanding

As you continue to read the novel *Tangerine*, take notes in your double-entry journal by applying the SIFT strategy. Pay particular attention to recurring symbols, imagery, and themes that are possible motifs.

Same Sport, Different School

Learning Targets
- Identify evidence to support a prediction.
- Write a compare-contrast paragraph.

LEARNING STRATEGIES:
Graphic Organizer,
Think-Pair-Share, Close
Reading

1. Take out the double-entry journal notes you created for Part 1 in your Reader/Writer Notebook. Select the entry that you think represents the most significant choice in Part 1, and copy it into the first row below. Find at least three people in your class who have recorded different choices. Take notes as they share their entries.

Textual evidence of a choice made by a character	Page #	Commentary on the consequences of that choice and the possible impact on Paul

Same Sport, Different School

Check Your Understanding

Consider the choice Paul made at the end of Part 1 to transfer to Tangerine Middle School. What does he think will be the consequence of this choice? Do you agree? Predict other possible consequences and write them below.

2. As you read the entries for "September 18 and 19," use the graphic organizer below to compare and contrast Lake Windsor Middle School and Tangerine Middle School. Write details shared by both schools in the middle space, details specific to Lake Windsor in the left space, and details specific to Tangerine in the right space.

Lake Windsor Middle School   **Both**   **Tangerine Middle School**

Expository Writing Prompt: Write a paragraph that focuses on the differences between the two schools. Think about how to structure sentences with adverbial clauses and coordinating conjunctions. Be sure to:

- Create a topic sentence about the differences.
- Provide supporting detail and commentary.
- Use transition words and a variety of sentence structures.

My Notes

3. After reading the journal entries for "September 18 and 19," reconsider Paul's decision to transfer to Tangerine Middle School. Choose two of the consequences that you predicted as a result of this choice. Explain whether or not you think your predictions are still correct, and cite textual evidence to support your conclusions. Compare with a partner.

Prediction 1:

Correct?

Textual evidence:

Prediction 2:

Correct?

Textual evidence:

A Good Sport

LEARNING STRATEGIES:
Quickwrite, Graphic Organizer,
Discussion Groups

My Notes

Learning Targets
* Identify a motif in a text.
* Write an effective introduction and conclusion on a thesis about sportsmanship in *Tangerine*.

1. **Quickwrite:** Consider the following quotes about sportsmanship. Which one do you agree with most, and why?

   "The moment of victory is much too short to live for that and nothing else."
   —*Martina Navratilova*, tennis player

   "If winning isn't everything, why do they keep score?"—*Vince Lombardi*, football coach

   "Victory isn't defined by wins or losses. It is defined by effort. If you can truthfully say, 'I did the best I could, I gave everything I had,' then you're a winner."
   —*Wolfgang Schadler*, Olympic luge competitor and coach

2. After reading the entries for "September" in Part 2 of *Tangerine*, complete the graphic organizer to evaluate the sportsmanship of different characters, providing textual evidence from the novel.

Character	Good or Bad Sport?	Textual Evidence
Paul Fisher		
Eric Fisher		
Victor Guzman		
Joey Costello		

3. Work with your class to craft and revise a thesis statement about sportsmanship in the novel *Tangerine*.

Copy it here:

Expository Writing Prompt: Write an introduction to an essay about the motif of sportsmanship in *Tangerine*. You can use one of the quotes from the Quickwrite exercise as a hook or write your own. Be sure to:

- Begin with a quote as a hook.
- **Interpret** the quote and connect it to the text.
- End with a thesis statement that organizes the ideas.

4. Prepare for a collaborative discussion on sportsmanship in *Tangerine*. With your class, identify the expectations for each of the following roles:

Leader:

Recorder:

Manager:

Presenter:

5. Write three questions about sportsmanship in *Tangerine* to contribute to your group discussion. Good discussion questions about literature are typically at the interpretive level of questioning (see Activity 3.3 to review Levels of Questions) and involve elements such as plot, setting, conflict, motifs, and characters.

My Notes

ACADEMIC VOCABULARY
To **interpret** is to explain the meaning of something. Thus, an *interpretation* is an explanation of meaning.

A Good Sport

My Notes

6. After your small group discussion, identify one example, opinion, or insight about sportsmanship for each of the categories in the graphic organizer below. As each group's presenter shares with the class, add to your notes.

Sportsmanship in *Tangerine*

Sportsmanship in youth or school sports

Expository Writing Prompt: Use your class discussion notes to help you draft a conclusion to an essay about the motif of sportsmanship in the novel *Tangerine*. Be sure to:

- Begin with a restatement of the thesis. (Literal)
- Evaluate the author's purpose (what you think Bloor was trying to say about sportsmanship). (Interpretive)
- Discuss the larger issues and the importance of sportsmanship in real life. (Universal)

Check Your Understanding

If you were writing a literary analysis essay about the motif of sportsmanship in the novel *Tangerine*, which two characters would you use as examples of good and bad sportsmanship? What textual evidence would you provide as support?

Seeing Is Believing

Learning Targets

• Identify literal and figurative meanings in multiple texts.

• Write a character analysis, analyzing a character in relation to a motif of the novel.

LEARNING STRATEGIES:
Quickwrite, Graphic
Organizer, Discussion
Groups

1. The verse below uses the imagery of sight and blindness. How is the use of this imagery similar to the use of the imagery in *Tangerine*?

> Amazing grace! how sweet the sound
> That sav'd a wretch like me!
> I once was lost, but now am found,
> Was blind, but now I see.

My Notes

2. What are the literal meanings of the imagery of sight and blindness? What are possible figurative or symbolic meanings?

Literal:

Figurative:

3. Reread the flashback at the end of Paul's entry for October 5 starting with "I stared hard into the backyard." When is Paul referring to "seeing" in a literal sense, and when do you think he is being figurative?

Literal:

Figurative:

4. Who Sees? Who Doesn't See?

After reviewing your double-entry journal entries for Part 2, think about the word *see* and its meanings, both literal and figurative, and how it is used as a motif in the novel. Your teacher will either assign a character from the novel *Tangerine* or ask you to choose one. In one lens of the glasses, list or draw the things the character sees or understands; in the other lens, list or draw the things the character does not see or understand (or refuses to see).

Character Name: _____

Seeing Is Believing

My Notes

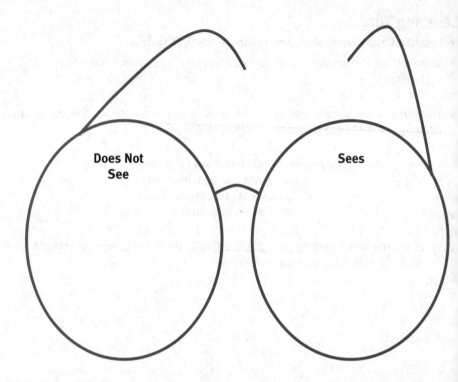

Does Not
See

Sees

5. After you have worked on the graphic organizer, meet with others who chose the same character. Compare and discuss what your character sees and doesn't see, and add details or images to your graphic organizer.

6. Next, meet in a group of three or four others, each of whom chose a different character, and compare notes and interpretations about characters with contrasting points of view about the events of the novel. Take notes on one other character besides the one upon which you have focused.

Expository Writing Prompt: On a separate page, draft a paragraph about your character's ability "to see," based on the details in your graphic organizer. Be sure to:

- Include a topic sentence about what your character does or does not "see."
- Provide supporting details, textual evidence, and commentary.
- Use a variety of sentence structures.

Language and Writer's Craft: Active versus Passive Voice

Verbs change form to show **active voice** or **passive voice**. A verb is in the active voice when the subject of the sentence performs the action. A verb is in the passive voice when the subject receives the action; that is, has something done to it. Writers—and readers—generally prefer the active voice because it is more lively, concise, and easier to understand.

Active voice: The goalie *deflected* the ball.
In this example, the subject (the goalie) is performing the action of deflecting.

Passive voice: The ball was *deflected* by the goalie.
In this example, the subject (the ball) is receiving the action of deflecting.

You can recognize passive voice because the verb phrase includes a form of *to be,* such as *am, is, was, were, are,* or *been.* Another way to recognize sentences with verbs in the passive voice is that they may include a "by ..." phrase after the verb.

7. Revise this sentence:

   Passive voice: The game **was won b**y the Tangerine War Eagles.

   Active voice:

8. Check the paragraph you wrote about a character's ability to "see." If necessary, revise any passive voice verbs to active voice.

Conflicts and Consequences

LEARNING STRATEGIES:
Graphic Organizer, Think-Pair-Share, Drafting

Learning Targets

- Identify conflicts in the novel's plot and subplot.
- Make predictions about the resolution of conflicts in the novel in an expository paragraph.

1. Take out the double-entry journal notes you created for Part 2 in your Reader/Writer Notebook. Select the entry that you think represents the most significant choice in Part 2. Copy it onto the graphic organizer below. Find at least two people in your class who selected different choices, and take notes as they share.

Part 2: Monday, September 18– Friday, November 10

Textual evidence of a choice made by a character	Page #	Commentary on the consequences of that choice and the possible impact on Paul

2. A novel is composed of many **conflicts** and plots. The major conflict involves the protagonist and drives the main plot. In the graphic below, state the main conflict of *Tangerine*, and list the details of that conflict.

Literary Terms
A **conflict** is a struggle between opposing forces. A **subplot** is a secondary plot that occurs along with the main plot.

Main Conflict

Individual vs. Self

My Notes

3. Each of the other types of conflicts in *Tangerine* is represented in a **subplot**. Give specifics that characterize each type of conflict.

Additional Conflicts

Man vs. Man

Man vs. Nature

Man vs. Society

4. Of the additional conflicts or subplots in this novel, which of them most directly affects Paul's conflict with himself?

Expository Writing Prompt: Choose one of the subplots in *Tangerine* in which the conflict has not been resolved. Write a literary analysis paragraph describing the conflict of the subplot and predicting how it might relate to Paul's conflict. Be sure to:

* Use a topic sentence that identifies a conflict and subplot and how it relates to the main conflict.
* Provide supporting details, textual evidence, and commentary.
* Use active voice and a variety of sentence structures.

Check Your Understanding

Scan Part 3 of Tangerine and note the length of the entries for this time period. Why do you think Paul wrote this much at this time? Read the first sentence for "Monday, November 20." Predict what will happen when the science-project group comes to Paul's house.

Independent Practice: As you read Part 3, continue to identify the conflicts and subplots in your double-entry journal. Also, make predictions about how the conflicts might be resolved. After reading, reflect on the accuracy of your predictions.

Mourning and Night

Learning Targets
- Analyze the diction and imagery of a poem to identify tone and theme.
- Make connections between the purpose and techniques of different genres.

Before Reading

1. Work with a partner to review the concepts of connotation and imagery, as well as the definitions of tone and theme.

During Reading

2. As you read the poem on the next page, do the following:
   - Mark the text by highlighting words that create visual images.
   - Underline words that relate to death and dying.
   - Draw a box around unfamiliar words or images.

After Reading

3. In *Tangerine*, on "December 1" Mr. Donnelly "read some lines from a poem called 'To an Athlete Dying Young.'" Read the poem again carefully. What lines do you think Donnelly read? Which lines would be most appropriate to memorialize Mike's death?

Check Your Understanding

On "December 1" the memorial for Mike Costello includes an **allusion** to "To an Athlete Dying Young" and the dedication of a laurel oak tree. Why are both appropriate tributes to Mike?

ABOUT THE AUTHOR
British poet A. E. Housman (1859–1936) spent most of his life as a teacher and a scholar. His poems are known for capturing deep feeling.

LEARNING STRATEGIES:
Note-taking, Choral Reading, Visualizing

My Notes

Literary Terms
An **allusion** is a brief, usually indirect, reference to a person, place, or event that is real or fictional.

My Notes

Poetry

To an Athlete Dying Young

by A. E. Housman

The time you won your town the race
We chaired you through the market-place;
Man and boy stood cheering by,
And home we brought you shoulder-high.

5   Today, the road all runners come,
Shoulder-high we bring you home,
And set you at your threshold down,
Townsman of a stiller town.

Smart lad, to slip betimes away
10 From fields where glory does not stay,
And early though the laurel grows
It withers quicker than the rose.

Eyes the shady night has shut
Cannot see the record cut,
15 And silence sounds no worse than cheers
After earth has stopped the ears:

Now you will not swell the rout
Of lads that wore their honours out,
Runners whom renown outran
20 And the name died before the man.

So set, before its echoes fade,
The fleet foot on the sill of shade,
And hold to the low lintel up
The still-defended challenge-cup.

25 And round that early-laurelled head
Will flock to gaze the strengthless dead,
And find unwithered on its curls
The garland briefer than a girl's.

KEY IDEAS AND DETAILS
What image is created by using the word "chaired"? How has this image changed in the second stanza?

KEY IDEAS AND DETAILS
According to the speaker, what is the advantage of dying young?

KEY IDEAS AND DETAILS
An **allusion** is a reference to a well-known person, place, event, or practice from literature or history. What is the poet alluding to when he uses the term "laurel" and "early-laurelled head"?

The Final Score

Learning Targets
- Outline support for a literary analysis essay on a topic from Part 3 of *Tangerine*.
- Analyze motif and theme in the novel *Tangerine*.

1. Take out the double-entry journal notes you created for Part 3 in your Reader/ Writer Notebook. Select the entry that you think represents the most significant choice in Part 3. Copy it onto the graphic organizer below. Find someone in your class who selected a different choice, and take notes as they share.

Part 3: Monday, November 20–Wednesday, December 6

Textual evidence of a choice made by a character	Page #	Commentary on the consequences of that choice and the possible impact on Paul

LEARNING STRATEGIES:
Graphic Organizer, Outlining, Visualizing

My Notes

The Final Score

2. Review all the notes you made about choices in your double-entry journals and in Activities 3.4, 3.9, and 3.12. Choose one character whose choices had significant consequences in the development of Paul's character. Select three or more of the character's choices and add them to the outline below in a logical order. Consider arranging them in one of these three organizational patterns:

   - least important to most important
   - types of choices made (good, bad)
   - chronological order (first to last)

3. Choose and follow an organizational pattern to complete the outline below that explains and evaluates your character's choices.

The Choices _____ Made

I. A choice made by _____ and how it affected Paul:

   A. Describe the choice.

   B. Why this choice was made: _____

   C. How Paul reacted to the choice and its effect on him.

II. Another choice made by _____ and how it affected Paul:

   A. Describe the choice.

   B. Why this choice was made: _____

   C. How Paul reacted to the choice and its effect on him.

III. Another choice made by _____ and how it affected Paul:

   A. Describe the choice.

   B. Why this choice was made: _____

   C. How Paul reacted to the choice and its effect on him.

Check Your Understanding

Write an explanation of how Paul shows his growing self-awareness and confidence in the choices he makes.

4. **Exploring Motif:** Consider the different motifs that Edward Bloor uses in *Tangerine*. In your home base group, assign a different motif to each person. Follow your teacher's directions to form an expert group with those who were assigned the same motif as you. Work together to complete one row of the chart below by finding examples of your motif in different parts of the novel.

Motif	Textual Evidence from Part 1	Textual Evidence from Part 2	Textual Evidence from Part 3
Sight			
Brothers			
Weather			
Sportsman-ship			

5. With your expert group, create a thesis statement about your motif. It should answer the question: How does the motif of _____ help to develop the conflict of the main character of *Tangerine*?

6. **Redesigning the Book Cover:** Review the information on the front and back covers of *Tangerine*, and consider what alterations or modifications you would make—and why—if you were redesigning the cover to emphasize the motif and theme you explored with your group. Create an original cover incorporating some of your ideas. You can give the novel a new title, use different imagery, include reviews of the novel from your classmates, and so on.

Front Cover: Revised Title, Visual Representation	**Back Cover:** Brief Synopsis of the Novel, Brag Page, and Review/Critique

7. Return to your home base group. Share your book cover designs. As your group members share the results from their expert groups, complete the remaining rows in the chart on the previous page with examples of how the different motifs were developed in the novel *Tangerine*.

Writing a Literary Analysis Essay

Assignment

Your assignment is to write a multi-paragraph literary analysis essay in response to the following prompt (or another provided by your teacher):

> In Edward Bloor's novel *Tangerine*, how did one character's choices and the consequences of these choices affect the development of the main character?

Planning and Prewriting: Take time to make a plan for your essay.

- How will you respond to the prompt in a clear thesis statement?

- How will you use the notes you have taken to find textual evidence to support your thesis?

- Will you organize your supporting ideas by importance, type, or time?

Drafting: Write a multi-paragraph essay that effectively organizes your ideas.

- How will you use an outline to help you draft your essay?

- How will your introduction engage the reader with a hook, summarize the novel, and state your thesis?

- How will you integrate topic sentences, transitions, details, textual evidence, and commentary in your support paragraphs?

- How will your conclusion include your thesis as well as an interpretation of the author's purpose and a connection to a larger issue?

Evaluating and Revising the Draft: Create opportunities to review and revise your work.

- During the process of writing, when can you pause to share and respond with others?

- What is your plan to include suggestions and revision ideas into your draft?

- How will you be sure to use precise, academic language and a variety of sentence structures?

- How can the Scoring Guide help you evaluate how well your draft meets the requirements of the assignment?

Checking and Editing for Publication: Confirm your final draft is ready for publication.

- How will you proofread and edit your draft to demonstrate command of the conventions of standard English, capitalization, punctuation, spelling, grammar, and usage?

- Have you put page numbers in parentheses wherever you quoted directly from the text?

- What would be an engaging title for your essay?

Reflection

After completing this Embedded Assessment, think about how you went about accomplishing this task, and respond to the following:

- How did the Reading and Note-taking strategies that you used during this unit help prepare you to write a literary analysis essay?

My Notes

Writing a Literary Analysis Essay

SCORING GUIDE

Scoring Criteria	Exemplary	Proficient	Emerging	Incomplete
Ideas	The essay • has a focused, insightful thesis that addresses the prompt fully and precisely • uses well-selected textual evidence • provides precise and insightful commentary showing the relationship between the evidence and the thesis.	The essay • has a focused thesis that addresses the prompt • uses textual evidence that is relevant and sufficient • provides relevant and clear commentary.	The essay • has a thesis that may address some part of the prompt • uses some textual evidence to support the thesis • provides little relevant commentary.	The essay • does not have a thesis appropriate for a multi-paragraph essay • is missing textual evidence or the evidence does not support the thesis • is missing commentary or the commentary is not related to the overall concept.
Structure	The essay • presents a strong introduction with a hook and clear thesis • is coherent with well-developed body paragraphs that use effective transitions • presents an insightful and compelling conclusion that follows directly from the ideas of the thesis.	The essay • presents a focused introduction with a clear thesis • contains body paragraphs that develop ideas of the thesis and establish cohesion with transitions • has a conclusion that follows from the ideas of the thesis.	The essay • presents an introduction without a strong thesis • contains body paragraphs that do little to develop the thesis • has a minimal conclusion that may not relate to the thesis.	The essay • may be lacking an introduction or thesis • may be missing body paragraphs or the paragraphs are not developed • may not have a conclusion or the conclusion may be only a summary statement.
Use of Language	The essay • shows a sophisticated variety of sentence types used appropriately • uses formal style and precise academic language • contains so few errors in grammar, spelling, capitalization, and punctuation that they do not detract from excellence.	The essay • uses a variety of well-chosen sentence types • uses formal and academic language appropriately • contains only a few errors in spelling and grammar.	The essay • shows little variety in sentence types • shows difficulty with the conventions of formal language and academic vocabulary • contains some errors in grammar and spelling that interfere with meaning.	The essay • shows serious flaws in the construction of purposeful sentence to convey ideas • has language that is confused or confusing • contains errors in grammar, spelling, and conventions that interfere with meaning.

Learning Targets

- Identify the knowledge and skills needed to complete Embedded Assessment 2 successfully and reflect on prior learning that supports the knowledge and skills needed.

- Interpret quotations, make inferences, and generate research questions.

Making Connections

In the first part of this unit, you read the novel *Tangerine* and analyzed its characters, setting, and mood. You also learned to predict future actions based on the author's use of foreshadowing. Describe one of the activities in the first half of the unit that helped prepare you to do well on Embedded Assessment 1. What did you do and learn in the activity, and how did it prepare you for success?

Developing Vocabulary

Look at your Reader/Writer Notebook and review the new vocabulary you learned as you studied the novel and its analysis. Which words do you know completely, and which do you need to learn more about?

Essential Questions

Now that you have read the novel *Tangerine* and analyzed the choices made by characters and the resulting consequences, how would you change your answer to the first Essential Question: What is the relationship between choices and consequences?

Unpacking Embedded Assessment 2

Read the assignment below for Embedded Assessment 2: Creating a Biographical Presentation, found on page 242.

> Your assignment is to work with a research group to create a biographical multimedia presentation of a great leader whose choices had positive consequences for society.

In your own words, summarize what you will need to know to complete this assessment successfully. With your class, create a graphic organizer to represent the skills and knowledge you will need to complete the tasks identified in the Embedded Assessment.

LEARNING STRATEGIES:
Discussion Groups, Graphic Organizer, Think-Pair-Share

My Notes

INDEPENDENT READING LINK
With help from your teacher, librarian, and peers, find a biography, autobiography, or work of historical fiction about a leader who has had a positive impact on society.

Previewing Embedded Assessment 2 and Analyzing Words That Inspire

1. In your discussion group, read each of the following quotes. Record your interpretation for each quote. In the final column, list what you know, inferences you can make, and/or questions you have about the quote's author.

Quote	Interpretation	Biography, inferences, research questions
Education is the most powerful weapon which you can use to change the world. —Nelson Mandela		
As we look ahead into the next century, leaders will be those who empower others. —Bill Gates		
No one can make you feel inferior without your consent. —Eleanor Roosevelt		
He who is not courageous enough to take risks will accomplish nothing in life. —Muhammad Ali		
Failure is simply the opportunity to begin again more intelligently. —Henry Ford		
In this life we cannot always do great things. But we can do small things with great love. —Mother Theresa		

2. Which of these leaders would you like to know more about, and why? How and where would you find more information? Is there another leader you would like to research?

Nelson Mandela in Hollywood

Learning Targets
- Analyze how biographical and historical facts are presented in a media text.
- Evaluate a leader's choices to understand how those choices can have positive consequences for society

LEARNING STRATEGIES:
Quickwrite, Graphic
Organizer, Discussion
Groups

Before Viewing

1. As you preview the first minute of the film *Invictus*, use the My Notes space on this page to take notes on the images you see. Which images stand out? What inferences and predictions can you make?

2. Read the following summary of the film excerpted from the DVD's back cover, and discuss how the imagery of the film clip helped prepare the viewer.

   "He was imprisoned 27 years for his heroic fight against apartheid. So what does Nelson Mandela do after he is elected President of South Africa? He rejects revenge, forgives his oppressors and finds hope of national unity in an unlikely place: the rugby field."

3. In your home base group, review each of the three sections of the chart on the following page. Make predictions about Nelson Mandela as a person and leader, events from his life, and the setting of South Africa.

4. Assign one section of the chart to each group member. You will next form a new group with other students who have been assigned the same section. This group will be the "expert" group. Share your predictions and consider any questions you might have before viewing the film.

During Viewing

5. At the end of each film clip, share your notes with the other students in your expert group. Add their ideas to your chart, as well as questions and answers that come up as you watch the film.

My Notes

WORD
CONNECTIONS

Foreign Words

Apartheid is an Afrikaans word meaning "separate." Apartheid was a policy of segregating people on the basis of race. It was the law in the Republic of South Africa until 1991.

Nelson Mandela in Hollywood

Invictus

Clip 1: A New South Africa	Clip 2: Bodyguards and Rugby	Clip 3: A Symbol of Apartheid

Section 1: Questions about Nelson Mandela and other characters in the film:

Details from Clip 1:	Details from Clip 2:	Details from Clip 3:

Section 2: Questions about events and incidents from the film:

Details from Clip 1:	Details from Clip 2:	Details from Clip 3:

Section 3: Questions about South Africa and specific settings from the film:

Details from Clip 1:	Details from Clip 2:	Details from Clip 3:

After Viewing

6. Discuss your notes for all three clips with your expert group, and then return to your home base group. Choose the best examples from each clip relating to your section to present your insights to the group. As each group member presents, take notes.

Check Your Understanding

Reflective Prompt: With your group, discuss how Nelson Mandela's choices show his courage and intelligence as a leader. What is he trying to do for the country of South Africa?

Research and Independent Reading

For Embedded Assessment 2, you will need to create and deliver a biographical presentation of a great leader of your choice. Choose the leader you want to present, and begin doing independent reading and research on his or her life. As you complete the next several activities, add to your research and consider additional questions, topics, or visuals to explore.

My Notes

A Long Walk to Peace

LEARNING STRATEGIES:
KWHL, Marking the Text,
Chunking the Text

Learning Targets

- Evaluate biographical information in response to research questions.
- Compare the features of a biography and an autobiography.

1. Begin the KWHL chart below by adding prior knowledge that you have of Nelson Mandela to the first two columns.

Nelson Mandela			
K: What I know	W: What I want to know	H: How I will find out	L: What I learned
		Nobel Prize Biography	
		Autobiographical Excerpt	

Literary Terms
A **biography** is an account of a person's life written by someone else. An **autobiography** is an account of a person's life written by the person. Both are genres of nonfiction.

During Reading

2. In 1993, Nelson Mandela was awarded the Nobel Peace Prize along with F. W. de Klerk. As you read the following biography from the Nobel Prize website, mark the text using metacognitive markers.

- ?: Put a question mark next to something that you do not understand.
- *: Put an asterisk next to information that is new or interesting.
- !: Put an exclamation mark next to something surprising.

Biography

The Nobel Peace Prize 1993, Biography of **Nelson Mandela**

My Notes

Nelson Rolihlahla Mandela was born in Transkei, South Africa on July 18, 1918. His father was Chief Henry Mandela of the Tembu Tribe. Mandela himself was educated at University College of Fort Hare and the University of Witwatersrand and qualified in law in 1942. He joined the African National Congress in 1944 and was engaged in resistance against the ruling National Party's apartheid policies after 1948. He went on trial for treason in 1956–1961 and was acquitted in 1961.

After the banning of the ANC in 1960, Nelson Mandela argued for the setting up of a military wing within the ANC. In June 1961, the ANC executive considered his proposal on the use of violent tactics and agreed that those members who wished to involve themselves in Mandela's campaign would not be stopped from doing so by the ANC. This led to the formation of *Umkhonto we Sizwe*. Mandela was arrested in 1962 and sentenced to five years' imprisonment with hard labour. In 1963, when many fellow leaders of the ANC and the *Umkhonto we Sizwe* were arrested, Mandela was brought to stand trial with them for plotting to overthrow the government by violence. His statement from the dock received considerable international publicity. On June 12, 1964, eight of the accused, including Mandela, were sentenced to life imprisonment. From 1964 to 1982, he was incarcerated at Robben Island Prison, off Cape Town; thereafter, he was at Pollsmoor Prison, nearby on the mainland.

During his years in prison, Nelson Mandela's reputation grew steadily. He was widely accepted as the most significant black leader in South Africa and became a potent symbol of resistance as the anti-apartheid movement gathered strength. He consistently refused to compromise his political position to obtain his freedom.

Nelson Mandela was released on February 11, 1990. After his release, he plunged himself wholeheartedly into his life's work, striving to attain the goals he and others had set out almost four decades earlier. In 1991, at the first national conference of the ANC held inside South Africa after the organization had been banned in 1960, Mandela was elected President of the ANC while his lifelong friend and colleague, Oliver Tambo, became the organisation's National Chairperson.

Source: Nobel Prize website, **http://www.nobelprize.org/nobel_prizes/peace/laureates/1993/mandela-bio.html**

KEY IDEAS AND DETAILS
What experiences in Mandela's life before he was imprisoned could you say contributed to his reputation?

After Reading

3. Use your text markings and notes to add to your KWHL chart as follows:

   • Add new questions to your "W" column.

   • Add new information to your "L" column.

   • In the "H" column, describe how this source was helpful in understanding what kind of leader Nelson Mandela was.

A Long Walk to Peace

My Notes

_____

_____

_____

_____

_____

_____

_____

_____

_____

_____

_____

During Reading

4. In 1995, Nelson Mandela published his autobiography *Long Walk to Freedom: The Autobiography of Nelson Mandela.* As you read the following excerpt, take notes in the "My Notes" section by summarizing the main idea of each chunk after marking the text for the following:

- Underline one key sentence or phrase in each chunk.
- Put an asterisk next to vivid imagery.
- Circle the words *free*, *freedom*, and *hunger*.

Autobiography

From **Long Walk to Freedom:** The Autobiography of Nelson Mandela

by Nelson Mandela

KEY IDEAS AND DETAILS
Mandela talks about his three stages of thinking about freedom. What are they?

Chunk 1

I was not born with a hunger to be free. I was born free—free in every way that I could know. Free to run in the fields near my mother's hut, free to swim in the clear stream that ran through my village, free to roast mealies under the stars and ride the broad backs of slow-moving bulls. As long as I obeyed my father and abided by the customs of my tribe, I was not troubled by the laws of man or God.

Chunk 2

It was only when I began to learn that my boyhood freedom was an illusion, when I discovered as a young man that my freedom had already been taken from me, that I began to hunger for it. At first, as a student, I wanted freedom only for myself, the transitory[1] freedoms of being able to stay out at night, read what I pleased, and go where I chose. Later, as a young man in Johannesburg, I yearned for the basic and honorable freedoms of achieving my potential, of earning my keep, of marrying and having a family—the freedom not to be obstructed in a lawful life.

Chunk 3

But then I slowly saw that not only was I not free, but my brothers and sisters were not free. I saw that it was not just my freedom that was curtailed,[2] but the freedom of everyone who looked like I did. That is when I joined the African National Congress, and that is when the hunger for my own freedom became the greater hunger for the freedom of my people. It was this desire for the freedom of my people to live their lives with dignity and self-respect that animated[3] my life, that transformed a frightened young man into a bold one, that drove a

GRAMMAR & USAGE
Correlative Conjunctions

Correlative conjunctions are a pair of conjunctions that work together to connect parts of sentences. In English, the primary correlative conjunctions are the following:

both ... and
either ... or
neither ... nor
not ... but
not only ... but (also)

For example, in the first paragraph of Chunk 3, Mandela uses correlative conjunctions in the sentence "... *not only* was I not free, *but* my brothers ..."

---

[1] **transitory:** temporary, not permanent
[2] **curtailed:** reduced or restricted
[3] **animated:** giving energy and purpose to

law-abiding attorney to become a criminal, that turned a family-loving husband into a man without a home, that forced a life-loving man to live like a monk. I am no more virtuous or self-sacrificing than the next man, but I found that I could not even enjoy the poor and limited freedoms I was allowed when I knew my people were not free. Freedom is indivisible; the chains on any one of my people were the chains on all of them, the chains on all of my people were the chains on me.

Chunk 4

It was during those long and lonely years that my hunger for the freedom of my own people became a hunger for the freedom of all people, white and black. I knew as well as I knew anything that the oppressor must be liberated just as surely as the oppressed. A man who takes away another man's freedom is a prisoner of hatred, he is locked behind the bars of prejudice and narrow-mindedness. I am not truly free if I am taking away someone else's freedom, just as surely as I am not free when my freedom is taken from me. The oppressed and the oppressor alike are robbed of their humanity.

Chunk 5

When I walked out of prison, that was my mission, to liberate the oppressed and the oppressor both. Some say that has now been achieved. But I know that that is not the case. The truth is that we are not yet free; we have merely achieved the freedom to be free, the right not to be oppressed. We have not taken the final step of our journey, but the first step on a longer and even more difficult road. For to be free is not merely to cast off one's chains, but to live in a way that respects and enhances the freedom of others. The true test of our devotion to freedom is just beginning.

Chunk 6

I have walked that long walk to freedom. I have tried not to falter; I have made missteps along the way. But I have discovered the secret that after climbing a great hill, one only finds that there are many more hills to climb. I have taken a moment here to rest, to steal a view of the glorious vista that surrounds me, to look back on the distance I have come. But I can rest only for a moment, for with freedom comes responsibilities, and I dare not linger, for my long walk is not yet ended.

After Reading

5. Choose one of the examples of vivid imagery that you marked on the text. Visualize and sketch it in the margins. Then, discuss how the imagery helped you understand Nelson Mandela's tone, voice, or personality.

6. Use your text markings and notes to add to your KWHL chart as follows:

   • Add new questions to your "W" column.

   • Add new information to your "L" column.

   • In the "H" column, describe how helpful this source was in helping you understand what kind of leader Nelson Mandela was.

My Notes

KEY IDEAS AND DETAILS
Quote the part of this text in which Mandela describes what true freedom is. After you quote the text, show your understanding by putting it in your own words.

KEY IDEAS AND DETAILS
Reread and compare the last paragraph of the biographical excerpt to the information in Chunk 5 of Mandela's autobiography. How does each passage interpret his mission once out of prison?

A Long Walk to Peace

My Notes

Check Your Understanding

Based on the two different versions of Nelson Mandela's life that you have read, analyze how biographical and autobiographical sources emphasize different evidence and interpret facts differently. Also think about the benefits and limits of each. Make one observation in each section of the chart below, and then add to or modify your response during class discussion.

Genre	Biography	Autobiography
How Evidence Is Emphasized		
How Facts Are Interpreted		
Benefits of the Genre		
Limits of the Genre		

7. **Brainstorm:** Besides print texts of biography and autobiography, what other kinds of sources could you use to answer your questions about Nelson Mandela? Where would you find them?

INDEPENDENT READING LINK
Identify the genre of the text you are reading independently and consider its benefits and limitations. Find another source online about the same person or time period, and create a graphic organizer to compare and contrast the information.

Language and Writer's Craft: Adjectival and Prepositional Phrases

You have studied the differences between clauses and phrases and have practiced with adverbial clauses and appositive phrases. In this activity, you will practice working with phrases that are used to modify nouns. "Modify" means "to describe," and using adjectives well helps you create visual images for your reader. Look at these examples:

I petted the dog.

I petted the growling dog.

Notice that the adjective "growling" modifies, or describes, the dog. Prepositional phrases can also be used as adjectives to describe nouns.

The book *on the bathroom floor* is swollen from shower steam.

The sweet potatoes *in the vegetable bin* are green with mold.

The hunger *for my own freedom* became the hunger *for the freedom of all*.

8. In these sentences, adjectives in the form of prepositional phrases come after the nouns they are describing. Circle the nouns being described.

9. Now, create your own prepositional phrases used as adjectives. Be sure each phrase begins with a preposition. Write your sentences in the My Notes space.

Phrases used as adjectives are known as adjectival phrases. For example:

His long, curly, dark hair was pulled back in a ponytail.

He commented on the cold, bleak, biting weather.

Dr. Richards was a hearty, healthy, dapper, red-faced gentleman.

Notice that these examples are **adjectives in a series** that make up the adjectival phrase. The adjectives are separated by commas and come before the noun they describe. Circle the noun described in each sentence.

10. Create your own adjectival phrases that include a series of adjectives. You can use the same nouns above or create your own sentences. Be sure to punctuate correctly. Write your sentences in the My Notes space.

11. Return to the excerpt from Mandela's autobiography and reread Chunk 3. As you read, look for adjective phrases and prepositional phrases used as adjectives. Notice especially the effect of adjectives. Mandela uses them to create a clearer, more detailed vision of the idea of freedom. Be careful; prepositional phrases can be used as adverbs too!

My Notes

Planning for Research and Citing Sources

LEARNING STRATEGIES:
Previewing, KWHL, Note-taking

Learning Targets
- Generate research questions and an annotated bibliography.
- Collaborate with and present research to your peers.

My Notes

1. In a later activity, you will be comparing text to film versions of *Invictus*. Look at the list of background topics below. Mark each as follows:
   - Put a question mark (?) next to subjects you have never heard of.
   - Put an asterisk (*) next to subjects you know something about.
   - Put an exclamation point (!) next to subjects you find interesting.

   Nelson Mandela

   Apartheid in South Africa

   African National Congress

   Afrikaners/Afrikaans

   South Africa Sport Boycott

   1995 Rugby World Cup

   Rugby

   Springboks

2. Follow your teacher's instructions to form a research group of two to three students and choose a topic or topics. On paper, create an individual KWHL chart and complete the first two columns by recording prior knowledge and generating research questions.

3. Collaborate with your research group to identify at least one different research question for each group member. In the "H" column of your KWHL chart, list search terms that you might use and types of sources that you might find online to answer your question(s).

4. Use the Internet Source Evaluation Chart on the following page to evaluate three different sources that might answer your question(s). A "yes" answer to many of the questions indicates that your source has a high degree of reliability and is a good source.

5. Choose the best source, based on the results of your evaluation. Copy the Web address (URL) here:

Internet Source Evaluation Chart

- Use a search engine to locate a website for your topic or research question.
- In column #1, answer each question with a "yes," "no," or N/A (not applicable).
- Do the same in columns #2 and #3 for two more websites. Write the URLs of the websites you researched in the space to the right, and label each as #1, #2, or #3.

Criteria	Question	#1	#2	#3
Accuracy	Is the site free from grammatical and typographical errors?			
	Do the links and graphics operate properly?			
	Was the information verified by a third party?			
Validity or Objectivity	Does the information appear to be well researched?			
	Is there a bibliography or list of sources?			
	Is there a statement about the purpose of the site?			
	Is there a place to note and communicate errors on the site?			
	Does the site appear to be free from bias or a single position?			
Authority	Are the author's name and qualifications clearly identified?			
	Does the URL address match the site's name?			
	Does the site identify itself as a .gov site in its address?			
	Does the author appear to be well qualified to write on the subject?			
	Does this site identify itself as an .edu site in its address?			
Currency and Uniqueness	Does the date the site was last updated appear?			
	Has the site been updated recently?			
	Are any parts of the site "under construction"?			
	Are the majority of the articles on the site a part of that site (as opposed to links to other sites)?			
Coverage	Does the site seem to cover the topic fully?			
	Are there other, related topics discussed on the site?			
	Is there a resources section with links to other sites?			

Planning for Research and Citing Sources

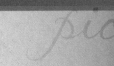

My Notes

6. Create a note card to record your findings from the website you chose. On the side of the note card without lines, write the complete bibliographical citation. Use the Internet, a word processing program, or a print reference to review the Modern Language Association (MLA) format for a citation. You may also want to try out a program that allows your group to record and share information using a computer.

Sample citation information:

"Nelson Mandela—Biography." Nobelprize.org, 1993. Web. 14 Feb. 2012. ‹http://www.nobelprize.org/nobel_prizes/peace/laureates/1993/mandela-bio.html›

ACADEMIC VOCABULARY
You may know that a **bibliography** is a list of the sources used in research and that **annotations** are notes. An **annotated bibliography** combines the two with a summary and/or evaluation of each source used to research a topic.

7. An **annotated bibliography** provides both the citation information and a brief explanation or summary of the source as well. On the back (lined) side of your notecard, write an annotation. Include the following:

- A brief summary of the content of the site
- An evaluation of the site's accuracy, validity, usefulness, etc.
- How this site helped you answer your research question

Sample annotation:

This site provides a brief biography of Nelson Mandela in order to give an overview of the events that led to his selection as a Nobel Peace Prize winner. While the site has validity and authority, it does not cover Mandela's life in very much detail. It answers the question "Why did he go to jail?" by explaining that he was accused of plotting to overthrow the government during his protest of apartheid.

8. Share your findings with your research partner or group. Prepare a brief summary of your findings to present to a larger group. When you present, be sure to:

- Remain focused on the main points of your summary.
- Use appropriate eye contact, adequate volume, and clear pronunciation.

As you listen to your peers, take notes in the "L" column of your KWHL chart.

Check Your Understanding

Quickwrite: What makes an effective research presentation? What elements were present in the summaries you heard today? What elements would have made them more interesting and engaging?

Research and Independent Reading

Review the information you have researched so far on the leader you have chosen for Embedded Assessment 2. Write any additional research questions that you want to explore here:

My Notes

Visual Impact

LEARNING STRATEGIES:
Graphic Organizer, Outlining,
Visualizing

Learning Targets

- Analyze photos, posters, charts, tables, and graphs to determine how visuals can enhance presentations.
- Create visuals that represent research about apartheid and Nelson Mandela.

My Notes

1. **Quickwrite:** Respond to the image of Nelson Mandela below by discussing your observations and making inferences. Write a caption for the photo.

Caption:

2. The pie charts below represent voting and unemployment statistics in South Africa under apartheid. What conclusions can you draw about the political and economic rights of black people in South Africa during apartheid? Write your responses in the space under the charts.

Voter Turnout in South Africa

1989

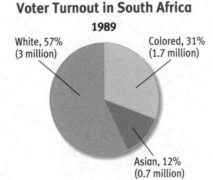

White, 57% (3 million)

Colored, 31% (1.7 million)

Asian, 12% (0.7 million)

Unemployed South Africans

1987

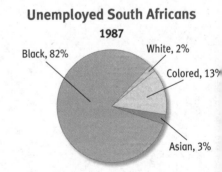

Black, 82%

White, 2%

Colored, 13%

Asian, 3%

3. **Discuss:** The poster below has both images and text. What do you observe about the images? What information does the text add? Write at least one question that you have about the poster.

4. Based on the graph below, how did American companies respond to the South African government's apartheid policies? What questions do you still have about the information in the graph?

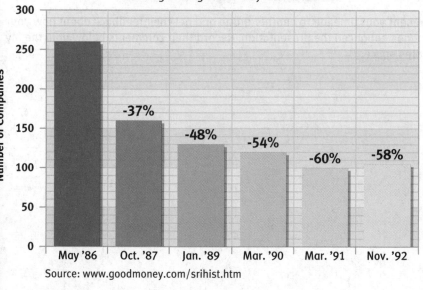

Changes in the Number of U.S. Companies Doing Business in South Africa

Percentage change since May '86 above bars.

Source: www.goodmoney.com/srihist.htm

Visual Impact

TECHNOLOGY TIP
If possible, use a computer
program to create your
timeline and add visuals. Also,
experiment with an online
document-sharing program
to collaborate with group
members on this project.

My Notes

5. Use the information from the table below to create your own bar graph or pie chart comparing the lives of blacks and whites in South Africa under apartheid. You may draw your chart, or use technology if you have access to a computer. Remember to place a title on your chart and label it appropriately.

A 1978 Snapshot of South Africa Under Apartheid	Blacks	Whites
Population	19 million	4.5 million
Ownership of Land	13 percent	87 percent
Share of National Income	< 20 percent	75 percent
Ratio of Average Earnings	1	14
Minimum Taxable Income	360 rands	750 rands
Annual Expenditure on Education per Pupil	$45	$696
Teacher/Pupil Ratio	1/60	1/22

6. What inferences might you make about the presentation of data in a table versus a chart?

7. On the following page, you will find a timeline of important events in Nelson Mandela's life. Work with a partner or small group to create an illustrated timeline that includes at least five key events from the timeline. For each event, include a date, a caption, and a visual image.

8. Present your timeline to another group and get their feedback about how your images enhanced the presentation. Record their comments below or in the My Notes space.

Informational Text

Landmarks of
Nelson Mandela's Life

BBC News

Early Days

1918 – Rolihlahla Dalibhunga Mandela is born into a tribal clan in a small village in South Africa's Eastern Cape. He is later given his English name, Nelson, by a teacher at his school.

1919 – His father is dispossessed on the orders of a white magistrate, losing most of his cattle, land and income.

Campaign Begins

1943 – Joins the African National Congress (ANC), initially as an activist.

1944 – With close friends Oliver Tambo and Walter Sislu, Mr Mandela forms the Youth League of the ANC. Marries his first wife, Evelyn Mase. They were divorced in 1957 after having three children.

1955 – The Freedom Charter is adopted at the Congress of the People, calling for equal rights and equal share of wealth with the country's white population.

1956 – Mr Mandela, along with 155 other political activists, is accused of conspiring to overthrow the South African state by violent means, and is charged with high treason. But the charges are dropped after a four-year trial.

1960 – Police open fire on men, women and children in Sharpeville protesting the new Pass Laws which limited the movement of blacks, killing 69 of them. The ANC is banned and Mandela forms an underground military wing.

Life Sentence

1964 – Captured by police after more than a year on the run, he is convicted of sabotage and treason in June and sentenced to life imprisonment, initially on Robben Island. His wife Winnie spearheads a campaign for his release.

1968 and 1969 – His mother dies and his eldest son is killed in a car crash. Mandela is not allowed to attend the funerals.

1980 – His friend Mr Tambo, who is in exile, launches an international campaign for his release.

My Notes

KEY IDEAS AND DETAILS
What do you notice about the way the timeline presents information? How do the headings and the years in boldface type help organize the content and guide the reader?

Visual Impact

My Notes

1986 – The international community tightens sanctions against South Africa. It is estimated that, between 1988 and 1990, the economic embargoes cost the country's treasury more than $4bn in revenue.

Changing Times

1990 – Bowing to the pressure, President FW de Klerk lifts the ban on the ANC and Mr. Mandela is released from prison. The ANC and the white National Party soon begin talks on forming a multi-racial democracy for South Africa.

1993 – Mr. Mandela and Mr. de Klerk are awarded the Nobel Peace Prize for their efforts to transform South Africa against a backdrop of bloodshed.

1994 – In the first multi-racial democratic elections in South Africa's history, Mr. Mandela is elected president. The ANC won 252 of the 400 seats in the national assembly.

1995 – South Africa wins the Rugby Union World Cup, and Mr Mandela is publicly presented with a team jersey by the team captain, seen as a highly symbolic gesture of unity between blacks and whites.

Source: **http://news.bbc.co.uk/2/hi/Africa/1502427.stm**

Check Your Understanding

Reflect on the use of images in a presentation by responding to the questions in the diagram.

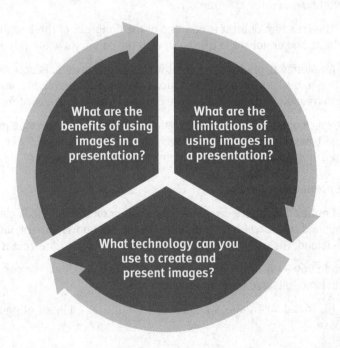

What are the benefits of using images in a presentation?

What are the limitations of using images in a presentation?

What technology can you use to create and present images?

Comparing Text and Film

Learning Targets

- Infer connections between a poem's theme and events in the life of a great leader.
- Analyze and compare a film text and a nonfiction text on a similar subject.

Before Reading

1. Read the information in "About the Author." In a small group, plan a choral reading of the poem "Invictus." As you listen to the poem, highlight words that you think express Henley's attitude about overcoming personal challenges.

> **LEARNING STRATEGIES:**
> Choral Reading, Marking the Text, Graphic Organizer

> **ABOUT THE AUTHOR**
> William Ernest Henley (1849 –1903) was a British poet. As a child, Henley contracted tuberculosis of the bone and had to have his foot and part of his leg amputated. He spent much time in hospitals and wrote 'Invictus' while recovering from a second surgery.

Poetry

invictus[1]

by William Ernest Henley

Out of the night that covers me,
Black as the Pit from pole to pole,
I thank whatever gods may be
For my unconquerable soul.

5 In the fell[2] clutch of circumstance
I have not winced nor cried aloud.
Under the bludgeonings[3] of chance
My head is bloody, but unbowed.

Beyond this place of wrath[4] and tears
10 Looms but the Horror of the shade,
And yet the menace of the years
Finds, and shall find, me unafraid.

It matters not how strait the gate,
How charged with punishments the scroll.
15 I am the master of my fate:
I am the captain of my soul.

> **My Notes**

> **KEY IDEAS AND DETAILS**
> How does each stanza set up a contrast?

---

[1] **Invictus:** Latin, meaning "unconquered, unconquerable, undefeated"
[2] **fell:** destructive or deadly
[3] **bludgeoning:** beating
[4] **wrath:** anger

Comparing Text and Film

My Notes

After Reading

2. After hearing the poem several times, work with your group to write a one-sentence summary of each stanza in the margins. Identify and discuss the theme of the poem.

3. **Discuss:** Based on your knowledge of Nelson Mandela's personal history, why might this poem have been important to him? What connections can you make between his life and the ideas in the poem?

Reading a Nonfiction Text

In Activity 3.16, you analyzed clips from *Invictus*, a film that is based on a true story as described in the book *Playing the Enemy: Nelson Mandela and the Game That Made a Nation* by John Carlin. In this next part of the activity, you will compare clips from the film with excerpts from the book.

During Reading

4. As you read the following excerpt from John Carlin's book, mark the text by highlighting or underlining phrases that help you understand the characters and emotions of the two main characters: Nelson Mandela and Francois Pienaar, the captain of the rugby team, Springbok.

ABOUT THE AUTHOR

John Carlin (b. 1956) is an English author who writes about sports and politics. During his early years, he lived in Argentina but returned to England for much of his school years. Carlin has worked as a journalist for numerous newspapers in various parts of the world, including South Africa. He has also written the scripts for documentary films and other television broadcasts about Nelson Mandela and South Africa.

Nonfiction

From **Playing the Enemy:**
Nelson Mandela and the Game That Made a Nation

by John Carlin

The President and the Captain:

Dressed in a dark suit and tie, Pienaar entered through a small door at the buildings' west wing, ducked through a metal detector, and presented himself before two policemen waiting for him at a desk behind a green-tinted window of thick bulletproof glass. Both being Afrikaners,[1] they immediately started engaging him animatedly on rugby.[2] The policemen dropped him off at a small waiting room, bare save for a table and some leather chairs, into which stepped Mandela's personal assistant, a tall imposing black lady called Mary Mxadana who asked him to take a seat and wait a moment. He sat in the room alone for five minutes, his palms sweating. "I was incredibly tense as the moment arrived when I would meet him," he recalled. "I was really in awe of him. I kept thinking, 'What do I say? What do I ask him?'"

***

Pienaar looked around the large wood-paneled office, vaguely registering a blend of décor old South African and new; ox-wagon watercolors side by side with shields of leather hide and wooden African sculptures. Mandela broke in. "Do you take milk, Francois?"

In less than five minutes Pienaar's mood had been transformed. "It's more than just being comfortable in his presence," Pienaar recalled. "You have a feeling when you are with him that you are safe."

***

Pienaar would not have guessed it at the time, but winning him over—and through him, enlisting the rest of the Springbok team—was an important objective for Mandela. For what Mandela had reckoned, in that half instinctive, half calculating way of his, was that the World Cup might prove helpful in the great challenge of national unification that still lay ahead.

Mandela never made his purpose overt[3] in that first meeting with Pienaar, but he did edge closer to the main theme when he switched the conversation to his memories of the Barcelona Olympic Games, which he had attended in 1992 and recalled with great enthusiasm. "He talked about the power that sport had to move people and how he had seen this not long after his release in the Barcelona

---

[1] **Afrikaner:** a South African of European descent
[2] **rugby:** a type of football game with 15 players on each team
[3] **overt:** open, not secret

My Notes

KEY IDEAS AND DETAILS
Choose a quote that indicates Pienaar's attitude toward his meeting with Mandela.

KEY IDEAS AND DETAILS
What is Mandela's purpose in meeting with Pienaar, the captain of the rugby team? Choose a quote that answers the question and explain.

Comparing Text and Film

Olympics, which he especially remembered for one particular moment when he said he stood up and he felt the whole stadium reverberating," said Pienaar, in whose mind Mandela was seeking to plant the first seeds of a political idea.

"Francois Pienaar was the captain of rugby and if I wanted to use rugby, I had to work with him," Mandela said. "I concentrated in our meeting on complimenting him for the role which he was playing and which he could play. And I briefed him on what I was doing about sports and why I was doing so. And I found him a highly intelligent person." The time had come, as Mandela explained to his guest, to abandon the old perception of the Springbok rugby team as "enemies" and see them as compatriots and friends. His message was, "Let us use sport for the purpose of nation-building and promoting all the ideas which we think will lead to peace and stability in our country."

After Reading

5. In the graphic organizer below, add key details from the text that you can use to make predictions about how the scene will look on film. After viewing the film clip, make comments in the third column evaluating the accuracy of your predictions. In some cases, the film portrays the facts just as Carlin's book recorded them. In others, you will notice that the film alters the facts.

Details from the text that help me visualize the film	How I predict the film will show character and emotion	Comments after viewing the film clip
Nelson Mandela		
Francois Peinaar		

6. **Discussion:** Compare and contrast the film and text versions. How were they similar and different? Why do you think some of the facts were altered in the film version?

Reading *Playing the Enemy: Nelson Mandela and the Game That Made a Nation*

The next section is also an excerpt from the book by John Carlin. When a film like *Invictus* is "based on a true story," the screenwriters and directors often change characters and events to make the story more dramatic or easier to understand. Sometimes the filmmakers change the facts of an event in an attempt to capture the mood of a scene. Or they may have one character represent the actions and personality of two or more people in real life.

During Reading

As you read the following excerpt from *Playing the Enemy: Nelson Mandela and the Game That Made a Nation*, make predictions in the margins about changes the filmmakers might make to this scene. Highlight or underline phrases that you would include if you were doing a biographical presentation on Nelson Mandela.

Robben Island

[The Springbok players] found themselves on a ferry bound for Robben Island. It had been Morne Du Plessis's idea. Du Plessis [the Springbok team manager] had begun to see just how enormous the impact of this "One Team, One Country" business was, not only in terms of the good it would do the country, but the good it would do the team.

"There was a cause-and-effect connection between the Mandela factor and our performance in the field," Du Plessis said. "It was a cause and effect on a thousand fronts. In players overcoming the pain barrier, in a superior desire to win, in luck going your way because you make your own luck, in all kinds of tiny details that go together or separately mark the difference between winning and losing. It all came perfectly together. Our willingness to be the nation's team and Mandela's desire to make the team the national team."

Robben Island was still being used as a prison and all the prisoners there were either Black or Coloured. Part of the day's events involved meeting them, but first the players took turns viewing the cell where Mandela had spent eighteen of his twenty-seven years in captivity. The players entered the cell one or two at a time; it couldn't hold any more than that. Having just met Mandela, they knew he was a tall man like most of them if not as broad. It required no great mental leap to picture the challenges, physical and psychological, of being confined in a box so small for so long.

***

After Mandela's cell the Springbok players went outside to the yard where Mandela had once been obliged to break stones. Waiting for them was a group of prisoners.

KEY IDEAS AND DETAILS
What effect does meeting with the prisoners have on the team members? Choose a quote and explain how it shows the effect.

Comparing Text and Film

"They were so happy to see us," Pienaar said. "Despite being confined here they were obviously so proud of our team. I spoke to them about our sense that we were representing the whole country now, them included, and then they sang us a song. James Small—I'll never forget this—stood in a corner, tears streaming out. James lived very close to the sword and I think he must have felt, 'I could have been here.' Yes, he felt his life could so easily have gone down another path. But," Pienaar added, recalling the bruising fights he would get into when he was younger, the time he thought he had killed a man, "… but mine too, eh? I could have ended up there too."

Small remembered the episode. "The prisoners not only sang for us, they gave us a huge cheer and I … I just burst into tears," he said, his eyes reddening again at the recollection. "That was where the sense really took hold in me that I belonged to the new South Africa, and where I really got a sense of the responsibility of my position as a Springbok. There I was, hearing the applause for me, and at the same time thinking about Mandela's cell and how he spent twenty-seven years in prison and came out with love and friendship. All that washed over me, that huge realization, and the tears just rolled down my face."

After Reading

7. After viewing the film clip, work with a partner or small group to record differences between the text and film. Make inferences about why you think the changes were made.

How the text was changed in the film	Effect of the change on the audience

Check Your Understanding

Did the film version of the scene capture the emotional spirit of the text version? Explain your opinion using evidence from the film and book.

Viewing the Film *Invictus*

Imagine trying to effectively capture the spirit of a sporting event on film. What would the challenges be? How might a filmmaker deal with these challenges? Can you think of any films that have done this well?

As you watch the final clip from *Invictus*, take notes on the effects of the filmmaker's choices regarding images and dialogue. You may choose to divide the work with a partner and share notes after viewing the film clip.

Images:	Effect on the audience:

Dialogue:	Effect on the audience:

On the next page, you will read a final excerpt from *Playing the Enemy: Nelson Mandela and the Game That Made a Nation*. This section describes the scene at the end of the World Cup game. Highlight or underline words or images that were portrayed similarly (or exactly the same) in the film version.

Comparing Text and Film

My Notes

The Rugby World Cup

"When the game ended," Morne Du Plessis said, "I turned and started running towards the tunnel and there was Edward Griffiths, who had invented the 'One Team, One Country' slogan, and he said to me, 'Things are never going to be the same again.' And I agreed instantly, because I knew right there that the best was behind, that life could offer nothing better. I said to him 'We've seen it all today.'"

But Du Plessis was wrong. There was more. There was Mandela going down onto the pitch, with his jersey on, with his cap on his head to hand over the cup to his friend Francois. And there was the crowd again—"Nelson! Nelson! Nelson!"—enraptured, as Mandela appeared at the touchline, smiling from ear to ear, waving to the crowd, as he prepared to walk toward a little podium that had been placed on the field where he would hand the world cup trophy to Francois Pienaar.

***

The gods at that moment were Mandela and Pienaar, the old man in green, crowned king of all South Africa, handing the cup to Pienaar, the young man in green, anointed that day as the spiritual head of born-again Afrikanerdom.

As the captain held the cup, Mandela put his left hand on his right shoulder, fixed him with a fond gaze, shook his right hand and said, "Francois, thank you very much for what you have done for our country."

Pienaar, meeting Mandela's eyes, replied, "No, Mr. President. Thank you for what you have done for our country."

Had he been preparing for this moment all his life, he could not have struck a truer chord. As Desmond Tutu said, "That response was made in heaven. We human beings do our best, but those words at that moment, well … you couldn't have scripted it."

Maybe a Hollywood scriptwriter would have had them giving each other a hug. It was an impulse Pienaar confessed later that he only barely restrained. Instead the two just looked at each other and laughed. Morne du Plessis, standing close by, looked at Mandela and the Afrikaner prodigal together, he saw Pienaar raise the cup high above his shoulders as Mandela, laughing, pumped his fists in the air, and he struggled to believe what his eyes were seeing. "I've never seen such complete joy," Du Plessis said. "He is looking at Francois and just, sort of, keeps laughing … and Francois is looking at Mandela and … the bond between them!"

It was all too much for the tough-minded Slabbert, hard-nosed veteran of a thousand political battles. "When Francois said that into the microphone, with Mandela there listening, laughing, and waving to the crowd and raising his cap to them, well," said Slabbert, "*everybody* was weeping. There wasn't a dry eye in the house."

There wasn't a dry eye in the country.

KEY IDEAS AND DETAILS
What evidence is there in this passage that sport had the effect that Mandela was counting upon to unite his country?

Check Your Understanding

The text suggests that a Hollywood scriptwriter would change the final scene. Why do you think they did not? What responsibilities do you think an author has when portraying a true event?

Follow the Leader

Learning Targets
- Analyze a speech to identify how the speaker shows himself to be a world leader.
- Generate a list of possible subjects for a biographical presentation.

Before Reading

1. **Quickwrite:** What are some of the character traits that great leaders have in common? Who are some historical or modern figures that you consider to be great leaders?

During Reading

As you read the following speech excerpt, mark the text by underlining words and phrases that reveal what he will do in the future to help all people. Use the My Notes space to take notes describing the emotions, values, or personality traits revealed by his words.

My Notes

Speech

From Nelson Mandela's Nobel Prize Acceptance Speech

We do not believe that this Nobel Peace Prize is intended as a commendation for matters that have happened and passed.

We hear the voices which say that it is an appeal from all those, throughout the universe, who sought an end to the system of apartheid.

We understand their call, that we devote what remains of our lives to the use of our country's unique and painful experience to demonstrate, in practice, that the normal condition for human existence is democracy, justice, peace, non-racism, non-sexism, prosperity for everybody, a healthy environment and equality and solidarity among the peoples.

Moved by that appeal and inspired by the eminence you have thrust upon us, we undertake that we too will do what we can to contribute to the renewal of our world so that none should, in future, be described as the "wretched of the earth."

Let it never be said by future generations that indifference, cynicism or selfishness made us fail to live up to the ideals of humanism which the Nobel Peace Prize encapsulates.

Let the strivings of us all, prove Martin Luther King Jr. to have been correct, when he said that humanity can no longer be tragically bound to the starless midnight of racism and war.

Let the efforts of us all, prove that he was not a mere dreamer when he spoke of the beauty of genuine brotherhood and peace being more precious than diamonds or silver or gold.

Let a new age dawn!

KEY IDEAS AND DETAILS
Note the **imagery** of the last three paragraphs. Choose one of the images and explain why Mandela included it in his speech.

Follow the Leader

After Reading

2. **Discussion:** What made Nelson Mandela a great leader?

3. As you explore speeches by other great leaders, complete the following graphic organizer to evaluate the character revealed by their words. Think of their potential as a possible subject for your biographical presentation.

Name of speaker and quote from speech	Character traits revealed by speaker's words	Why I might be interested in researching this speaker

4. Meet with your research group or partner and compare notes to generate a list of potential subjects for your biographical presentation. Consider subjects from your independent reading, from famous quotes, and from this activity. Remember to select a leader whose choices had positive consequences for society.

Language and Writer's Craft: Dangling and Misplaced Modifiers

As you prepare to complete Embedded Assessment 2, think about how you will use language for your presentation and on your visuals. Careful writers create sentences that are vivid and powerful. They are also careful not to create confusion in their sentences with misplaced modifiers.

Which sentence below has a misplaced modifier? Be prepared to say why.

1. She saw a moose on the way to the store.

2. On the way to the store, she saw a moose.

The key to avoiding this kind of confusion is to be sure the noun or pronoun comes immediately after the descriptive phrase. If not, the description "dangles," the connection is sloppy or unclear, and the sentence may confuse the reader.

Revise each sentence below to put the modifier where it belongs.

1. When we opened the leather woman's purse, we found the missing keys.

2. Driving down the street, the car's striking paint job made everyone gasp.

3. Running late for school, a bowl of cold cereal was all the child ate.

4. Her only full-time paid employee is a pleasant young woman with a nose ring named Rebecca, who sits at the front desk.

5. Vicious smelly creatures with huge tusks, the ship's crew were reluctant to drive the male walruses from the beach.

6. John was photographed at the mall with his girlfriend dressed in a car mechanic's overalls last week.

Creating a Biographical Presentation

Assignment

Work with a research group to create and deliver a biographical multimedia presentation of a great leader whose choices have had positive consequences for society.

Planning and Prewriting: Take time to collaborate on a plan for your presentation.

- Who are some possible subjects, that is, great leaders who have contributed to positive change?
- What research strategies (such as KWHL) will help your group generate research questions?
- What visuals will you need to find or create?

Researching: Gather information from a variety of reliable sources.

- How will you gather a variety of useful sources, and what criteria will you use to determine reliability?
- How will you create note cards to record each source's bibliographic information as well as the information that answers your research questions?
- How will you revise your search and generate new research questions based on what you learn?

Drafting and Creating: Create a multimedia project and annotated bibliography.

- How will you create an annotated list with a citation, summary, and evaluation of each source?
- How will you use multimedia to present your subject's history, character, choices, actions, and words to justify your selection of that person as a great leader?
- How can the Scoring Guide help you evaluate how well your project meets the requirements of the assignment?

Rehearsing and Presenting: Refine your communication skills as a speaker and listener.

- How and when will you present your project to another group for feedback and suggestions?
- How and when will you present your multimedia project to the class?
- How will you take notes on your observations, reflections, and questions during the other class presentations?

Reflection

After completing this Embedded Assessment, think about how you went about accomplishing this task, and respond to the following:

- What were the challenges of creating a collaborative multimedia presentation? How did you and your group confront these challenges?

Technology TIP:

Use a presentation tool such as PowerPoint or Prezi to organize the multimedia and visual aspects of your presentation.

SCORING GUIDE

Scoring Criteria	Exemplary	Proficient	Emerging	Incomplete
Ideas	The presentation • clearly describes in detail the subject's character and personal history and includes specific examples of the choices, actions, and words that made him or her a great leader • shows extensive evidence of research conducted • maintains focus on the main points of the summary and effectively communicates to the intended audience.	The presentation: • describes the subject's character and personal history and includes examples of the choices, actions, and/or words that made him or her a great leader • contains evidence of research conducted • focuses on the main points and clearly communicates to the intended audience.	The presentation • contains little information and neglects to make clear what distinguishes the subject as a great leader • contains minimal evidence of research conducted.	The presentation • provides no clear sense of what distinguishes the subject as a great leader • contains no evidence of research conducted.
Structure	The presentation • uses well-chosen and relevant visuals with explanatory captions, and includes photos, tables, and/or charts created and interpreted by students • shows collaborative group work to present the project, using all members effectively • contains a precise annotated bibliography, a well-written summary of relevant source information, and a description of how each source was evaluated and assisted the research.	The presentation • uses a variety of relevant visuals created or interpreted by the students • shows collaborative group work to present the project with equal division of work • contains an annotated bibliography of sources with few errors, a summary of source information, and a description of how each source was evaluated and assisted the research.	The presentation • contains few visuals or visuals that are not clear in their purpose • shows that the group did not work collaboratively to present the project • may be missing sources or have incorrect citations (multiple errors in conventions and/or spelling), a minimal summary of the information contained in the source, and/or an inadequate description of how each source assisted the research.	The presentation • may be lacking visuals • shows little or no collaboration among group members • is missing sources or has numerous errors in citations, a minimal or no summary of the information contained in sources, and/or no description of how each source assisted the research.

Creating a Biographical Presentation

SCORING GUIDE

Scoring Criteria	Exemplary	Proficient	Emerging	Incomplete
Use of Language	Each presenter • uses appropriate eye contact, adequate volume, and clear pronunciation • displays a sophisticated variety of sentence types used appropriately • uses formal style and precise academic language • displays few errors in grammar, spelling, capitalization, and punctuation that do not detract from excellence.	Each presenter • connects with the audience through adequate volume, eye contact and pronunciation • uses a variety of well-chosen sentence types • uses formal and academic language appropriately • displays only a few errors in spelling and grammar.	Each presenter • fails to maintain connection to audience with effective eye contact, volume and or speech clarity • shows little variety in sentence types • shows difficulty with the conventions of formal language and academic vocabulary • includes some errors in grammar and spelling.	Each presenter • shows serious flaws in the ability to construct purposeful sentences to convey ideas • uses language that is confused or confusing • includes errors in grammar, spelling, and conventions that interfere with meaning.

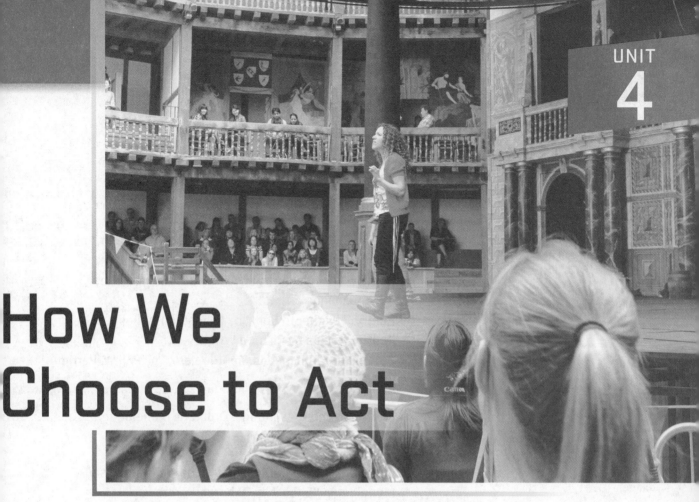

How We Choose to Act

Visual Prompt: Study the scene in the photo. How does this scene relate to a monologue?

Unit Overview

In this unit, you will discover that writers make choices about their use of language based on their intended effect, just like a performer or presenter makes choices about oral and physical delivery. To prepare for Embedded Assessment 1, you will practice reading and analyzing poetry as well as portraying various characters in group and individual performances. The unit will finish with an opportunity for you to perform a scene from a Shakespearean comedy.

How We Choose to Act

GOALS:
- To increase textual analysis skills across genres
- To strengthen verbal and nonverbal communication skills
- To improve oral fluency and presentation skills
- To collaborate on a Shakespearean performance

ACADEMIC VOCABULARY
precise
structure
modify
romantic
realistic
improvise
represent
diagram

Literary Terms
persona
oral interpretation
rhyme
rhyme scheme
alliteration
assonance
consonance
monologue
pantomime
syntax
verse
prose
poetic devices
internal rhyme
parody
vocal delivery
visual delivery
dialogue
stage directions

Contents

Activities

Texts not included in these materials.

Previewing the Unit

LEARNING STRATEGIES:
QHT, Marking the Text,
Skimming/Scanning

My Notes

Learning Targets
- Identify the skills and knowledge needed to complete Embedded Assessment 1 successfully.
- Preview and choose a text for independent reading and set goals in an independent reading plan.

Making Connections
In this unit, you will study oral presentations and performance. You will be making creative choices about how to write and present a monologue. You will also present a scene from Shakespeare and will make choices about how to address your audience as a performer.

Essential Questions
Based on your current knowledge, how would you answer these questions?

1. How do writers and speakers use language for effect?

2. How do performers communicate meaning to an audience?

Developing Vocabulary
Look through the Table of Contents, and use a QHT chart to sort the Academic Vocabulary and Literary Terms. One academic goal is to move all words to the **"T"** column by the end of the unit.

Unpacking Embedded Assessment 1
Do a close reading of Embedded Assessment 1. Underline or highlight key skills and knowledge you will need to be successful with the assignment.

> Your assignment is to write and present a monologue about a topic that sparks a strong emotion (e.g. amusement, regret, disappointment, excitement, joy, sadness, contentment, or anger). You may choose to speak as yourself, or you may adopt a **persona**.

You will work with your class to paraphrase the expectations and create a graphic organizer to use as a visual reminder of the required concepts and skills. After each activity, use this graphic to guide reflection about what you have learned and what you still need to learn to be successful on the Embedded Assessment.

Creating an Independent Reading Plan
The unit focuses on literary text analysis, using language for effect, and presentation skills. Throughout the unit, you will be asked to transform chunks of your selected Independent Reading text into monologue format, and you will practice delivering your text orally in front of your peers. After choosing a text, make a plan for when you will read and how many pages you will read each day.

Literary Terms
A **persona** is the voice or character speaking or narrating a story.

INDEPENDENT READING LINK
In the first part of this unit, you will be reading and creating monologues. Choose a work of fiction written from a first-person point of view. Preview possible choices by reading a few pages to make sure the text is interesting to you.

Analyzing and Transforming "Casey at the Bat"

Learning Targets
- Analyze a narrative poem.
- Transform the text into a monologue and deliver an effective presentation of it.

Before Reading

1. In your expert group, define and provide an example of each of your assigned words from the poem "Casey at the Bat." Then, in your jigsaw group, teach the meaning of each word.

2. **Warm up:** Complete an open word sort to help you study the definitions of all of the words before you play Vocabulary Baseball.

A

brilliant
bearing
patron
doff (doffed)
straggling (straggle)
applauded
despair

B

writhing (writhe)
preceded (precede)
defiance
latter
sneer
stricken
sphere

C

multitude
haughty
melancholy
grandeur
wonderment
unheeded (heed)
despised

D

muffled
occurred
stern
lusty
charity
recoiled
visage

E

tumult
scornful
spheroid
awed (awe, *v.*)
clenched (clench)
shattered (shatter)
favored (favor, *v.*)

LEARNING STRATEGIES:
Manipulatives, Word Sort, Diffusing, Questioning the Text, Marking the Text, Rereading, Visualizing, RAFT, Discussion Groups, Sharing and Responding, Rehearsing

My Notes

WORD CONNECTIONS

Prefixes

Prefixes can help you determine meaning. Some common prefixes and their meanings are:
multi-: many
pre-: before
de-: remove from or reverse of
un-: opposite of

Analyzing and Transforming "Casey at the Bat"

Play Vocabulary Baseball!

Choose a captain, a pitcher, and a scorekeeper for your team, and name your team. Your teacher is the umpire. Team members must define words as they are "pitched" or called out by the pitcher. Each correct answer will move a player forward one base. Words defined incorrectly are "outs." The game is over when time is called or when all the words have been "pitched."

BATTER UP!

My Notes

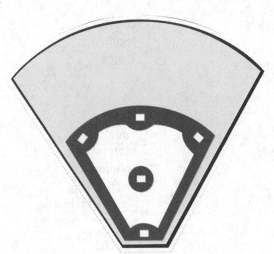

Vocabulary Word Bank

brilliant	despised	sphere	awed	multitude
patron	occurred	haughty	clenched	melancholy
straggling	lusty	grandeur	shattered	writhing
despair	recoiled	unheeded	favored	defiance
preceded	bearing	muffled	wonderment	visage
latter	doffed	stern	sneer	tumult
stricken	applauded	charity	spheroid	defiance

During Reading

3. Diffuse the text by circling and defining unfamiliar words.

ABOUT THE AUTHOR

Ernest Lawrence Thayer (1863–1940) wrote light verse while he was on the editorial staff of the *San Francisco Examiner*. "Casey at the Bat," his best-known poem, became a popular choice for oral recitation in schools and theaters.

Poetry

Casey at the Bat

by Ernest Lawrence Thayer

1 The outlook wasn't brilliant for the Mudville nine that day;
   The score stood four to two, with but one inning more to play,
   And then when Cooney died at first, and Burrows did the same,
   A pall-like silence fell upon the patrons of the game.

2 A straggling few got up to go in deep despair. The rest
   Clung to that hope which springs eternal in the human breast;
   They thought, "If only Casey could but get a whack at that —
   We'd put up even money now, with Casey at the bat."

3 But Flynn preceded Casey, as did also Jimmy Blake,
   And the former was a hoodoo, while the latter was a fake;
   So upon that stricken multitude grim melancholy sat;
   For there seemed but little chance of Casey getting to the bat.

4 But Flynn let drive a single, to the wonderment of all,
   And Blake, the much despised, tore the cover off the ball;
   And when the dust had lifted, and men saw what had occurred,
   There was Jimmy safe at second and Flynn a-hugging third

5 Then from five thousand throats and more there rose a lusty yell;
   It rumbled through the valley, it rattled in the dell;
   It pounded on the mountain and recoiled upon the flat,
   For Casey, mighty Casey, was advancing to the bat.

My Notes

My Notes

6   There was ease in Casey's manner as he stepped into his place;
    There was pride in Casey's bearing and a smile lit Casey's face.
    And when, responding to the cheers, he lightly doffed his hat,
    No stranger in the crowd could doubt 'twas Casey at the bat.

7   Ten thousand eyes were on him as he rubbed his hands with dirt.
    Five thousand tongues applauded when he wiped them on his shirt.
    Then while the writhing pitcher ground the ball into his hip,
    Defiance flashed in Casey's eye, a sneer curled Casey's lip.

8   And now the leather-covered sphere came hurtling through the air,
    And Casey stood a-watching it in haughty grandeur there.
    Close by the sturdy batsman the ball unheeded sped —
    "That ain't my style," said Casey. "Strike one!" the umpire said.

9   From the benches, black with people, there went up a muffled roar,
    Like the beating of the storm-waves on a stern and distant shore;
    "Kill him! Kill the umpire!" shouted someone on the stand;
    And it's likely they'd have killed him had not Casey raised his hand.

10 With a smile of Christian charity great Casey's visage shone;
    He stilled the rising tumult; he bade the game go on;
    He signaled to the pitcher, and once more the spheroid flew;
    But Casey still ignored it, and the umpire said "Strike two!"

11 "Fraud!" cried the maddened thousands, and echo answered "Fraud!"
    But one scornful look from Casey and the audience was awed.
    They saw his face grow stern and cold, they saw his muscles strain,
    And they knew that Casey wouldn't let that ball go by again.

12 The sneer has fled from Casey's lip, the teeth are clenched in hate;
    He pounds with cruel violence his bat upon the plate.
    And now the pitcher holds the ball, and now he lets it go,
    And now the air is shattered by the force of Casey's blow.

13 Oh, somewhere in this favored land the sun is shining bright,
    The band is playing somewhere, and somewhere hearts are light,
    And somewhere men are laughing, and little children shout;
    But there is no joy in Mudville — mighty Casey has struck out.

Introducing the Strategy: RAFT

RAFT is a strategy that is primarily used to create new texts by manipulating elements of a text during prewriting and drafting. This strategy helps you create or substitute various roles, audiences, formats, and topics as a way to focus your thinking about a new text.

After Reading

4. Your teacher will assign you a stanza to transform into a monologue, which you will present to the class. Reread the text multiple times to accurately visualize your assigned chunk. Be sure to make the setting, characters, and action clear and to capture how the characters are feeling.

5. Use the RAFT strategy to transform your assigned text into a monologue about the loss at Mudville. You may choose from the suggestions below or brainstorm more options for the role and audience.

Role: What is your perspective?	Audience: Who is the target audience for this text?	Format: What is the best format to capture your ideas?	Topic: What is the topic?
1. Casey	• News reporter	• Monologue	• To respond to the events leading up to the loss at Mudville
2. Fan	• Interviewer		
3. Mudville team member			• To describe the feelings and thoughts experienced before, during, and after the loss
4. Visiting team member			
5. Spectator from the crowd			

Preparing for the Presentation

6. Mark the text to indicate effective volume, rate (speed), pitch (high or low), inflection (emphasis on specific words for effect), and tone (speaker's attitude toward the subject) throughout the monologue.

7. Also mark the text to indicate appropriate eye contact, facial expressions, and movement. These elements should support your tone.

8. Brainstorm creative yet simple ideas for pantomime and props, and record your ideas next to appropriate sections in the monologue.

9. Rehearse your presentation.

- Practice delivering your lines fluently.
- Practice delivering your lines with an effective volume, rate, pitch, inflection, and tone.
- Practice using eye contact, facial expressions, and movement appropriate for your lines.

My Notes

Analyzing and Transforming "Casey at the Bat"

During the Presentation

10. When it is your turn, present your monologue.

11. When you are in the audience, listen to evaluate and compare and contrast presentations using Scoring Guide criteria.

After the Presentation

12. Reflect on the process and product:

   a. Are you satisfied with your presentation? Explain.

   b. What helped you plan and prepare your presentation? Did anything interfere with your planning and preparation? Explain.

   c. How did your presentation skills improve? What do you still need to work on?

   d. What are your goals for next time?

13. Revisit your monologue word map and add another layer of information and examples relating to successful monologues. Record ideas for your personal monologue. Be sure to identify specific emotions associated with each idea.

Language and Writer's Craft: Dangling and Misplaced Modifiers

A **modifier** is a word, phrase, or clause that describes, clarifies, or gives more detail about a concept in a sentence.

Example: Casey, *who everyone thinks is the team's best hitter, unexpectedly* struck out. (clause modifies *Casey*)

A **dangling modifier** modifies a word not clearly stated in the sentence.

Incorrect: Now stepping up to the plate, the pitcher hurled the ball. (phrase seems to modify *pitcher*)

Correct: Now stepping up to the plate, Casey waited calmly as the pitcher hurled the ball. (phrase now modifies *Casey*)

A misplaced modifier is a modifier that is placed too far away from the word or phrase it modifies, resulting in confusion.

Incorrect: *Chanting out his name*, the slugger turned to the crowd and doffed his cap. (the slugger is not chanting his own name; the crowd is)

Correct: *Chanting out his name*, the crowd watched as the slugger doffed his cap. (modifier now properly modifies *crowd*)

Strategies for revising dangling and misplaced modifiers:

• Make sure the word or phrase the modifier refers to is named in the sentence.

• Make sure the modifier is close to the word or phrase it modifies, with no intervening words that can be confused as the target.

Practice: Revisit the monologue you wrote in Activity 4.6, and revise it to improve your use of modifiers and to change any dangling modifiers.

ACADEMIC VOCABULARY

To **modify** something is to change or alter it. A change is called a **modification**. In grammar, a **modifier** changes or alters the meaning of a word it modifies, just as the words *green* and *three-toed*, in "green three-toed frog," **modify** the word *frog* to alter its meaning slightly.

My Notes

Using Language to Develop Theme

My Notes

Learning Target

• Analyze a narrative poem and explain how a writer uses language for effect.

Before Reading

1. Complete the anticipation guide below by writing an **A** (agree) or a **D** (disagree) next to each statement below.

   • _____ Criminals can never be heroes.

   • _____ You should be willing to sacrifice your life to save the person you love.

   • _____ People in authority are always right.

2. As you read the following informational text, diffuse the vocabulary and summarize central ideas.

Informational Text

The *Highwaymen* of Hounslow Heath

1 Once part of the extensive Forest of Middlesex, and now largely buried beneath the runways of London Airport, Hounslow Heath[1] was for more than 200 years the most dangerous place in Britain. Between the 17th and early 19th centuries, the Heath occupied perhaps 25 square miles. No one was really certain where its boundaries lay, and no one cared, for it was a tract of country to be crossed as quickly as possible. Though Hounslow itself was not large, it was after London the most important of coaching centres. Across the Heath ran the Bath Road and the Exeter Road, along which travelled wealthy visitors to West Country resorts and courtiers travelling to Windsor. All provided rich pickings for highwaymen lurking in copses[2] bordering the lonely ways.

2 The first of the legendary highwaymen were Royalist[3] officers who "took to the road" when they were outlawed under the Commonwealth. These were men familiar with the relatively newfangled pistols, which gave them an advantage over their victims, usually only armed with swords.

3 Perhaps because they concentrated on the wealthy, the highwaymen became popular heroes. No one, except the victims, grieved when the dukes of Northumberland and St Albans were held up on the Heath at the end of the 17th century. And when one audacious villain pasted notices on the doors of rich Londoners telling them they should not venture forth with less than a watch and 10 guineas, the whole town was convulsed with laughter.

---

[1] **Heath:** area of open, uncultivated land

[2] **copses:** group of small trees

[3] **Royalist:** person who believes in a monarchy

Famous Highwaymen on the Heath

4   While many of the highwaymen were thugs pure and simple, it cannot be denied that some of them had a certain flair. There was Twysden, Bishop of Raphoe, who was shot and killed while carrying out a robbery on the Heath—though it was later given out that he had died of "an inflammation." Others returned money to needy victims and released women and children unmolested, including the children of the Prince of Wales, held up at Hounslow in 1741. There are even accounts of robberies in which the victim is referred to as "a man" and the robber as "a gentleman." To be robbed by a famous highwayman was regarded as something of an honor.

5   When James Maclaine accidentally wounded Horace Walpole while attempting to rob him, the antiquarian[4] bore no grudge and wrote to tell him so. In June 1750, Maclaine also held up Lord Eglington, taking 50 guineas and his lordship's blunderbuss[5]. Dick Turpin is credited with having stayed in most old pubs in the Hounslow area, but in fact he mostly confined his activities to Essex, North London, and Yorkshire. The most gallant of the Heath's highwaymen was probably the French-born Claude Duval, who danced with a beautiful victim on the Heath and let her wealthy husband go for £100.

6   Despite the inefficiency of the authorities, few highwaymen survived beyond their early twenties. Betrayed for blood-money or by their own carelessness, most of them ended their short lives on Tyburn Tree, where felons were hanged. Most died well, and when they were dead, their bodies were returned to the scene of their crimes, there to hang rotting as a lesson to others. So plentiful were the gibbets[6] on Hounslow Heath that they came to be regarded as landmarks and even figured on 18th century maps.

KEY IDEAS AND DETAILS
Summarize the reality and the more romantic view of the activities of the highwaymen as presented in paragraphs 3 and 4.

My Notes

---

[4] **antiquarian:** one who collects antiques

[5] **blunderbuss:** gun

[6] **gibbets:** wooden scaffold where people were executed by hanging

Using Language to Develop Theme

ACADEMIC VOCABULARY
Romantic and **realistic** are often used as opposites. **Realism** is characterized by a concern for the actual or real, whereas a **romantic** view or an emphasis on **romance** is characterized by an appeal to what is heroic, adventurous, remote, mysterious, or idealized.

Check Your Understanding

3. In an era when the term "gentleman" indicated a member of the upper class, highwaymen were sometimes called "gentlemen of the roads." Write a paragraph explaining how they came to be seen as more than common thieves, and how realistic this view was. Support your idea with information from the text.

My Notes

During Reading of "The Highwayman"

4. Work to make meaning of the challenging text by using the following strategies:
   - Diffuse the text to define unfamiliar words.
   - Visualize each chunk by describing the characters and plot using sensory detail. Pretend you are a witness and you are reporting your account of what happened: What do you see? Hear? Feel? Smell?

ABOUT THE AUTHOR
English poet Alfred Noyes (1880–1958) wrote more than five volumes of poetry, many of them long narrative poems or epic poems. He is best known for "The Highwayman" and *Drake*, which is a 200-page epic. Noyes published his first volume of poetry at age 21. His poetry was clearly influenced by Romantic poets such as Wordsworth and Tennyson. Noyes spent time in the United States as a professor of literature at Princeton University from 1914 to 1923, and he also he lived in Canada and the United States during World War II. He returned to Great Britain in 1949.

My Notes

Poetry

The Highwayman

by Alfred Noyes

Part One

1   The wind was a torrent of darkness upon the gusty trees,
    The moon was a ghostly galleon[1] tossed upon cloudy seas,
    The road was a ribbon of moonlight looping the purple moor,
    And the highwayman came riding—
    Riding—riding—
    The highwayman came riding, up to the old inn door.

2   He'd a French cocked hat on his forehead, a bunch of lace at his chin;
    A coat of the claret[2] velvet, and breeches of fine doe-skin.
    They fitted with never a wrinkle. His boots were up to the thigh.
    And he rode with a jeweled twinkle,
       His pistol butts a-twinkle,
    His rapier[3] hilt a-twinkle, under the jeweled sky.

---

[1] **galleon:** a sailing ship used from the 15th to 17th centuries
[2] **claret:** a deep red
[3] **rapier:** a thin sword with a very sharp tip

Using Language to Develop Theme

KEY IDEAS AND DETAILS
What images in the second
stanza create the impression
that this highwayman is a
"romantic" character?

My Notes

3   Over the cobbles he clattered and clashed in the dark inn-yard.
    He tapped with his whip on the shutters, but all was locked and barred.
    He whistled a tune to the window, and who should be waiting there
    But the landlord's black-eyed daughter,
        Bess, the landlord's daughter,
    Plaiting a dark red love-knot into her long black hair.

4   And dark in the dark old inn-yard a stable-wicket[4] creaked
    Where Tim the ostler[5] listened. His face was white and peaked.
    His eyes were hollows of madness, his hair like mouldy hay,
    But he loved the landlord's daughter,
        The landlord's red-lipped daughter.
    Dumb as a dog he listened, and he heard the robber say—

5   "One kiss, my bonny sweetheart, I'm after a prize tonight,
    But I shall be back with the yellow gold before the morning light.
    Yet if they press me sharply, and harry[6] me through the day,
    Then look for me by moonlight,
        Watch for me by moonlight,
    I'll come to thee by moonlight, though hell should bar the way."

6   He rose upright in the stirrups. He scarce could reach her hand,
    But she loosened her hair in the casement.[7] His face burnt like a brand
    As the black cascade of perfume came tumbling over his breast;
    And he kissed its waves in the moonlight,
        (O, sweet, black waves in the moonlight!)
    Then he tugged at his rein in the moonlight, and galloped away to the west.

Part Two

7   He did not come in the dawning. He did not come at noon;
    And out of the tawny sunset, before the rise of the moon,
    When the road was a gypsy's ribbon, looping the purple moor,
    A red-coat troop came marching—
        Marching—marching—
    King George's men came marching, up to the old inn-door.

---

[4] **stable-wicket:** a small door or gate
[5] **ostler:** a person employed by a stable to care for horses
[6] **harry:** to carry out attacks on someone
[7] **casement:** a type of window that opens on hinges

KEY IDEAS AND DETAILS
Pay special attention to poetic musical devices. In addition to the rhyme scheme, identify examples of alliteration and onomatopoeia.

8 They said no word to the landlord. They drank his ale instead.
   But they gagged his daughter, and bound her, to the foot of her narrow bed.
   Two of them knelt at her casement, with muskets at their side!
   There was death at every window;
       And hell at one dark window;
   For Bess could see, through her casement, the road that he would ride.

9 They had tied her up to attention, with many a sniggering jest,
   They had bound a musket beside her, with the barrel beneath her breast!
   "Now, keep good watch!" and they kissed her. She heard the doomed man say—
   Look for me by moonlight;
       Watch for me by moonlight;
   I'll come to thee by moonlight, though hell should bar the way!

10 She twisted her hands behind her; but all the knots held good!
   She writhed her hands till her fingers were wet with sweat or blood!
   They stretched and strained in the darkness, and the hours crawled by like years,
   Till, now, on the stroke of midnight,
       Cold, on the stroke of midnight,
   The tip of one finger touched it! The trigger at least was hers!

11 The tip of one finger touched it. She strove no more for the rest.
   Up, she stood up to attention, with the muzzle beneath her breast.
   She would not risk their hearing, she would not strive again;
   For the road lay bare in the moonlight;
       Blank and bare in the moonlight;
   And the blood in her veins, in the moonlight, throbbed to her love's refrain.

12 *Tlot tlot; tlot tlot!* Had they heard it? The horsehoofs, ringing clear;
   Tlot tlot, tlot tlot, in the distance? Were they deaf that they did not hear?
   Down the ribbon of moonlight, over the brow of the hill,
   The highwayman came riding—
       Riding—riding—
   The red-coats looked to their priming![8] She stood up, straight and still.

My Notes

---

[8] **priming:** to prepare a gun for firing

Using Language to Develop Theme

13 *Tlot tlot*, in the frosty silence! *Tlot tlot*, in the echoing night!
Nearer he came and nearer. Her face was like a light.
Her eyes grew wide for a moment; she drew one last deep breath,
Then her finger moved in the moonlight,
    Her musket shattered the moonlight,
Shattered her breast in the moonlight and warned him—with her death.

14 He turned. He spurred to the west; he did not know who stood
Bowed, with her head o'er the musket, drenched with her own blood!
Not till the dawn he heard it, and his face grew grey to hear
How Bess, the landlord's daughter,
    The landlord's black-eyed daughter,
Had watched for her love in the moonlight, and died in the darkness there.

15 Back, he spurred like a madman, shouting a curse to the sky,
With the white road smoking behind him and his rapier brandished high.
Blood-red were his spurs in the golden noon; wine-red was his velvet coat;
When they shot him down on the highway,
    Down like a dog on the highway,
And he lay in his blood on the highway, with a bunch of lace at his throat.

16 *And still of a winter's night, they say, when the wind is in the trees,*
When the moon is a ghostly galleon tossed upon cloudy seas,
When the road is a ribbon of moonlight over the purple moor,
A highwayman comes riding—
    Riding—riding—
    A highwayman comes riding, up to the old inn-door.

17 *Over the cobbles he clatters and clangs in the dark inn-yard.*
He taps with his whip on the shutters, but all is locked and barred.
He whistles a tune to the window, and who should be waiting there
But the landlord's black-eyed daughter,
    Bess, the landlord's daughter,
Plaiting a dark red love-knot into her long black hair.

After Reading

5. How does the information from Gillian Spragg's text on *Outlaws and Highwaymen* help you understand the poem "The Highwayman"?

6. By the time Alfred Noyes wrote "The Highwayman," these thieves no longer existed. Does the poet use a realistic or a romanticized version of this figure from English history? Compare and contrast the historical character with the fictional character.

Creative Writing Prompt: Create a monologue from the point of view of one of the characters from "The Highwayman." Imagine what he or she might say about the events of the story as it is. You do not have to write a rhyming poem. Be sure to:

- Review the elements of monologues to decide what to include.
- Use diction, syntax, and punctuation to create a persona and a dramatic effect.
- Vary the length and complexity of your sentence structure (syntax) for effect.
- Carefully sequence the narrative you are retelling.

My Notes

Creating and Presenting a Monologue

Assignment

Your assignment is to write and present a monologue about a topic that sparks a strong emotion (e.g., amusement, regret, disappointment, excitement, joy, sadness, contentment, or anger). You may choose to speak as yourself, or you may adopt a persona.

Planning and Prewriting: Take time to make a plan for your monologue.

- How will you use your notes from your Reader/Writer Notebook and the activities in this unit to generate ideas?

- How can you use prewriting strategies (such as RAFT or a web) to organize your ideas?

- What tone would be appropriate, and should it shift or remain constant?

Drafting and Revising: Write and revise your monologue in the proper structure and format.

- How will you use your understanding of narrative techniques to be sure that your monologue has a strong beginning, middle, and end?

- How will you use diction, syntax, and devices effectively for your purpose, audience, and tone?

- How can you effectively share and respond in your discussion group, and how will you use the feedback?

Rehearsing: Plan and rehearse the performance with your partner and others.

- How will you mark your monologue to indicate key aspects of your oral and physical delivery?

- How can you enhance your monologue with a costume and/or prop?

- How can the Scoring Guide help you evaluate how well your and your peers' presentations meet the requirements of the assignment?

Presenting and Listening: Present your monologue and take notes on your classmates' performances.

- How will you use pantomime, eye contact, facial expressions, and movement to engage your audience?

- How will you evaluate and compare/contrast presentations using the Scoring Guide criteria?

Reflection

After completing this Embedded Assessment, think about how you went about accomplishing this task, and respond to the following:

- How have your writing and speaking skills improved during this unit?

- You observed many other monologues. If you were to do this assessment again, what would you do differently?

Technology TIP:

As part of the rehearsal process, consider making an audio recording of your performance.

SCORING GUIDE

Scoring Criteria	Exemplary	Proficient	Emerging	Incomplete
Ideas	The presenter • uses narrative techniques skillfully and smoothly weaves details into the story to create interest and develop a believable persona • uses clever props, facial expressions, and movement to create meaning for the audience • shows excellent oral delivery with volume, rate, pitch, and inflection that add to the interpretation.	The presenter • uses narrative techniques and details to create interest and develop a persona • uses appropriate props, delivery techniques, facial expressions, and/or movement to aid audience understanding and engagement • delivers fluently with appropriate volume, rate, pitch, and inflection.	The presenter • follows only some narrative techniques and provides few details to develop a persona • uses some props and/or movement to aid audience understanding • delivers with little expression or change in volume, rate, pitch, and inflection.	The presenter • follows few narrative techniques and provides few or no details to develop a persona • uses no props and/or movement to aid audience understanding • delivers with little expression or change in volume, rate, pitch, and inflection.
Structure	The monologue • engages and orients the audience with a creative hook that sets the tone and establishes context and point of view • follows a careful sequence and provides a clever ending • uses transitions smoothly to convey sequence and signal shifts.	The monologue • engages and orients the audience with a hook that establishes context and point of view • follows a logical sequence and provides a conclusive ending • uses a variety of transitions to convey sequence and signal shifts.	The monologue • attempts to create a hook, but it does not clearly establish a context or point of view • does not follow a logical sequence and/or provide a conclusive end • includes few transitions.	The monologue • begins without a hook to establish a context and point of view for the audience • is disorganized and difficult to follow • includes no transitions.
Use of Language	The monologue • uses specific language to communicate tone • creates imagery with figurative language and sensory details • uses multiple sentence types • cleverly uses literary devices and punctuation for meaning, reader interest, and style.	The monologue • creates tone with language used for effect • creates imagery with figurative language and sensory details • uses a variety of sentence types • uses literary devices and punctuation for meaning, reader interest, and style.	The monologue • attempts to create tone but it is not clear • uses some figurative language and sensory details • uses few sentence types • uses few literary devices or punctuation to aid meaning, reader interest, and style.	The monologue • does not use effective language to create tone • uses little figurative language or sensory details • uses few sentence types • uses few or no literary devices or punctuation to aid meaning, reader interest, and style.

Previewing Embedded Assessment 2 and Performing Shakespeare

My Notes

Learning Targets

- Identify the skills and knowledge needed to be successful on Embedded Assessment 2.
- Explain previous learning and make connections to new learning.

Making Connections

In the first part of this unit you studied, wrote, and performed several monologues and oral interpretations. Along the way you learned various techniques and devices that authors employ when they use language for effect. In this part of the unit you will focus on analyzing a Shakespearean play, *Twelfth Night*, as you further study dramatic monologues and prepare for a performance of a dramatic dialogue.

Essential Questions

Now that you have studied how writers and poets use language and have completed several oral interpretations yourself, reflect on your current understanding of the first Essential Question: How do writers and speakers use language for effect?

1. How has your understanding of language changed over the course of this unit? Consider using the sentence frame below to guide your writing.

    At the beginning of the unit, _____, but
    now _____.

2. What did you learn in the first half of the unit that has prepared you for the second Essential Question: How do performers communicate meaning to an audience?

Developing Vocabulary

Use the QHT strategy to re-sort the vocabulary you have studied in the first part of this unit. Compare this sort with your original sort. How has your understanding changed? Select a word from the chart and write a concise statement about your learning. How has your understanding of this word changed over the course of this unit?

Unpacking Embedded Assessment 2

Closely read the below assignment for Embedded Assessment 2.

> Your assignment is to work collaboratively with a partner to plan, rehearse, and perform a dialogue from William Shakespeare's *Twelfth Night*.

Write down five things you believe you willl need to know in order to complete this assignment successfully. Then, work with your class to paraphrase the expectations in the Scoring Guide and create a graphic organizer to use as a visual reminder of the required concepts (what you need to know) and skills (what you need to do). Copy the graphic organizer for future reference.

After each activity in this part of the unit, use the graphic you have created to guide reflection about what you have learned and what you still need to learn in order to be successful on the Embedded Assessment.

Making Oral Presentations

Whether you are presenting a speech or interpreting a scene from a Shakespeare drama, all presentations are a performance. All performances have certain elements in common, such as needing to appeal to the audience and be interesting.

3. What live performances have you ever attended? Name one or more performances, if possible, and tell what type each performance was (musical concert, drama, etc.). Tell whether you thought the performance was enjoyable and successful or not.

4. Now think about a performance you judged to be enjoyable and successful. Name as many factors as possible that you think would contribute to making a successful performance.

5. Discuss your responses with a partner or small group, and add to the elements you listed above to create a definitive list of factors.

My Notes

INDEPENDENT READING LINK
To support your learning in the second half of the unit, you may want to choose a drama or novel in which characters are concealing something about their identity. Ask your teacher or librarian for suggestions.

Putting on the Mask

LEARNING STRATEGIES:
Brainstorming, Discussion
Groups, Marking the Text, SIFT,
Rereading, Rehearsing

My Notes

Learning Targets
- Analyze a poem about masks, using the SIFT strategy.
- Create a mask that uses symbols and imagery to convey tone.

Before Reading

1. Look at the people in a variety of magazine advertisements. Describe some of the emotions you see on their faces.

2. With a partner or small group, choose one advertisement and brainstorm what really might have been going through the model's mind as he or she was posing for this advertisement.

3. Reflect: How do models and actors put on "masks" even when nothing is covering their faces? How do people in real life "mask" their true feelings and emotions?

During Reading

4. As you read the poem "We Wear the Mask," by Paul Laurence Dunbar, highlight words that describe emotions or that have strong connotations.

5. Take notes in the margin as you work with your class to apply the SIFT strategy to the poem.

ABOUT THE AUTHOR
The son of former slaves, Paul Laurence Dunbar (1872–1907) was the first African American writer to earn his living solely by writing poetry and fiction. He was also the first to gain a national audience of mostly white readers.

Poetry

We Wear the Mask

by Paul Laurence Dunbar

We wear the mask that grins and lies,
It hides our cheeks and shades our eyes,—
This debt we pay to human guile[1];
With torn and bleeding hearts we smile,
5 And mouth with myriad[2] subtleties.

Why should the world be over-wise,
In counting all our tears and sighs?
Nay, let them only see us, while
　　We wear the mask.

10 We smile, but, O great Christ, our cries
To thee from tortured souls arise.
We sing, but oh the clay is vile[3]
Beneath our feet, and long the mile;
But let the world dream otherwise,
15　　We wear the mask!

---

[1] **guile:** deception
[2] **myriad:** numerous, countless
[3] **vile:** repulsive or wretched

My Notes

Symbols:

Imagery:

Figurative Language:

Tone/Theme:

Putting on the Mask

After Reading

6. Reread the "About the Author" text, and then reread the poem. How does the poet's personal history help you understand the poem further?

7. Create a mask to represent a tone. Decorate your mask with symbols and imagery, including colors and details that you associate with the chosen emotion or attitude.

8. Choose one of the quotes about acting (below) to memorize. Wearing your mask, deliver your line to your peers. As you observe and listen to other students, try to guess the tone of each mask.

9. Reflect: Could you identify the tone of each mask? Did the mask change how you interpreted the different quotes?

Quotes About Acting

Seneca: "Life's like a play: it's not the length, but the excellence of the acting that matters."

George Burns: "Acting is all about honesty. If you can fake that, you've got it made."

Katharine Hepburn: "Acting is a nice childish profession—pretending you're someone else and, at the same time, selling yourself."

Johnny Depp: "With any part you play, there is a certain amount of yourself in it. There has to be, otherwise it's just not acting. It's lying."

Claire Danes: "Acting is the greatest answer to my loneliness that I have found."

Aristotle: "Men acquire a particular quality by constantly acting in a particular way."

Improvisation

Learning Targets
- Explore plot through role playing.
- Create a visual representation of key events or characters.

LEARNING STRATEGIES:
Predicting, Role Playing,
Rehearsal, Brainstorming,
Visualizing, Sketching

1. The plot of *Twelfth Night* centers on a character who masks her true identity and pretends to be something that she is not. Think of other examples from real life, literature, or film, and brainstorm reasons why someone would disguise his or her true identity.

My Notes

2. In *Twelfth Night*, Viola is a young woman who disguises herself as a man. Predict why she might have done this and what difficulties might arise from her decision:

3. Read one of the plot summaries on the next page and work with a partner to role play the scene through **improvisation**. Rehearse your improvisation several times before presenting it to a group of your peers. Be sure to:
   - Say the characters' real names frequently in your presentation: "Hey, *Viola*, do you think ..." "Sure, *Olivia*, but ..."
   - Include specific details from the plot summary.
   - Use pantomime and gestures to enhance your performance.

4. After each of your peers' performances, ask questions to clarify what happened in the scene and which characters were involved. Take notes under each plot summary to describe the performance and record memorable details.

ACADEMIC VOCABULARY
When you **improvise**, you perform with little or no preparation and usually without a script. **Improvisation** means you are inventing as you perform.

Improvisation

Twelfth Night Plot Summaries for Role Play

1. **Viola** and **the Captain** are washed up onshore after a shipwreck. Viola is worried about her twin brother (Sebastian) who was lost at sea. The Captain tells her that they have landed in Illyria, a land ruled by Duke Orsino. Viola decides to dress up as a male to go work for Orsino.

   Performance Notes:

2. **Duke Orsino** is talking to his servant **Cesario** (who is really a young woman named Viola in disguise). Orsino tells Cesario about his love for a woman (Olivia) who will not date him. Orsino wants Cesario to convince Olivia to go out with him. Cesario doesn't want to, but agrees anyway.

   Performance Notes:

3. **Olivia** meets **Cesario** (who is really a young woman named Viola in disguise). Cesario is trying to convince Olivia to date his boss, Duke Orsino. Unfortunately, Olivia has no interest in Duke Orsino, and actually starts flirting with Cesario, which makes Cesario uncomfortable.

   Performance Notes:

4. **Duke Orsino** complains to **Cesario**, his servant, about Olivia—the woman he loves. (Cesario is really a young woman named Viola who is in love with Duke Orsino.) Cesario tries to convince Orsino to try other women, but Orsino says no woman can truly love. Cesario disagrees.

   Performance Notes:

5. **Olivia** decides she is in love with **Cesario** (who is really a young woman named Viola—in disguise.) Cesario tries to hint that he is not really the man Olivia thinks he is, and tries to convince Olivia to give her boss (Duke Orsino) a chance. Olivia keeps flirting with Cesario.

Performance Notes:

6. **Sebastian** meets **Olivia** in the streets of Illyria. Olivia immediately declares her love for Sebastian, thinking that he is Cesario (Sebastian's twin sister Viola in disguise). Sebastian is confused but feels pretty lucky that this beautiful, rich woman wants him, so he marries her.

Performance Notes:

Check Your Understanding

Use what you learned from the role plays to create a visual representation of *Twelfth Night*. You may want to explore the key events in a plot diagram (see Unit 1) or create a graphic organizer that represents the characters' relationships to each other. Include both images and text. Use your notes and the plot summaries as guides.

As you view the other visual representations created by your class, discuss which ones are the most effective at helping you understand the plot and characters. What makes them effective?

My Notes

Analyzing and Delivering a Shakespearean Monologue

LEARNING STRATEGIES:
Summarizing, Diffusing, Marking the Text, Brainstorming, Choral Reading, Discussion Groups, Rehearsal

Literary Terms

Vocal delivery refers to the ways words are expressed on stage through tone, pitch, volume, rate (or speed) of speech, pauses, or emphasis.

Visual delivery refers to the way plot, character, and conflict are expressed on stage through gestures, movement, and facial expression.

My Notes

Learning Targets

- Analyze and rehearse a monologue.
- Deliver a choral reading of a Shakespearean monologue with appropriate vocal and visual delivery.

Before Reading

1. Play the following drama game with a small group or with a partner: Choose a simple question, such as "What are you doing?" and a response such as "Nothing important." Sitting in a circle, have one student ask the question in a happy tone of voice and the student to the left respond in a happy tone. Then, have the responder repeat the question in a different tone. Keep moving clockwise around the circle until you run out of different emotions.

2. Describe the tone you would expect in a monologue by a man who is in love with a woman who refuses to see him.

During Reading

3. Diffuse the text by identifying and defining unfamiliar words.

4. Mark the text by highlighting powerful diction and words that convey the speaker's tone.

5. Work with a partner or small group to summarize how the speaker feels about love.

ABOUT THE AUTHOR

Little is known about the early life of William Shakespeare (1564–1616) except that he was born and grew up in Stratford-upon-Avon, England. Shakespeare moved to London to become an actor, playwright, and poet. He wrote 37 plays (comedies, tragedies, and histories) and 154 sonnets (poems). Shakespeare is considered one of the world's greatest dramatists, and performances of his plays continue in theaters around the world.

Drama

Monologue from *Twelfth Night*

by William Shakespeare

Duke Orsino:

My Notes

If music be the food of love, play on;
Give me excess of it, that, surfeiting,
The appetite may sicken, and so die.
That strain again, it had a dying fall:

5 O, it came o'er my ear like the sweet sound,
That breathes upon a bank of violets,
Stealing and giving odor! Enough; no more:
'Tis not so sweet now as it was before.
O spirit of love, how quick and fresh art thou,

10 That, notwithstanding thy capacity
Receiveth as the sea, nought enters there,
Of what validity and pitch soe'er,
But falls into abatement and low price,
Even in a minute: so full of shapes is fancy

15 That it alone is high fantastical.

KEY IDEAS AND DETAILS
When and how does the tone shift in the monologue?

After Reading

5. View an actor performing the monologue and take notes on the actor's vocal and visual delivery.

Vocal delivery: tone, pitch, volume, rate, pauses, emphasis	Visual delivery: gestures, movement, facial expressions

Analyzing and Delivering a Shakespearean Monologue

7. Plan and rehearse a choral reading of the monologue. Include some of the following techniques to enhance the monologue:

   • Read some lines as a group, some with a partner, and some alone.
   • Use pantomime and gestures to enhance visual delivery.
   • Deliver lines fluently with appropriate vocal delivery.

8. After observing several choral readings, reflect on the different interpretations. Which ones were effective, and why? How did seeing and hearing the monologue help you understand Shakespeare's language?

9. What are some visual and vocal techniques that you might use in an oral presentation?

Check Your Understanding

Think back to the monologues presented in the first part of the unit and the choral reading of the scene from Shakespeare. How were they different, and how were they alike? What visual and vocal techniques did you observe, and how were they effective in communicating meaning to an audience?

Acting for Understanding

Learning Targets

- Annotate a dialogue by paraphrasing lines.
- Plan and rehearse a performance that communicates meaning to an audience through vocal and visual delivery.

Before Reading

1. Play the following drama game with a small group or with a partner:

   Have one student act as the silent "athlete" while the other student is the "commentator." The athlete should pantomime playing a sport while the commentator describes the action. Both students will have to respond to each other's choices: For example, if the athlete falls down, the commentator should make up a reason why; likewise, if the commentator describes a ball flying at the athlete's face, the athlete should react.

2. What kind of vocal and visual delivery would you expect from a character who has just washed up onshore after a terrible shipwreck?

During Reading

3. Paraphrase the text of the **dialogue** below by rendering each sentence in plain English.

4. Conduct an oral reading with a small group, reading your paraphrases first, then the original text.

5. Once you have chosen roles, go back and annotate each of your character's lines with notes for vocal and visual delivery.

> **LEARNING STRATEGIES:**
> Drama Games, Paraphrasing, Marking the Text, Oral Reading, Rereading, Discussion Groups, Rehearsal

My Notes

> **Literary Terms**
> A **dialogue** is a conversation between two characters in a play.

Drama

adapted from
Twelfth Night
Act 1, Scene 2

by William Shakespeare

Viola: What country, friends, is this?

Captain: This is Illyria, lady.

Viola: And what should I do in Illyria?

My brother he is in Elysium.

Perchance he is not drown'd: what think you, sailors?

> **KEY IDEAS AND DETAILS**
> *Elysium* in Greek mythology refers to a heavenly afterlife. What does Viola think happened to her brother?

Acting for Understanding

My Notes

KEY IDEAS AND DETAILS
What do you think the Captain means by "'twas fresh in murmur" that Orsino loves Olivia?

Captain: To comfort you with chance,

Assure yourself, after our ship did split,

I saw your brother bind himself

To a strong mast that lived upon the sea.

Viola: For saying so, there's gold:

Know'st thou this country?

Captain: Ay, madam, well; for I was bred and born

Not three hours' travel from this very place.

Viola: Who governs here?

Captain: A noble duke, in nature as in name.

Viola: What is the name?

Captain: Orsino.

Viola: Orsino! I have heard my father name him:

He was a bachelor then.

Captain: And so is now, or was so very late;

For but a month ago I went from hence,

And then 'twas fresh in murmur

That he did seek the love of fair Olivia.

Viola: I prithee, and I'll pay thee bounteously,

Conceal me what I am, and be my aid

For such disguise as haply shall become

The form of my intent. I'll serve this duke.

Captain: Be you his servant, and your mute I'll be:

When my tongue blabs, then let mine eyes not see.

Viola: I thank thee: lead me on.

After Reading
Check Your Understanding

6. Perform the dialogue with at least three different people who prepared the other character's lines.

7. Reflect on the effectiveness of your own and other students' delivery. What aspects of the performances would help communicate meaning to an audience?

Interpreting Character
in Performance

Learning Targets

- Analyze and perform a dialogue.
- Write an expository interpretation of a character in a performance.

Before Reading

1. Play the following drama game with a small group or partner:

   Have each group member create an imaginary character by writing down the person's age, gender, name, personality type, physical characteristics, hobbies, and interests. Also jot down something important that just happened to your character: car crash, marriage, lottery win, a new baby. … Do not tell your partner/group about your character. Have one person start by sitting down at a "bus stop." When the second person arrives, improvise their conversation and interactions. Continue with a third character who will take over as the first person "boards the bus" and leaves the scene.

2. After you have finished the drama game, have group members share the written descriptions of their character. Which parts of the character were evident in the game, and which parts were not brought up?

3. Reflect: Why is it important to understand your character if you are acting in a play?

During Reading

4. With a partner, choose one of the dialogues on the following pages, and then select your roles.

5. Meet with a group of students who are performing the same dialogue. Work together to diffuse the text and paraphrase the lines.

6. Divide your group in two so that you are working only with students who have the same role. Work together to annotate your scene for vocal and visual delivery.

LEARNING STRATEGIES:
Drama Games, Diffusing, Marking the Text, Paraphrasing, Sketching, Discussion Groups, Rehearsal

My Notes

Interpreting Character in Performance

My Notes

KEY IDEAS AND DETAILS
How does Orsino's physical description of Cesario reveal that Viola's disguise is not completely successful?

Dialogue 1

adapted from
Twelfth Night
Act 1, Scene 4

by William Shakespeare

Viola (*disguised as the servant Cesario, speaking to herself*):
If the duke continue these favours towards you,
Cesario, you are like to be much advanced: he hath
known you but three days, and already you are no stranger.
Here comes the count. (*Enter DUKE ORSINO*)

Duke Orsino: Who saw Cesario, ho?

Viola: On your attendance, my lord; here.

Duke Orsino: Cesario, Thou know'st no less but all; I have unclasp'd
To thee the book even of my secret soul:
Therefore, good youth, address thy gait unto her;
Be not denied access, stand at her doors,
And tell them, there thy fixed foot shall grow
Till thou have audience.

Viola: Sure, my noble lord,
If she be so abandon'd to her sorrow
As it is spoke, she never will admit me.

Duke Orsino: Be clamorous and leap all civil bounds
Rather than make unprofited return.

Viola: Say I do speak with her, my lord, what then?

Duke Orsino: O, then unfold the passion of my love,
Surprise her with discourse of my dear faith:
It shall become thee well to act my woes;
She will attend it better in thy youth
Than in a nuncio's of more grave aspect.

Viola: I think not so, my lord.

Duke Orsino: Dear lad, believe it;
For they shall yet belie thy happy years,
That say thou art a man: Diana's lip
Is not more smooth and rubious; thy small pipe
Is as the maiden's organ, shrill and sound,
And all is semblative a woman's part.
I know thy constellation is right apt for this affair.

Viola: I'll do my best
To woo your lady:
(*Aside*) yet, a barful strife!
Whoe'er I woo, myself would be his wife.

Dialogue 2

adapted from
Twelfth Night
Act 1, Scene 5

by William Shakespeare

KEY IDEAS AND DETAILS
Why do you think Olivia throws a veil over her face?

My Notes

Olivia (*to herself*): Give me my veil. Come, throw it o'er my face.

Viola: Are you the lady of the house?

Olivia: If I do not usurp myself, I am.

Viola: Most certain, if you are she, you do usurp yourself; for what is yours to bestow is not yours to reserve. I will on with my speech in your praise, and then show you the heart of my message.

Olivia: Come to what is important in't: I forgive you the praise.

Viola: Alas, I took great pains to study it, and 'tis poetical.

Olivia: It is the more like to be feigned: I pray you, if you have reason, be brief. Speak your office.

Viola: Good madam, let me see your face.

Olivia: We will draw the curtain and show you the picture. Look you, sir, is't not well done? (*Unveiling*)

Viola: Lady, you are the cruell'st she alive, If you will lead these graces to the grave And leave the world no copy.

Olivia: Were you sent hither to praise me?

Viola: I see you what you are, you are too proud; But, my lord and master loves you.

Olivia: Your lord does know my mind; I cannot love him: He might have took his answer long ago. I cannot love him: let him send no more; Unless, perchance, you come to me again.

Viola: Farewell, fair cruelty. (*Exits*)

Olivia: Thy tongue, thy face, thy limbs, actions and spirit, Do give thee five-fold blazon. How now! Even so quickly may one catch the plague? Methinks I feel this youth's perfections With an invisible and subtle stealth To creep in at mine eyes. Well, let it be.

KEY IDEAS AND DETAILS
Why does Viola think that Olivia is "too proud"?

Interpreting Character in Performance

ACADEMIC VOCABULARY

A **representation** is a verbal or visual portrait of something or someone. The stem of this word, *represent*, is commonly used to describe a lawyer acting for a client. In a court case, you might hear a judge ask whether a defendant has representation.

My Notes

After Reading

7. Work with your group to create a visual **representation** of your character from the dialogue. Draw a stick figure or outline, and annotate the image with words and other images to describe your character. Add significant quotes from your dialogue and any information that you have from the role playing in Activity 4.12.

   Visual Representation of My Character:

8. Meet with your original partner to rehearse your dialogue together. Perform your dialogue for at least one other group who rehearsed a different dialogue.

Check Your Understanding

Expository Writing Prompt: Explain how you used vocal and visual delivery to interpret your character in a performance. Be sure to:

* Identify specific character traits that your character possesses.
* Provide textual evidence of characterization: thoughts, appearance, emotions, and actions.
* Explain how you portrayed the character in your performance.

Comparing Film and Text

Learning Targets
- Compare film and text versions of two scenes.
- Revise a performance plan based on new ideas for vocal and visual delivery.

LEARNING STRATEGIES:
Graphic Organizer,
Note-taking, Marking the
Text, Revising, Rereading,
Discussion Groups, Rehearsal

Before Reading

1. As you view the scene between Orsino and Viola (Cesario), take notes in the graphic organizer below on the vocal and visual delivery of each character.

	Vocal delivery: tone, pitch, volume, rate, pauses, emphasis	Visual delivery: gestures, movement, facial expressions
Viola		
Orsino		

2. Based on your observations, what is the purpose of this scene? What is happening between these characters? How do they feel about each other? What emotions are they feeling, and why?

My Notes

_____

_____

_____

_____

_____

_____

_____

_____

_____

_____

_____

_____

_____

_____

During Reading

3. Work with a partner or small group to read and mark the text of the scene, on the following page, between Viola and Orsino. Add annotations for vocal and visual delivery, using your notes from the graphic organizer.

4. Rehearse the scene with a partner, and then perform it for your group. Reflect: How are your performances different from those of the actors in the film?

5. Read the scene between Olivia and Viola, adding annotations for vocal and visual delivery.

My Notes

KEY IDEAS AND DETAILS
What is Viola's response to Orsino's accusation about female love?

Drama
adapted from
Twelfth Night,
Act 2, Scene 4

by William Shakespeare

Duke Orsino: Once more, Cesario,
Get thee to yond same sovereign cruelty.

Viola: But if she cannot love you, sir?

Duke Orsino: I cannot be so answer'd.

Viola: Sooth, but you must.
Say that some lady, as perhaps there is,
Hath for your love a great a pang of heart
As you have for Olivia: you cannot love her;
You tell her so; must she not then be answer'd?

Duke Orsino: There is no woman's sides
Can bide the beating of so strong a passion
As love doth give my heart; no woman's heart
So big, to hold so much; make no compare
Between that love a woman can bear me
And that I owe Olivia.

Viola: Ay, but I know—

Duke Orsino: What dost thou know?

Viola: Too well what love women to men may owe:
In faith, they are as true of heart as we.
My father had a daughter loved a man,
As it might be, perhaps, were I a woman,
I should your lordship.

Duke Orsino: And what's her history?

Viola: A blank, my lord. She never told her love,
But let concealment, like a worm i' the bud,
Feed on her damask cheek: she pined in thought,
Smiling at grief. Was not this love indeed?
We men may say more, swear more: but indeed
Our shows are more than will; for still we prove
Much in our vows, but little in our love.

Duke Orsino: But died thy sister of her love, my boy?

Viola: I am all the daughters of my father's house,
And all the brothers too: and yet I know not.

Drama
adapted from

Twelfth Night,
Act 3, Scene 1

by William Shakespeare

Olivia: What might you think?
Have you not set mine honour at the stake.

Viola: I pity you.

Olivia: That's a degree to love.

Viola: No, not a grize; for 'tis a vulgar proof,
That very oft we pity enemies.

Olivia: Why, then, methinks 'tis time to smile again. (*Clock strikes*)
The clock upbraids me with the waste of time.
Be not afraid, good youth, I will not have you:
There lies your way, due west.

Viola: Then westward-ho! Grace and good disposition
Attend your ladyship!
You'll nothing, madam, to my lord by me?

Olivia: Stay, I prithee, tell me what thou thinkest of me.

Viola: That you do think you are not what you are.

Olivia: If I think so, I think the same of you.

Viola: Then think you right: I am not what I am.

Olivia: I would you were as I would have you be!

Viola: Would it be better, madam, than I am?
I wish it might, for now I am your fool.

Olivia: O, what a deal of scorn looks beautiful
In the contempt and anger of his lip!
Cesario, by the roses of the spring,
By maidhood, honour, truth and every thing,
I love thee so, that, maugre all thy pride,
Nor wit nor reason can my passion hide.

Viola: By innocence I swear, and by my youth
I have one heart, one bosom and one truth,
And that no woman has; nor never none
Shall mistress be of it, save I alone.
And so adieu, good madam: never more
Will I my master's tears to you deplore.

KEY IDEAS AND DETAILS
Why does Viola say that
pity is not a kind of love?

My Notes

KEY IDEAS AND DETAILS
What hints does Viola give
Olivia that she is not really
a man?

Comparing Film and Text

After Reading

6. As you view the film version of Olivia and Viola's scene, add notes to your own scene about the actors' visual and vocal delivery.

7. Compare and contrast the film version of the scene with Olivia and Viola and the text you have read.

   • Did the director's version of the scene match your understanding of the scene based on reading it? Did the director change the scene?

   • How did the visual and vocal techniques in the film help you to understand Shakespeare's text?

8. Revise your original performance plan to incorporate ideas from the film actors' interpretation, and then rehearse and perform this scene for your peers.

Check Your Understanding

Describe how reading a text and viewing it in a different medium changes or enhances your perception of the text.

Stage Directions

Learning Target

- Plan and rehearse a scene with stage movement and character interaction.

Before Reading

1. What does the play *Twelfth Night* have to do with the theme of choices? What important choices have different characters made so far? What do you think Shakespeare is saying about the role choice plays when two people fall in love?

2. Consider the film scenes that you viewed in the previous activity. How would these scenes have been different on a stage? How does a stage limit the choices actors have in terms of how they move and position their bodies?

3. Review the image of the stage diagram on the following page. Note that **stage directions** are always from the actor's perspective. You learned in Activity 4.3 that stage directions are the instructions to actors in a drama script. In a small group, practice using and following stage directions by taking turns playing director and calling out directions to the actors, such as "Viola, move downstage left" or "Orsino, enter stage right."

During Reading

4. Mark the text of the following scene for any clues about how the characters might move onstage. Use the margin to take notes on ideas you have for how they would be interacting with each other.

5. Using the image of the stage **diagram** as a guide, work with a small group to annotate the scene with stage directions. Note that there are actually two scenes, so decide how the characters will enter and exit each scene. Sketch a plan on the graphic organizer, using arrows to indicate movement.

LEARNING STRATEGIES:
Summarizing, Diffusing, Marking the Text, Brainstorming, Rereading, Discussion Groups, Rehearsal

My Notes

Literary Terms

Stage directions are the instructions an author places in a script to tell the actors how to perform a scene. Stage directions often include telling actors which area of the stage to enter or exit from, where to stand, and the like."

ACADEMIC VOCABULARY

Diagram has many different meanings. It can be a verb and a noun; in this case it is used to describe a kind of pictorial representation.

Stage Directions

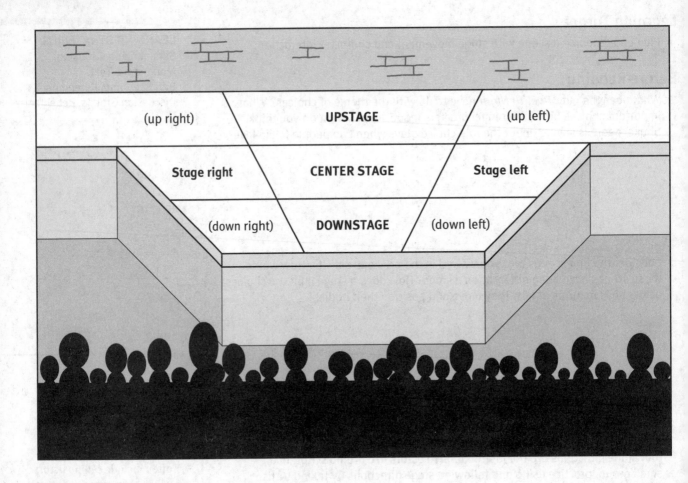

(up right) **UPSTAGE** (up left)

Stage right **CENTER STAGE** **Stage left**

(down right) **DOWNSTAGE** (down left)

Staging Graphic Organizer:

Up Right	Upstage	Up Left
Stage Right	Center Stage	Stage Left
Down Right	Downstage	Down Left

Audience

Drama
adapted from
Twelfth Night
Act 4, Scenes 1–2

by William Shakespeare

Olivia: Be not offended, dear Cesario. I prithee, gentle friend,
Go with me to my house. Do not deny.

Sebastian: What relish is in this? how runs the stream?
Or I am mad, or else this is a dream:
Let fancy still my sense in Lethe steep;
If it be thus to dream, still let me sleep!

Olivia: Nay, come, I prithee; would thou'ldst be ruled by me!

Sebastian: Madam, I will.

Olivia: O, say so, and so be!

***

Sebastian: This is the air; that is the glorious sun;
This pearl she gave me, I do feel't and see't;
And though 'tis wonder that enwraps me thus,
Yet 'tis not madness.
For though my soul disputes well with my sense,
That this may be some error, but no madness,
Yet doth this accident and flood of fortune
So far exceed all instance, all discourse,
That I am ready to distrust mine eyes
And wrangle with my reason that persuades me
To any other trust but that I am mad
Or else the lady's mad; there's something in't
That is deceiveable. But here the lady comes.

Olivia: Blame not this haste of mine. If you mean well,
Now go with me and with this holy man
Into the chantry by: there, before him,
And underneath that consecrated roof,
Plight me the full assurance of your faith;
That my most jealous and too doubtful soul
May live at peace. He shall conceal it
Whiles you are willing it shall come to note,
What time we will our celebration keep
According to my birth. What do you say?

Sebastian: I'll follow this good man, and go with you;
And, having sworn truth, ever will be true.

Olivia: Then lead the way, good father; and heavens so shine,
That they may fairly note this act of mine!

My Notes

KEY IDEAS AND DETAILS
What are the possible explanations Sebastian comes up with for Olivia's love for him?

Stage Directions

After Reading

6. Rehearse the scene, revising the stage directions as needed. Remember to do the following:

   - Always face the audience: when two characters are having a conversation, they should stand at an angle toward the audience.

   - Use physical interactions between the characters, such as linking arms or shaking hands.

   - Respond with appropriate facial expressions and gestures while the other character is speaking.

7. Perform your scene for at least two other groups. Give each other feedback on the effectiveness of each performance's staging and movement. Make notes here on feedback you want to give.

   Group Performance Feedback:

Check Your Understanding

Write a brief description of what you need to do to prepare for presenting a scene. Include the things you have learned to do to enhance a performance, such as analyzing a character, considering elements of visual and vocal delivery, and planning the staging (props, etc.).

Exploring Theatrical Elements

Learning Target
• Create a performance plan that includes theatrical elements.

Before Reading
1. As you view the film clip, take notes on the theatrical elements used by the filmmakers.

LEARNING STRATEGIES:
Summarizing, Diffusing, Marking the Text, Brainstorming, Rereading, Discussion Groups, Rehearsal

Theatrical Elements	Effect on the Scene
Masks/Costuming:	
Set Design/Setting	
Props	
Music	

My Notes

Exploring Theatrical Elements

My Notes

_____

_____

_____

_____

During Reading

2. Annotate the scene with ideas for how you could use theatrical elements if you were performing this scene in class. Consider the following:

- What kinds of costumes could you create out of clothing that you already own?
- What could you draw or collect to create a setting?
- What props could you create or assemble?
- What songs do you know of that capture the emotions in your scene?

KEY IDEAS AND DETAILS
How do Olivia, Viola, and Orsino represent a perfect love triangle?

_____

_____

_____

_____

_____

_____

_____

Drama

from

Twelfth Night,
Act 5, Scene 1

by William Shakespeare

Duke Orsino: Here comes the countess: now heaven walks on earth.

Olivia: What would my lord, but that he may not have,
Wherein Olivia may seem serviceable?
Cesario, you do not keep promise with me.

Viola: Madam!

Duke Orsino: Gracious Olivia,—

Olivia: What do you say, Cesario? Good my lord,—

Viola: My lord would speak; my duty hushes me.

Olivia: If it be aught to the old tune, my lord,
It is as fat and fulsome to mine ear
As howling after music.

Duke Orsino: Still so cruel?

Olivia: Still so constant, lord.

Duke Orsino: What, to perverseness? you uncivil lady,
What shall I do?

Olivia: Even what it please my lord, that shall become him.

Duke Orsino: Why should I not, had I the heart to do it,
Kill what I love?
Come, boy, with me; my thoughts are ripe in mischief:
I'll sacrifice the lamb that I do love,
To spite a raven's heart within a dove.

Viola: And I, most jocund, apt and willingly,
To do you rest, a thousand deaths would die.

KEY IDEAS AND DETAILS
How does Viola respond to Orsino's threats to kill her just to get back at Olivia?

Olivia: Where goes Cesario?

Viola: After him I love
More than I love these eyes, more than my life,
More, by all mores, than e'er I shall love wife.

Olivia: Ay me, detested! how am I beguiled!

Viola: Who does beguile you? who does do you wrong?

Olivia: Hast thou forgot thyself? is it so long?
Call forth the holy father.

Duke Orsino: Come, away!

Olivia: Whither, my lord? Cesario, husband, stay.

Duke Orsino: Husband!

Olivia: Ay, husband: can he that deny?

Duke Orsino: Her husband, sirrah!

Viola: No, my lord, not I.

Olivia: Fear not, Cesario; take thy fortunes up:
A contract of eternal bond of love.

Duke Orsino: O thou dissembling cub!
Farewell, and take her; but direct thy feet
Where thou and I henceforth may never meet.

Viola: My lord, I do protest—

Olivia: O, do not swear!
Hold little faith, though thou hast too much fear. (*Enter Sebastian*)

Sebastian: Pardon me, sweet one, even for the vows
We made each other but so late ago.

Duke Orsino: One face, one voice, one habit, and two persons,
A natural perspective, that is and is not!
How have you made division of yourself?
An apple, cleft in two, is not more twin
Than these two creatures.

Olivia: Most wonderful!

Sebastian: Do I stand there? I never had a brother;
I had a sister,
Whom the blind waves and surges have devour'd.
Of charity, what kin are you to me?
What countryman? what name? what parentage?

Viola: Of Messaline: Sebastian was my father;
Such a Sebastian was my brother too,
So went he suited to his watery tomb.

My Notes

_____

_____

_____

KEY IDEAS AND DETAILS
Why does Olivia think
Cesario is afraid?

_____

_____

_____

_____

_____

_____

KEY IDEAS AND DETAILS
How do Orsino and Olivia
react to Sebastian's
appearance?

_____

_____

_____

_____

_____

_____

_____

_____

_____

Exploring Theatrical Elements

My Notes

KEY IDEAS AND DETAILS
Why do you think it takes Viola and Sebastian so long to accept each other's identity?

KEY IDEAS AND DETAILS
How does Orsino respond to finding out about Viola's disguise?

Sebastian: Were you a woman, as the rest goes even,
I should my tears let fall upon your cheek,
And say 'Thrice-welcome, drowned Viola!'

Viola: My father had a mole upon his brow.

Sebastian: And so had mine.

Viola: And died that day when Viola from her birth
Had number'd thirteen years.

Sebastian: O, that record is lively in my soul!
He finished indeed his mortal act
That day that made my sister thirteen years.

Viola: If nothing lets to make us happy both
But this my masculine usurp'd attire,
I'll bring you to a captain in this town,
Where lie my maiden weeds; by whose gentle help
I was preserved to serve this noble count.

Sebastian (*To Olivia*): So comes it, lady, you have been mistook:
You would have been contracted to a maid;
Nor are you therein, by my life, deceived,
You are betroth'd both to a maid and man.

Duke Orsino: Be not amazed; right noble is his blood.
If this be so, as yet the glass seems true,
I shall have share in this most happy wreck. (*To Viola*)
Boy, thou hast said to me a thousand times
Thou never shouldst love woman like to me.

Viola: And all those sayings will I overswear.

Duke Orsino: Give me thy hand;
And let me see thee in thy woman's weeds.

Viola: The captain that did bring me first on shore
Hath my maid's garments.

Duke Orsino: Your master quits you;
And since you call'd me master for so long,
Here is my hand: you shall from this time be
Your master's mistress. Cesario, come;
For so you shall be, while you are a man;
But when in other habits you are seen,
Orsino's mistress and his fancy's queen.

After Reading

3. With a partner, select one of the dialogues from the previous activities.
   Begin your performance plan by brainstorming and annotating the scene for
   theatrical elements.

Performing a Shakespearean Dialogue

Assignment

Your assignment is to work collaboratively with a partner to plan, rehearse, and perform a dialogue from William Shakespeare's *Twelfth Night*.

Planning: Select and annotate one of the dialogues from *Twelfth Night*.

- What is the meaning of each of your character's lines?

- How will you use vocal delivery to express your character's thoughts and feelings?

- How will you use visual delivery and staging to interpret the scene and interact with your partner's character?

- How will you and your partner make notes and plan your performance?

Rehearsing: Memorize your lines and rehearse the performance with your partner and others.

- What are the "cues" in your partner's lines that will remind you of what to say?

- While your partner is speaking, how should your character react?

- How can you speak to your partner's character while both of you face the audience?

- How can you make the scene more understandable and interesting for your audience with facial expressions, vocal inflection, and gestures?

- How can you enhance your scene with at least one of the following theatrical elements: set design, masks, costumes, props, or music?

- How can the Scoring Guide help you evaluate how well your planned performance will meet the requirements of the assignment?

Performing and Listening: Perform your scene for an audience of your peers, and take notes on your classmates' performances:

- Who are the characters involved?

- What is the dialogue about?

- How did the performers help you understand and appreciate the scene?

Reflecting in Writing: Write a paragraph explaining the strengths and challenges of your performance.

- What would you do differently in a future performance?

- How did performing a dialogue help you understand Shakespearean language?

- What were the best performances you saw, and what made them effective?

Reflection

After completing this Embedded Assessment, think about how you went about accomplishing this task, and respond to the following:

- How did you feel about performing and speaking in front of others before this unit?

- How did this experience prepare you to be a confident oral presenter?

My Notes

Technology TIP:

As part of the rehearsal process, consider video recording your performance.

EMBEDDED
ASSESSMENT 2
continued

Performing a Shakespearean Dialogue

SCORING GUIDE

Scoring Criteria	Exemplary	Proficient	Emerging	Incomplete
Ideas	The performance • delivers an insightful interpretation, and meaning is cleverly communicated through tone, pauses, volume, facial expressions, movements, and gestures • includes several theatrical elements that expand meaning for the audience.	The performance • delivers an effective interpretation, and meaning is communicated through tone, pauses, volume, facial expressions, movements, and gestures • includes one or more theatrical elements.	The performance • delivers an acceptable interpretation, but meaning is not clearly communicated through tone, pauses, volume, facial expressions, movements, or gestures • includes a theatrical element, but it does not enhance the presentation.	The performance • delivers an unclear interpretation, and meaning is confused through inappropriate or inadequate tone, pauses, volume, facial expressions, movements, or gestures • includes no theatrical elements.
Structure	The performance • includes detailed scene annotations with performance notes and a creative plan for the performance • notes show excellent evidence of listening to and evaluating peer performances • reflection demonstrates insightful commentary on strengths, challenges, growth, and evaluation of performances.	The performance • includes an annotated scene with performance notes and a plan for the performance • notes show adequate evidence of listening to and evaluating peer performances • reflection demonstrates adequate commentary on strengths, challenges, growth, and evaluation of performances.	The performance • includes some scene annotations with some performance notes and elements of a plan for the performance • notes show some evidence of listening to and evaluating peer performances • reflection demonstrates little commentary on strengths, challenges, growth, and evaluation of performances.	The performance • includes few annotations and/or little planning for the performance • notes are missing or show little evidence of listening to and evaluating peer performances • reflection is missing or includes little or no commentary on strengths, challenges, growth, and evaluation of performances.
Use of Language	The performance • uses language that delivers a faithful and dramatic representation through visual and vocal delivery • effectively communicates meaning for the audience through gestures, inflection, volume, and pitch.	The performance • uses language that delivers a faithful representation with effective visual and vocal delivery • adequately communicates meaning for the audience.	The performance • includes mispronunciations, mumbled words, and/or language that does not correctly represent the scene • does not adequately communicate meaning for the audience.	The performance • does not include significant parts of the scene and/or shows unclear vocal delivery • does not communicate meaning for the audience.

332   SpringBoard® English Language Arts Grade 7

Grammar Handbook

Part 1: Grammar

Words, Word Groups, and Sentences

Words: Parts of Speech

Part of Speech	Function	Examples
Noun	names a person, place, thing, or idea	Taylor, mayor, ship, Missouri River, log, happiness
Pronoun	takes the place of a noun or other pronoun	I, you, she, us, they, himself, this, who, whom, that, which, each, none
Verb	expresses an action or state of being	go, be, startle, break, feel, do
Adjective	modifies a noun or pronoun	green, large, English, two
Adverb	modifies a verb, adjective, or other adverb	suddenly, awhile, yesterday, really
Preposition	relates one word to another word	in, on, to, above, before, with, between
Conjunction	joins words or word groups	and, or, but, so, either … or, because
Interjection	expresses emotion	ow, whew, uh-oh, hooray

Word Groups: Phrases

A **phrase** is a word group that functions as a specific part of speech and does NOT contain both a subject and its verb.

Kind of Phrase	Description	Examples
noun phrase	functions as a noun (names a person, place, thing, or idea)	**The cold, dark woods** looked like **a forbidding place to be.**
verb phrase	functions as a verb (expresses an action or state of being)	We **were looking** for his house, where the old parrot cage **was stored.**
adjective phrase	functions as an adjective (modifies a noun or pronoun)	The book **on the left** is the one **to read** if you are working on the report **assigned in class.**
adverb phrase	functions as an adverb (modifies a verb, adjective, or other adverb)	He turned **to the left** when he was ready **to leave.**
participial phrase	begins with a past or present participle and functions as an adjective (modifies a noun or pronoun)	The book **sitting on the shelf** is the one **given by Uncle Dan**; you can use it for the report **assigned in class.**
infinitive phrase	begins with an infinitive verb form (to + base form) and functions as a noun, adjective, or adverb	He wants **to leave the theater** whenever you are ready **to go home.**
gerund phrase	begins with an –*ing* verb form and functions as a noun	**Leaving the theater early** and **going home** are our next steps.
prepositional phrase	introduced by a preposition and usually acts as an adjective or adverb	The book **on the left** is the one to read if you are working **on the report** assigned **in class.**

(continued)

appositive phrase	renames or identifies another noun or pronoun	My best friends, **Meredith and Emily,** say that they are going to New Orleans, **my favorite city.**
absolute phrase	consists of a noun and its modifiers and functions as a modifier of a verb or whole clause.	**The sunset waning,** we decided to head back to camp. There, we found our friend Jackson, **his backpack leaning against the picnic table.**

Word Groups: Clauses

A **clause** is a word group that contains both a subject and its verb. An **independent clause** can stand alone as a sentence and expresses a complete thought. A **dependent clause,** or **subordinate clause,** does not express a complete thought and cannot stand alone as a sentence.

> Independent clause: **The pear tree grows.**
> Dependent clause: The pear tree **that Aunt Kim gave us** grows well.

Dependent clauses can function as nouns, adjectives, or adverbs.

> Noun clause: Do you know **who planted the tree**?
> Adjective clause: Do you see the birds **that are nesting**?
> Adverb clause: We'll start the mosaic **after Eric arrives**.

A **noun clause** functions as a noun does—for example, as the subject of a sentence or as a direct or indirect object.

> **Whoever wants a copy** should send me a message.

An **adjective clause,** or **relative clause,** modifies a noun or pronoun. Adjective clauses can be **restrictive** (essential to a sentence's meaning) or **nonrestrictive** (nonessential to the sentence's meaning). Nonrestrictive clauses are set off by commas.

> Restrictive: The boys **who want a copy** have added their names to the list.
> Nonrestrictive: The four broken containers, **which are stacked in the corner**, need to be returned.

Sentences

A **sentence** is a word group that has both a subject and a verb and that expresses a complete thought. Sentences are made of words, phrases, and clauses. A **phrase** is a word group that functions as a specific part of speech and does NOT contain both a subject and its verb. A **clause** is a word group that contains both a subject and its verb and that may act as a part of speech.

A **simple sentence** is made of one independent clause and no dependent clauses. It may contain any number of phrases.

> The pear tree grows.
> The pear tree given to us by Aunt Kim grows very well in that corner of the yard.

A **compound sentence** is made of two or more independent clauses and no dependent clauses. It may contain any number of phrases.

> The sun shines, and the pear tree grows.
> The pear tree given to us by Aunt Kim grows very well in that corner of the yard, and we may plant another one near it in the fall.

A **complex sentence** is made of one independent clause and at least one dependent clause. It may contain any number of phrases.

The pear tree that we planted last season grows well.
The pear tree that we planted last season and that Aunt Kim gave us grows well.

A **compound-complex sentence** is made of one independent clause and at least one dependent clause. It may contain any number of phrases.

The pear tree that we planted last season grows well, and so does the apple tree.
The pear tree that we planted last season and that Aunt Kim gave us grows well, and so does the apple tree.

Part 2: Usage

Subject-Verb Agreement

Compound Subjects
When the subject of a sentence is composed of two or more nouns or pronouns connected by *and*, use a plural verb.

Sara and **her sisters are** at the movie theater.

When two or more singular nouns or pronouns are connected by *or* or *nor*, use a singular verb.

Clive or **Penny is** in the yard.

When a compound subject contains both a singular and a plural noun or pronoun joined by *or* or *nor*, the verb should agree with the noun or pronoun that is nearer the verb.

George or **his teammates practice** daily.

Other Problems in Agreement
Doesn't is a contraction of *does not* and should be used with a singular subject. *Don't* is a contraction of *do not* and should be used with a plural subject. Exception: With the pronouns *I* and *you*, the contraction *don't* should be used.

He doesn't **like** it.
They don't **like** it.

Do not be misled by a phrase that comes between the subject and the verb. The verb agrees with the subject, not with a noun or pronoun in the interrupting phrase.

One of the stores **is** closed.
The **people** who love that band **are** many.
The **captain of the team**, as well as his rivals, **is** ready.
The **movie**, including all the trailers that come before, **is** very long.
A teenager with a skateboard and basketball **walks** past this bus stop each day.

The terms *each, each one, either, neither, everyone, everybody, anybody, anyone, nobody, somebody, someone,* and *no one* are singular and require a singular verb.

Each of these platters **is** full.
Everybody knows the answer.
Either is fine with me.

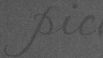

Some nouns that are plural in form, such as *civics*, *mathematics*, *measles*, and *news*, require singular verbs.

> **Measles is** a serious illness.

Some nouns, such as *scissors*, *tweezers*, *pants*, and *shears*, identify singular objects but name things that have two parts. These nouns take plural verbs.

> These **scissors are** sharp.
> Those **pants are** made of heavy fabric.

In sentences beginning with *there is* or *there are*, the subject follows the verb, but the verb must still agree with the subject.

> There **are** many **owls** in the woods.
> There **is** a **question**.

Collective nouns are words that can take a singular or plural verb, depending on if they refer to the group as a whole or to the group as a collection of different members or elements. Examples include *group*, *team*, *committee*, *class*, and *family*.

> The **family has** a long history.
> My **family have** never been able to agree.

Pronoun-Antecedent Agreement

When a pronoun takes the place of a singular noun, use a singular pronoun.

> **Incorrect:** If a student parks a car on campus, they have to buy a parking sticker.
> **Correct:** If a **student** parks a car on campus, **he or she** has to buy a parking sticker.

If using *he or she* sounds wordy, you can revise a sentence to use a plural form instead:

> **Students** who park on campus have to buy parking stickers for **their** cars.

The pronouns *each*, *each one*, *either*, *neither*, *everyone*, *everybody*, *anybody*, *anyone*, *nobody*, *somebody*, *someone*, and *no one* require a singular verb.

> **Everybody** ought to do **his or her** job.
> **Neither** of the girls brought **her** backpack.

Other Problems in Agreement

Agreement in Person

Pronouns should agree in person with their antecedents. Do not switch between first, second, and third person without reason.

> **Incorrect:** When a person comes to class, you should have your homework ready.
> **Correct:** A **person** arriving in class should have **his or her** homework ready.

Clear Reference

Pronouns should refer specifically and clearly to their antecedents. In some cases, you may need to reword or reorganize a sentence to make it clearer.

> **Ambiguous:** Although the car hit the building, it was not damaged. [Is *it* the car or the building?]
> **Revised:** Although it hit the building, the car was not damaged.
> **Ambiguous:** Stella told Kathryn that she ought to help build the set. [Does *she* refer to Stella or Kathryn?]
> **Revised:** According to Stella, Kathryn ought to help build the set.

Unclear: In the newspaper they say that the drought will last all summer. [Who are "they"?]

Revised: An article in the newspaper says that the drought will last all summer.

Unclear: Armand had a job as a ranger in a state forest last summer. This may be his life's work. [What word does this refer to?]

Revised: Armand had a job as a ranger in a state forest last summer. Protecting nature may be his life's work.

Pronoun Case

Pronouns have three cases.

- **Subjective (nominative) case:** pronouns used as subjects or predicate nominatives
- **Objective case:** pronouns used as objects of verbs or prepositions
- **Possessive case:** pronouns that express ownership

Subjective Case	Objective Case	Possessive Case
I	me	my (mine)
you	you	your (yours)
he, she, it	him, her, it	his, her (hers), it (its)
we	us	our (ours)
they	them	their (theirs)
who	whom	whose

Reflexive and Intensive Pronouns

	Singular	Plural
First person	myself	ourselves
Second person	yourself	yourselves
Third person	himself, herself, itself	themselves

A **reflexive pronoun** refers back to the subject of a clause or sentence. It functions as a complement or as the object of a preposition.

> I told myself to be brave. [The reflexive pronoun is the indirect object of *told*.]

An **intensive pronoun** emphasizes the word it refers to.

> I myself led the team to safety. [The reflexive pronoun emphasizes the subject.]

Compound Structures

In compound structures that include two pronouns or a noun and a pronoun, pay attention to pronoun case. Hint: If you're not sure which form to use, try each pronoun on its own in the sentence.

Incorrect: Dylan and me play soccer. [Would you say, "me play"?]
Correct: Dylan and I play soccer.

Incorrect: He gave the message to the faculty and I. [Would you say, "he gave the message to I"?]
Correct: He gave the message to the faculty and me.

Incorrect: Us musicians like the conductor. [Would you say, "us like the conductor"?]
Correct: We musicians like the conductor.

Comparisons

In comparisons, pay attention to pronoun case. Hint: You can finish the comparison, as shown below, to determine which case to use.

> Connor is more talented **than I** (am).
> This helps Eliot **as much as** (it helps) **me**.

Who and Whom

In formal writing, use *whom* and its related forms as an object of a verb or of a preposition.

> **Informal:** Who am I talking to?
> **Formal:** To **whom** am I talking?
> **Informal:** I will be sitting next to whoever Senator Gorm invites.
> **Formal:** I will be sitting next to **whomever** Senator Gorm invites.

Appositives

An **appositive** is a noun or pronoun that identifies or explains another noun or pronoun.

> Your friend **Bill** is in Dr. Levine's AP class.
> My sister's cat, **Chimmy**, doesn't like your dog.

An **appositive phrase** usually follows the word it explains or identifies, but it may also precede it.

> **A state known for its cold climate**, Alaska is closer to the North Pole than to Texas.

Some appositives are **restrictive**, or essential to a sentence's meaning. Restrictive appositives are not set off by punctuation.

> The civil rights leader **Martin Luther King, Jr.** is often quoted. [Without the appositive, we would not know who is often quoted.]

If the appositive is **nonrestrictive**, or not essential to a sentence's meaning, it is set off with commas.

> Martin Luther King, Jr. **a famous civil rights leader**, is often quoted. [Without the appositive, we would still know who is often quoted.]

Verbals

Gerunds and Gerund Phrases

A **gerund** is a verbal that ends in *–ing* and functions as a noun. Since a gerund functions as a noun, it can be used as a subject, direct object, subject complement, or object of preposition.

> **Traveling** might satisfy your desire for new experiences.
> Are you excited about **arriving**?

Gerund phrases include a gerund and any modifiers or complements of the gerund. A gerund phrase functions as a noun.

> **Traveling to Asia** might satisfy your desire for new experiences.
> Are you excited about **arriving tomorrow**?

Participles and Participial Phrases

A **participle** is a verbal that is used as an adjective and most often ends in *–ing* or *–ed*. Participles modify nouns or pronouns. Present participles end in *–ing*. Past participles end in *–ed*, *–d*, *–en*, *–t*, or *–n*, as in the words *used, beaten, dealt*, and *seen*.

The **dangling** toy caught the kitten's attention.
The **broken** shutter banged in the wind.

A **participial phrase** includes the participle and any modifiers or complements of the participle. A participial phrase modifies a noun or pronoun.

The toy **dangling off the sofa** caught the kitten's attention.
The shutter **broken in the winter storm** banged in the wind.

A participial phrase should clearly modify a word in the sentence and should be placed near the word it modifies.

Incorrect: Carrying a stack of plates, his foot caught on a step. [His foot was not carrying plates. This participial phrase is a **dangling modifier**; it does not clearly modify any word in the sentence.]
Correct: Carrying a stack of plates, he caught his foot on a step.
Incorrect: Flying across the sky, Eugene saw a huge flock of gorgeous birds. [Eugene was not flying. This participial phrase is a **misplaced modifier**; it appears to modify *Eugene* rather than *flock*.]
Correct: Eugene saw a huge flock of gorgeous birds **flying across the sky.**

Punctuating Participial Phrases

When a participial phrase begins a sentence, a comma should be placed after the phrase.

Arriving at the park, Tara found that it had just closed.
Exercising regularly, Miguel found that his health and his attitude both improved.

When a participial phrase comes in the middle of a sentence, it should be set off with commas only if the information in the phrase is not essential to the meaning of the sentence.

Gricelda, **performing in the play**, found that she enjoyed being onstage. [not essential]
The teenager **performing in the play** was very talented. [essential]

When a participial phrase comes at the end of a sentence, a comma usually precedes the phrase if it modifies an earlier word in the sentence but not if the phrase directly follows the word it modifies.

The rangers watched the caribou **heading toward the stream**. [The phrase modifies *caribou*.]
The rangers watched the caribou, **admiring the animals' beauty and strength**. [The phrase modifies *rangers*, not *caribou*.]

Infinitives and Infinitive Phrases

An infinitive is a verbal consisting of the word *to* and the base form of a verb. It can function as a noun, adjective, or adverb. The infinitive may function as a subject, direct object, subject complement, adjective, or adverb in a sentence.

To stay seemed rude. [subject]
Jerome wanted **to go**. [direct object]
Her preference was **to delay**. [predicate nominative]
He lacked the willingness **to insist**. [adjective]
They finally were ready **to depart**. [adverb]

Don't confuse an infinitive—a verbal consisting of *to* plus a verb—with a prepositional phrase beginning with *to*.

Infinitives: to paint, to become, to exit, to sit, to throw
Prepositional phrases: to Jason, to the field, to all of us, to the hour

An **infinitive phrase** includes an infinitive and its modifiers or complements.

> **To stay past 10:00 p.m.** seemed rude. [subject]
> Jerome wanted **to go right away.** [direct object]
> Her preference was **to delay till her aunt arrived**. [predicate nominative]
> He lacked the willingness **to insist that they say good night**. [adjective]
> They finally were ready **to depart around midnight**. [adverb]

Punctuating Infinitives and Infinitive Phrases

If an infinitive or infinitive phrase is used as an adverb and begins a sentence, it should be set off with a comma; otherwise, no punctuation is needed.

> **To convince me to read the book**, Jacob read me his favorite passages. [adverb]
> **To plant a garden** is my next goal. [noun]

Split Infinitives

Split infinitives occur when words come between *to* and the verb in an infinitive. Although splitting infinitives is sometimes acceptable, it is often awkward, and some readers find split infinitives overly informal. You may wish to avoid splitting infinitives in formal writing.

> **Awkward:** He began **to**, all of a sudden, **talk** excitedly about his new job.
> **Revised:** He began, all of a sudden, **to talk** excitedly about his new job.

Prepositions

Preposition Use: Expressions of Time

On is used with days:

> I will see Tim **on** Wednesday.

At is used with *noon, night, midnight,* and with the time of day:

> The movie is **at** noon.

In is used with other parts of the day, with months, with years, with seasons:

> We will gather **in** the afternoon.
> **In** the spring, we can visit Kansas.

To express continuing action, English uses the following prepositions: *since, for, by, from ... to, from ... until, during, (with)in.*

> The visitors have been here **since** yesterday.
> I'm going to Atlanta **for** two weeks.
> Mike's cousins were in Austin **from** August **to** October.

Preposition Use: Expressions of Place

English uses the following prepositions:

- to talk about a specific point or place: *in*
  There is an egg **in** the nest.
- to express something contained: *inside*
  What is **inside** that blue box?
- to talk about the surface: *on*
  What is **on** the counter?
- to talk about a general vicinity: *at*
  We left him **at** Antietam.

Preposition Use: Objects of Verbs

English uses the following prepositions to introduce objects of the following verbs.

At: *glance, laugh, look, rejoice, smile, stare*

> I'm laughing **at** the puppets' antics.
> The toddler smiled **at** you.

Of: *approve, consist, smell*

> Aunt Irene approves **of** your career choice.
> That smells **of** mildew.

Of (or about): *dream, think*

> Zac dreams **of** starting anew.
> Zeb thinks **about** leaving for Seattle.

For: *call, hope, look, wait, watch, wish*

> Caroline hopes **for** success.
> The stranded sailor waits and watches **for** rescue.

Sentence Construction: Connecting Clauses

Coordinating conjunctions and **conjunctive adverbs** can be used to connect independent clauses.

Coordinating Conjunctions: The coordinating conjunctions used to join independent clauses are *and, but, or, for, nor, so,* and *yet.* When the second independent clause in a sentence begins with a coordinating conjunction, a comma is needed before the coordinating conjunction:

> Ben wanted to play soccer, **but** Miles wanted to run track.

Conjunctive Adverbs: Some common conjunctive adverbs are *also, consequently, furthermore, however, moreover, nevertheless,* and *therefore.* A conjunctive adverb can begin an independent clause or can be used to join independent clauses. When the second independent clause in a sentence has a conjunctive adverb, a semicolon is needed before it.

> Ben wanted to play soccer; **however**, Miles wanted to run track.

Subordinating conjunctions can connect dependent clauses to independent clauses. Common subordinating conjunctions include *after, although, as, as if, because, before, even if, even though, if, in order to, since, though, unless, until, when, whenever, whether,* and *while.*

> **Even if** she does prefer vanilla, I think she will enjoy the coconut cake.
> I will help you with the dishes **whenever** you are ready.
> The chicken likes to roost outside **unless** it is raining.

Common Sentence Construction Errors

Comma Splices: A comma splice is the use of a comma to join two independent clauses. You can usually fix the error in one of these ways:

- changing the comma to a period and turning the two clauses into separate sentences
- changing the comma to a semicolon
- making one clause dependent by inserting a subordinating conjunction
- adding a coordinating conjunction after the comma

Incorrect:
I love that movie, I have watched it 10 times.
Correct:
I love that movie. I have watched it 10 times.
I love that movie; I have watched it 10 times.
Because I love that movie, I have watched it 10 times.
I love that movie, and I have watched it 10 times.

Fused Sentences: A fused sentence is two or more independent clauses run together with no punctuation. This error is also known as a run-on sentence. The error can sometimes be corrected by adding a period, semicolon, or colon between the clauses.

Incorrect: I love that movie I have watched it 10 times.
Correct: I love that movie. I have watched it 10 times.
Correct: I love that movie; I have watched it 10 times.
Correct: I love that movie: I have watched it 10 times.

Sentence Fragments: A sentence fragment is a word group that does not express a complete thought and cannot stand alone as a sentence. You can usually fix a fragment by combining it with another sentence to make a complete thought or by removing a subordinating conjunction.

Incorrect: Because today I have band practice.
Correct: Because today I have band practice, I won't be riding the bus.
Correct: Today I have band practice.

Using Verbs Correctly

Verbs express different times through tenses. Do not change tenses unnecessarily. Use tenses consistently unless you are deliberately expressing differences in time or sequence.

Inconsistent: I **was talking** to Roseanne, and I **say**, "Will you be in Florida in June?"
Consistent: I **was talking** to Roseanne, and I **said**, "Will you be in Florida in June?"

Sequence of Tenses
Present Perfect: They have walked.
Present: They walk.
Past Perfect: They had walked.
Past: They walked.
Future Perfect: They will have walked.
Future: They will walk.

Problems in sequencing tenses usually occur with the perfect tenses, which are formed by adding an auxiliary or auxiliaries to the past participle.

Verb	Past Form	Perfect Tenses
ring	rang	has/have/had rung; will have rung
walk	walked	has/have/had walked; will have walked

The most common auxiliaries are *can, do, may, must, ought, shall, will, has, have, had,* and forms of *be.*

Present Perfect: The present perfect consists of a past participle preceded by has or have. It expresses action that began in the past and that continues into the present.

Past: Ms. Gage **taught** for 10 years. [She no longer teaches.]
Present Perfect: Ms. Gage **has taught** for 10 years. [She is still teaching.]

Past Perfect: The past perfect tense expresses action in the past that is completed before another past action.

Past: Mr. Geiser played in a band for years.
Past Perfect: Mr. Geiser had played in a band for years before he went solo.

Future Perfect: The future perfect tense expresses action that will have been completed at a specified time in the future.

Future: Mr. Catalano will teach for 17 years.
Future Perfect: Mr. Catalano will have taught for 17 years this November.

Mood and Modal Forms

Mood refers to the form the verb takes to indicate the speaker's attitude. Avoid unnecessary shifts in mood.

Indicative mood expresses a fact or opinion. It is used in declarative sentences.

The Rogers family **raises** chickens.

Imperative mood expresses a command or request.

Bring me the eggs, please.

Subjunctive mood expresses a suggestion, necessity, condition contrary to fact, or a wish.

I recommend that you **be seated** now.
It is necessary that you **be seated**.
If I **were** you, I would be seated.
I wish I **were** seated already.

Interrogative sentences express a question.

Did you **go** to the farm?
Are they **raising** chickens?

Conditional verbs express actions or states of being that depend on other conditions.

If the sun had already set, we **would have gone** home.

Irregular Verbs

In English, verbs have a base form (the present), a past form, and a past participle. Regular verbs add –ed to the base form to make both the past form and past participle. Irregular verbs do not follow this pattern.

Present	Past	Past Participle
be	was, were	been
become	became	become
begin	began	begun
blow	blew	blown
break	broke	broken
bring	brought	brought
build	built	built

(continued)

burst	burst	burst
buy	bought	bought
catch	caught	caught
choose	chose	chosen
come	came	come
cut	cut	cut
deal	dealt	dealt
do	did	done
drink	drank	drunk
drive	drove	driven
eat	ate	eaten
fall	fell	fallen
feed	fed	fed
feel	felt	felt
fight	fought	fought
find	found	found
fly	flew	flown
forbid	forbade	forbidden
forget	forgot	forgotten
forgive	forgave	forgiven
freeze	froze	frozen
get	got	gotten
give	gave	given
go	went	gone
grow	grew	grown
have	had	had
hear	heard	heard
hide	hid	hidden
hold	held	held
hurt	hurt	hurt
keep	kept	kept
know	knew	known
lay	laid	laid
lead	led	led
leave	left	left
let	let	let
lie	lay	lain
lose	lost	lost
make	made	made
meet	met	met
pay	paid	paid

quit	quit	quit
read	read	read
ride	rode	ridden
run	ran	run
say	said	said
see	saw	seen
seek	sought	sought
sell	sold	sold
send	sent	sent
shake	shook	shaken
shine	shone	shone
sing	sang	sung
sit	sat	sat
sleep	slept	slept
speak	spoke	spoken
spend	spent	spent
spring	sprang	sprung
stand	stood	stood
steal	stole	stolen
swim	swam	swum
swing	swung	swung
take	took	taken
teach	taught	taught
tear	tore	torn
tell	told	told
think	thought	thought
throw	threw	thrown
understand	understood	understood
wake	woke (waked)	woken (waked)
wear	wore	worn
win	won	won
write	wrote	written

Commonly Confused Verbs

Lie vs. Lay		
Present	**Past**	**Past Participle**
lie, lying (to tell a falsehood)	I lied to no one.	I have lied to no one.
lie, lying (to recline)	I lay in bed because I was tired.	He has lain in bed all morning.
lay, laying (to put, place)	I laid the doll in the cradle.	We have laid the doll in the cradle.

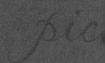

Sit vs. Set		
Present	**Past**	**Past Participle**
sit (to be seated or come to a resting position)	I sat on the curb to wait.	You have sat on the curb all afternoon.
set (to put or place)	I set my dish in the sink.	She has set her dishes in the sink.

Rise vs. Raise		
Present	**Past**	**Past Participle**
rise (steady or customary upward movement)	The helicopter rose into the air.	The helicopter has risen into the air.
raise (to cause to rise)	They raised their hands to give the answer.	I have raised my hands in class many times.

Part 3: Style

Parallel Structure

Parallel structure is the use of similar grammatical structures to show that two or more ideas are similar in importance or meaning or to provide emphasis. Words, phrases, and clauses can be parallel.

Words and Phrases

Not Parallel: Carla likes hik**ing**, swimm**ing**, and **to ride** a bicycle.
Parallel: Carla likes hik**ing**, swimm**ing**, and rid**ing** a bicycle.

Not Parallel: The manager wrote his report quick**ly**, accurate**ly**, and **in a detailed manner**.
Parallel: The manager wrote his report quick**ly**, accurate**ly**, and thorough**ly**.

Not Parallel: He wait**ed** until the last minute to study for the exam, completed his lab problems in a careless manner, and **his motivation was** low.
Parallel: He wait**ed** until the last minute to study for the exam, complet**ed** his lab problems in a careless manner, and lack**ed** motivation.

Clauses

Not Parallel: The teacher told the students **that they should get** a lot of sleep, **that they should not worry** too much, and **to go over their notes**.
Parallel: The teacher told the students **that they should get** a lot of sleep, **that they should not worry** too much, and **that they should go over their notes**.

Not Parallel: I asked **when the order would be ready, where the package should be delivered**, and **the name of the recipient**.
Parallel: I asked **when the order would be ready, where the package should be delivered,** and **who would receive the package**.

Lists

Be sure to keep the elements in a list parallel.

> **Not Parallel:** The tutorial covers how to **identify clauses**, **correct common errors**, and **proofreading for errors**.

Parallel: The tutorial covers how to **identify clauses**, **correct common errors**, and **proofread for errors**.

Bulleted items should be parallel.

Not Parallel:

The master gardener talked about these topics:
- compost
- wildflowers
- eradicating pests
- irrigation

Parallel:

The master gardener talked about these topics:
- compost
- wildflowers
- pests
- irrigation

Using Active Voice

In a sentence using **active voice,** the subject of the sentence performs the action expressed by the verb.

The girl **threw** the ball.
I **ate** three apples yesterday.

In a sentence using **passive voice,** the subject of the sentence receives the action expressed by the verb.

The ball **was thrown**.
Three apples **were eaten** yesterday.

	Active	Passive
Simple Present	Acme **ships** the widgets to many clients.	Widgets **are shipped** to many clients.
Present Progressive	The chef **is cooking** the beets.	The beets **are being** cooked.
Simple Past	I **mailed** a letter last Friday.	A letter **was mailed** last Friday.
Past Progressive	The principal **was making** announcements at the assembly.	Announcements **were being made** at the assembly.
Future	The president **will make** decisions.	Decisions **will be made** by the president.
Present Perfect	Kelli **has made** the appointment.	The appointment **has been made**.
Past Perfect	They **had baked** muffins for us.	Muffins **had been baked** for us.
Future Perfect	By Tuesday, we **will have completed** this project.	By Tuesday, this project **will have been completed**.

The active voice is more vigorous and direct. There are times when passive voice is useful or appropriate—for instance, when you want to be diplomatic and avoid naming names, or when you want to emphasize the recipient of the action. However, generally, you should use active voice most of the time. Avoid unnecessary shifts in voice.

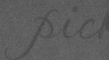

Part 4: Mechanics

Capitalization

Capitalize the first word of a sentence.

Do you have my schedule?

Capitalize the pronoun *I*.

When I sneeze, I try not to do so loudly.

Capitalize proper nouns (the names of specific people, places, organizations, and things).

Dreiser Company   Brooklyn Bridge
Supreme Court   Cleveland, Ohio
Indian Ocean   Federal Trade Commission

Capitalize proper names of family members.

I sent cookies to Grandma but not to Uncle Joe.
What did Father say?

Lowercase words for family members when they are preceded by *a*, *an*, *the*, or a possessive pronoun.

Carina is an aunt now.
I sent cookies to our grandmothers but not our uncles.
What did your father say?

Capitalize the names of specific deities, religious figures, and holy books.

God   Abraham
the Virgin Mary   Shiva
the Bible   Buddha
Mercury   Zeus
the Torah   the Koran

Exception: Do not capitalize the nonspecific use of the word *god*.

The Greek gods seem almost human at times.

Capitalize titles preceding names but not titles that follow names.

What do you think of Mayor Nagin?
I voted for Cecilia Guerra, the mayor of Nettontown.

Capitalize directions that are used as names of parts of the country.

The Rogers family has lived in the South for several generations.

Note: Do not capitalize directions when they are not used as names.

We are heading south next week.

Capitalize days of the week, months of the year, and holidays.

Easter   Monday
January   September
Friday   Thanksgiving

Capitalize the names of seasons only when they are part of a proper noun.

Brentwood Fall Festival
2016 Summer Olympics

Capitalize the names of countries, nationalities, and specific languages.

Paraguay   Russia
Spanish   Russian

Capitalize the first word in a sentence that is a direct quotation.

George Saunders said, "Grief is the bill that comes due for love."

Capitalize the first, last, and all important words in titles of literary and artistic works.
Do not capitalize short prepositions or the articles *a*, *an*, and *the* unless used as the first word of the title.

The Catcher in the Rye
"Nothing Gold Can Stay"
Starry Night

Capitalize the names of members of national, political, racial, social, civic, and athletic groups.

New Orleans Saints   Republicans
African Americans   Phi Beta Kappa
Golden State Warriors   Japanese

Capitalize historical periods and major events.

Edwardian Era   Boston Tea Party
Great Depression   Louisiana World Exposition

Note: Do not capitalize names of centuries.

sixteenth century
first century

Capitalize trademarked brand names.

Pepsi   IBM
Toyota   Nintendo

Punctuating Sentences
Here are basic sentence patterns and how they are punctuated.

Simple Sentence
This pattern is an example of a simple sentence.

Independent clause [.]
We went on an urban hike downtown.

Compound Sentence with a Comma and Coordinating Conjunction

This pattern is an example of a compound sentence with a coordinating conjunction.

Independent clause [,] **coordinating conjunction** *independent clause* [.]

These are the coordinating conjunctions: *and, but, for, or, nor, so, yet.* Note that *then* is not a coordinating conjunction and cannot be used with a comma to separate independent clauses.

We went on an urban hike downtown, and we took notes on the world around us.

Compound Sentence with a Semicolon

This pattern is an example of a compound sentence with a semicolon.

Independent clause [;] *independent clause* [.]

We went on an urban hike downtown; we took notes on the world around us.

Compound Sentence with a Conjunctive Adverb

This pattern is an example of a compound sentence with a conjunctive adverb.

Independent clause [;] **conjunctive adverb** [,] *independent clause* [.]

These are examples of conjunctive adverbs: *also, consequently, however, moreover, therefore, thus.*

We went on an urban hike downtown; also, we took notes on the world around us.

Complex Sentence Beginning with a Dependent Clause

This pattern is an example of a complex sentence. It begins with a subordinating conjunction and a subordinate (dependent) clause.

Subordinating conjunction *dependent clause* [,] *independent clause* [.]

These are examples of subordinating conjunctions: *after, although, as, as if, because, before, if, since, until, when, while.*

When we went on an urban hike downtown, we took notes on the world around us.

Complex Sentence Beginning with an Independent Clause

This pattern is an example of a complex sentence beginning with an independent clause.

Independent clause **subordinating conjunction** *dependent clause* [.]
We took notes on the world around us while we were on an urban hike downtown.

Independent Clause with an Embedded Nonessential Phrase or Clause

This pattern includes an independent clause with an embedded nonessential clause or phrase. A nonessential clause or phrase can be removed without changing the basic meaning of the sentence or making it ungrammatical. The nonessential clause or phrase provides extra information, but the sentence can stand alone without it.

First part of independent clause [,] **nonessential clause or phrase** [,] *rest of the independent clause* [.]
We took notes, some serious and some humorous, on the world around us.
We took notes, which we used later in reports, on the world around us.

Independent Clause with an Embedded Essential Phrase or Clause

This pattern includes an independent clause with an embedded essential clause or phrase. An essential clause or phrase cannot be removed without changing the basic meaning of the sentence.

> *First part of an independent clause* **essential clause or phrase** *rest of the independent clause* [.]
> The next hike that we will take will go along Main Street.
> The next hike through downtown will go along Main Street.

Commas

Commas are often used between grammatical elements and have many conventional uses. Here are essential rules for comma use.

Use a comma with a coordinating conjunction **to join two independent clauses** (*and, but, or, for, nor, so, yet*).

> Rain fell last weekend, but this weekend should be sunny.

Use a comma after an **introductory verbal phrase or an introductory adverb clause**.

> To see the meteors, you should go where there is less light pollution.
> Watching the meteors, we felt both excited and sleepy.
> Before we left, we packed extra snacks.

Use a comma after a long **introductory prepositional phrase** or after more than one prepositional phrase.

> By one o'clock in the morning, we were getting cold.

Use a comma after one short **introductory prepositional phrase** if needed for clarity or readability.

> In December, 17 meteors streaked above me as I watched. [Without the comma, it looks at first as if the sentence contains the date *December 17*.]

Use a comma to separate **items in a series**. For logic and consistency, it is helpful to include a final comma (called the serial comma, or Oxford comma) before the conjunction; however, it is usually not incorrect to omit it.

> The trail was long, dusty, and arduous.
> I like to read novels by George Eliot, Charles Dickens, and E. M. Forster.
> They invited my parents, Frank, and Peggy. [Note that without the serial comma, it would be unclear whether two or four people were invited.]

Use a comma to set off **nonessential phrases and clauses**.

> My hen, a Rhode Island Red, lays several eggs each week.
> Russell Hoban's novel *Riddley Walker*, which I am reading, is fascinating.

Use a comma between **coordinate adjectives** (adjectives that have equal weight and that can be reordered in the sentence).

> He turned in a concise, well-written essay.

If you cannot change the order of the adjectives without making the sentence sound awkward or unidiomatic, you may not need commas.

> His skateboard is the big green one. [You wouldn't say "green big one."]
> The routine involves an easy high kick. [You wouldn't say "high easy kick."]

Use a comma after a **transitional word or phrase**, such as *however, therefore, nonetheless, also, otherwise, finally, instead, thus, of course, above all, for example, in other words, as a result, on the other hand, in conclusion, in addition*.

> Nonetheless, we will proceed as planned.
> Otherwise, we will be stranded here without our phones.

Use a comma to set off **direct quotations and speech tags**.

> "Hey," Roy said, "I will be taking photos at the gallery reception."
> Emily replied, "I hope you get good pictures of Katherine and Alan."

Use commas to set off **items in a date**.

> She was born on October 27, 1962.
> That was due on Friday, April 12, 2013, but was turned in late.

Use commas to set off **thousands, millions, billions**, and so on.

> 27,000,000

Use commas to set off **personal titles and suffixes**. Note that in running text, a comma follows the title or suffix.

> Please welcome Michael Davidson, M.D., to the stage.
> The next speaker was Monica Sanchez, attorney at law, who once attended our school.

Use a comma to separate a **city name** from a state or country name. In running text, a comma follows the state or country name.

> I am from Salisbury, England, and she is from Edinburgh, Scotland.
> I ordered copies from a bookstore in Philadelphia, Pennsylvania, but they haven't arrived.

Semicolons

Use a semicolon to **join two independent clauses** when the second clause restates the first or when the two clauses are closely related.

> If you can arrive early, I will appreciate it; we'll have to set up the sound system.

Use a semicolon to join two independent clauses when the second clause begins with a conjunctive adverb, such as *however, therefore, moreover, furthermore, thus, meanwhile, nonetheless,* or *otherwise,* or a transition, such as *in fact, for example, that is, for instance, in addition, in other words, on the other hand,* or *even so*.

> The technician has already left; however, I think I have her cell number.

Use a semicolon to join items in a series when the items themselves include commas.

> My favorite cities are London, England; Dublin, Ireland; and Chicago, Illinois.

Colons

Use a colon to join two independent clauses when you want to emphasize the second clause.

> I'll ask you again: Would you please return the shirt you borrowed?

Use a colon after an independent clause when it introduces a list, a quotation, an appositive, or other idea directly related to the independent clause.

> We need supplies for the party: ice, beverages, cups, and snacks.
> This is Nelson's favorite quotation by George Eliot: "What do we live for, if it is not to make life less difficult for each other?"
> Tasha has an idea for the perfect classroom pet: a turtle.

Use a colon after the greeting of a business letter.

> To Whom It May Concern:

Use a colon to separate hours and minutes.

> 12:00 p.m.

Use a colon to separate the chapter and verse in a biblical reference.

> 1 John 4:7

Parentheses

Parentheses are used to set off explanatory content, especially if it is tangential. Use parentheses to set off nonessential, or nonrestrictive, information such as dates, clarifying information, or sources, from a sentence.

> David Foster Wallace (1962–2008) wrote both fiction and nonfiction.
> You can find us at 1802 Quentin Street (just behind Compson Middle School).

Use parentheses to enclose literary citations or explanations of acronyms.

> *The Wired Northwest* (Hirt, 2012) details the electrification of the Northwest.
> The scientists at NIH (National Institutes of Health) will issue a report.

Brackets

Brackets are used to clarify the meaning of quoted material.

> The biologist explained, "We were dismayed to find that it [the mantis shrimp] was capable of breaking the glass of the aquarium."
> Dr. Carlisle replied, "The reform bill of the [eighteen-]thirties was in some ways problematic."

Quotation Marks

Use quotation marks to enclose direct quotations. Note that commas and periods are placed inside closing quotation marks, while colons and semicolons are placed outside. The placement of question and exclamation marks depends on meaning.

> Monique asked, "What time does the plane land?" and Jay replied, "Right at noon."
> Monique said, "I'll bring the car"; Jay replied, "Great!"
> Did Jay really say, "I'm sure the plane will be late"?

Use quotation marks to indicate that a word is jargon, slang, or a new word, or is used ironically.

> That's what is known as a "culture capture."
> She raised an eyebrow at this "fair" decision but did not object.

Use quotation marks around the titles of short poems, songs, short stories, magazine or newspaper articles, essays, speeches, chapters, short films, and episodes of television or radio programs.

> "Nothing Gold Can Stay," by Robert Frost
> "Dizzy," by Tommy Roe
> "City Council to Reconsider Redevelopment Plan," an article in the newspaper

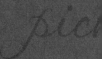

Italics

Italicize the titles of magazines, books, newspapers, films, television programs, long poems, plays, operas, music albums, works of art, and individual spacecraft, trains, planes, or ships.

> *TIME*
> *Julius Caesar* by William Shakespeare
> *Starry Night* by Vincent van Gogh
> *Enterprise* (space shuttle)

Italicize foreign words and phrases.

> *C'est la vie* means, "That's life."

Italicize a word or phrase to add emphasis. (This should be done sparingly.)

> I said we'd be there *late*, not *at eight*.

Italicize words referred to as words, letters referred to as letters, or numbers referred to as numbers.

> The word *curfew* comes from the French. It means "cover fire" and refers to the time of day when medieval families would bank their fires and go to bed.

> Are those *0*'s, *8*'s, or *o*'s?

Hyphens

Use a hyphen to divide a word at the end of a line, if necessary. Break words only between syllables.

> splen-did
> heart-felt
> class-i-fi-ca-tion

For line breaks, divide already hyphenated words only at the hyphen.

> half-
> dollar
> many-
> sided

Use a hyphen to join two or more words serving as a single adjective before a noun.

> hand-dipped chocolates
> well-loved book

However, when compound modifiers come after a noun, they are often not hyphenated.

> The chocolates were hand dipped.
> The book was well loved.

Use a hyphen between tens and ones in compound numbers.

> twenty-seven
> one hundred forty-four

Use a hyphen with the prefixes *ex-* (meaning former), *self-*, *all-*, and *half-*, and with the suffix *-elect*.

> ex-wife
> self-critical
> all-inclusive

half-life
president-elect

Use a hyphen between a prefix and a capitalized word.

mid-October
anti-American
pre-Reformation

Use a hyphen between figures and letters.

T-shirt
mid-1900s

Dashes

En dashes (–) are used between sequential numbers, such as page ranges and date ranges.

Chapters 1–3 are due tomorrow.
The show is onstage September 20–27.

Em dashes (—) are used to set off nonrestrictive or parenthetical information or to emphasize text. Dashes can be used to show pauses or breaks in thought. They are more emphatic than commas or parentheses.

Two of the plays—*Macbeth* and *Guest by Courtesy*—are Jamie's favorites.
If you peek over the edge—watch your footing—you can see far into the canyon.
There is room in the van for six people—not 16.

Use a dash to set off an appositive phrase that already includes commas.

Three cats—Penny, Clytie, and Penguin—are in the front room.

Apostrophes

The apostrophe is used "to:"

- form possessives of nouns
- show the omission of letters in contractions
- indicate plurals of certain lowercase letters

Possessives of Nouns

There are several rules for making the possessive forms of nouns.

Add an apostrophe and –s to:

- the singular form of a word (even if it already ends in –s)
  a dog**'s** collar
  Mr. Rogers**'s** pocket watch
- plural forms that do not end in –s
  those women**'s** books
  these sheep**'s** vaccinations
- the end of compound words
  attorney-general**'s** money
  president-elect**'s** agenda
- the last name of two in a pair to show joint possession
  Ben and Max**'s** wagon
- both names in a pair to show individual possession
  Ben**'s** and Max**'s** backpacks

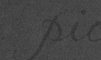

Add just an apostrophe to plural nouns that end in –s.

> four trees' leaves
> the Smiths' new house

Don't use apostrophes to make pronouns possessive or to make nouns plural.

> **Possessive pronouns:** *his, her, hers, its, my, your, yours, our, ours, their, theirs*
> **Incorrect:** That book is her's.
> **Correct:** That book is **hers**.
> **Incorrect:** Is that it's box?
> **Correct:** Is that **its** box?
> **Incorrect:** That book is your's.
> **Correct:** That book is **yours**.

Contractions

Apostrophes are used in contractions to show where one or more letters or numbers have been omitted.

> doesn't = does not
> we're = we are
> should've = should have
> '70s = 1970s

Ellipses

Use ellipses, three spaced periods (…), to show where text is left out of a quoted passage.

> "Four score and seven years ago our fathers brought forth on this continent, a new nation … dedicated to the proposition that all men are created equal."

Use ellipses to show a pause or break in thought.

> It's just that … I don't know … maybe you're right.

Resources

SpringBoard Learning Strategies

READING STRATEGIES

STRATEGY	DEFINITION	PURPOSE
Chunking the Text	Breaking the text into smaller, manageable units of sense (e.g., words, sentences, paragraphs, whole text) by numbering, separating phrases, drawing boxes	To reduce the intimidation factor when encountering long words, sentences, or whole texts; to increase comprehension of difficult or challenging text
Close Reading	Accessing small chunks of text to read, reread, mark, and annotate key passages, word-for-word, sentence-by-sentence, and line-by-line	To develop comprehensive understanding by engaging in one or more focused readings of a text
Diffusing	Reading a passage, noting unfamiliar words, discovering meaning of unfamiliar words using context clues, dictionaries, and/or thesauruses, and replacing unfamiliar words with familiar ones	To facilitate a close reading of text, the use of resources, an understanding of synonyms, and increased comprehension of text
Double-Entry Journal	Creating a two-column journal (also called Dialectical Journal) with a student-selected passage in one column and the student's response in the second column (e.g., asking questions of the text, forming personal responses, interpreting the text, reflecting on the process of making meaning of the text)	To assist in note-taking and organizing key textual elements and responses noted during reading in order to generate textual support that can be incorporated into a piece of writing at a later time
Graphic Organizer	Using a visual representation for the organization of information from the text	To facilitate increased comprehension and discussion
KWHL Chart	Setting up discussion that allows students to activate prior knowledge by answering "What do I know?"; sets a purpose by answering "What do I want to know?"; helps preview a task by answering "How will I learn it?"; and reflects on new knowledge by answering "What have I learned?"	To organize thinking, access prior knowledge, and reflect on learning to increase comprehension and engagement
Marking the Text	Selecting text by highlighting, underlining, and/or annotating for specific components, such as main idea, imagery, literary devices, and so on	To focus reading for specific purposes, such as author's craft, and to organize information from selections; to facilitate reexamination of a text
Metacognitive Markers	Responding to text with a system of cueing marks where students use a ? for questions about the text; a ! for reactions related to the text; and an * for comments ,about the text and underline to signal key ideas	To track responses to texts and use those responses as a point of departure for talking or writing about texts
OPTIC	**O** (Overview): Write notes on what the visual appears to be about. **P** (Parts): Zoom in on the parts of the visual and describe any elements or details that seem important. **T** (Title): Highlight the words of the title of the visual (if one is available). **I** (Interrelationships): Use the title as the theory and the parts of the visual as clues to detect and specify how the elements of the graphic are related.	To analyze graphic and visual images as forms of text

STRATEGY	DEFINITION	PURPOSE
OPTIC (continued)	**C** (Conclusion); Draw a conclusion about the visual as a whole. What does the visual mean? Summarize the message of the visual in one or two sentences.	
Predicting	Making guesses about the text by using the title and pictures and/or thinking ahead about events which may occur based on evidence in the text	To help students become actively involved, interested, and mentally prepared to understand ideas
Previewing	Making guesses about the text by using the title and pictures and/or thinking ahead about events which may occur based on evidence in the text	To gain familiarity with the text, make connections to the text, and extend prior knowledge to set a purpose for reading
QHT	Expanding prior knowledge of vocabulary words by marking words with a Q, H, or T (Q signals words students do not know; H signals words students have heard and might be able to identify; T signals words students know well enough to teach to their peers)	To allow students to build on their prior knowledge of words, to provide a forum for peer teaching and learning of new words, and to serve as a prereading exercise to aid in comprehension
Questioning the Text* The AP Vertical Teams Guide for English (109–112)	Developing levels of questions about text; that is, literal, interpretive, and universal questions that prompt deeper thinking about a text	To engage more actively with texts, read with greater purpose and focus, and ultimately answer questions to gain greater insight into the text; helps students to comprehend and interpret
Paraphrasing	Restating in one's own words the essential information expressed in a text, whether it be narration, dialogue, or informational text	To encourage and facilitate comprehension of challenging text.
RAFT	Primarily used to generate new text, this strategy can also be used to analyze a text by examining the role of the speaker (R), the intended audience (A), the format of the text (F), and the topic of the text (T).	To initiate reader response; to facilitate an analysis of a text to gain focus prior to creating a new text
Rereading	Encountering the same text with more than one reading.	To identify additional details; to clarify meaning and/or reinforce comprehension of texts
SIFT* The AP Vertical Teams Guide for English (17–20)	Analyzing a fictional text by examining stylistic elements, especially symbol, imagery, and figures of speech in order to show how all work together to reveal tone and theme	To focus and facilitate an analysis of a fictional text by examining the title and text for symbolism, identifying images and sensory details, analyzing figurative language and identifying how all these elements reveal tone and theme
Skimming/Scanning	Skimming by rapid or superficial reading of a text to form an overall impression or to obtain a general understanding of the material; scanning focuses on key words, phrases, or specific details and provides speedy recognition of information	To quickly form an overall impression prior to an in-depth study of a text; to answer specific questions or quickly locate targeted information or detail in a text
SMELL* The AP Vertical Teams Guide for English	• Sender-receiver relationship—What is the sender-receiver relationship? Who are the images and language meant to attract? Describe the speaker of the text. • Message—What is the message? Summarize the statement made in the text.	To analyze a persuasive speech or essay by focusing on five essential questions

STRATEGY	DEFINITION	PURPOSE
SMELL* (continued)	• Emotional Strategies—What is the desired effect? • Logical Strategies—What logic is operating? How does it (or its absence) affect the message? Consider the logic of the images as well as the words. • Language—What does the language of the text describe? How does it affect the meaning and effectiveness of the writing? Consider the language of the images as well as the words.	
SOAPSTone*	Analyzing text by discussing and identifying Speaker, Occasion, Audience, Purpose, Subject, and Tone	To facilitate the analysis of specific elements of non-fiction literary and informational texts and show the relationship among the elements to an understanding of the whole
Summarizing	Giving a brief statement of the main points or essential information expressed in a text, whether it be narration, dialogue, or informational text	To facilitate comprehension and recall of a text
Think Aloud	Talking through a difficult passage or task by using a form of metacognition whereby the reader expresses how he/she has made sense of the text	To reflect on how readers make meaning of challenging texts and facilitate comprehension
TP-CASTT* The AP Vertical Teams Guide for English (94–99)	Analyzing a poetic text by identifying and discussing Title, Paraphrase, Connotation, Attitude, Shift, Theme, and Title again	To facilitate the analysis of specific elements of a literary text, especially poetry. To show how the elements work together to create meaning
Visualizing	Forming a picture (mentally and/or literally) while reading a text	To increase reading comprehension and promote active engagement with text
Word Maps	Using a clearly defined graphic organizer such as concept circles or word webs to identify and reinforce word meanings	To provide a visual tool for identifying and remembering multiple aspects of words and word meanings

*Delineates AP strategy

WRITING STRATEGIES

STRATEGY	DEFINITION	PURPOSE
Adding	Making conscious choices to enhance a text by adding additional words, phrases, sentences, or ideas	To refine and clarify the writer's thoughts during revision and/or drafting
Brainstorming	Using a flexible but deliberate process of listing multiple ideas in a short period of time without excluding any idea from the preliminary list	To generate ideas, concepts, or key words that provide a focus and/or establish organization as part of the prewriting or revision process
Deleting	Providing clarity and cohesiveness for a text by eliminating words, phrases, sentences, or ideas	To refine and clarify the writer's thoughts during revision and/or drafting
Drafting	Composing a text in its initial form	To incorporate brainstormed or initial ideas into a written format

STRATEGY	DEFINITION	PURPOSE
Free writing	Write freely without constraints in order to capture thinking and convey the writer's purpose	To refine and clarify the writer's thoughts, spark new ideas, and/or generate content during revision and/or drafting
Generating Questions	Clarifying and developing ideas by asking questions of the draft. May be part of self-editing or peer editing	To clarify and develop ideas in a draft; used during drafting and as part of writer response
Graphic Organizer	Organizing ideas and information visually (e.g., Venn diagrams, flowcharts, cluster maps)	To provide a visual system for organizing multiple ideas, details, and/or textual support to be included in a piece of writing
Looping	After free writing, one section of a text is circled to promote elaboration or the generation of new ideas for that section. This process is repeated to further develop ideas from the newly generated segments	To refine and clarify the writer's thoughts, spark new ideas, and/or generate new content during revision and/or drafting
Mapping	Creating a graphic organizer that serves as a visual representation of the organizational plan for a written text	To generate ideas, concepts, or key words that provide a focus and/or establish organization during the prewriting, drafting, or revision process
Marking the Draft	Interacting with the draft version of a piece of writing by highlighting, underlining, color-coding, and annotating to indicate revision ideas	To encourage focused, reflective thinking about revising drafts
Note-taking	Making notes about ideas in response to text or discussions; one form is the double-entry journal in which textual evidence is recorded on the left side and personal commentary about the meaning of the evidence on the other side.	To assist in organizing key textual elements and responses noted during reading in order to generate textual support that can be incorporated into a piece of writing at a later time. Note-taking is also a reading and listening strategy.
Outlining	Using a system of numerals and letters in order to identify topics and supporting details and ensure an appropriate balance of ideas.	To generate ideas, concepts, or key words that provide a focus and/or establish organization prior to writing an initial draft and/or during the revision process
Quickwrite	Writing for a short, specific amount of time in response to a prompt provided	To generate multiple ideas in a quick fashion that could be turned into longer pieces of writing at a later time (May be considered as part of the drafting process)
RAFT	Generating a new text and/or transforming a text by identifying and manipulating its component parts of Role, Audience, Format, and Topic	To generate a new text by identifying the main elements of a text during the prewriting and drafting stages of the writing process
Rearranging	Selecting components of a text and moving them to another place within the text and/or modifying the order in which the author's ideas are presented	To refine and clarify the writer's thoughts during revision and/or drafting
Self-Editing/Peer Editing	Working individually or with a partner to examine a text closely in order to identify areas that might need to be corrected for grammar, punctuation, spelling	To facilitate a collaborative approach to generating ideas for and revising writing.

STRATEGY	DEFINITION	PURPOSE
Sharing and Responding	Communicating with another person or a small group of peers who respond to a piece of writing as focused readers (not necessarily as evaluators)	To make suggestions for improvement to the work of others and/or to receive appropriate and relevant feedback on the writer's own work, used during the drafting and revision process
Sketching	Drawing or sketching ideas or ordering of ideas. Includes storyboarding, visualizing	To generate and/or clarify ideas by visualizing them. May be part of prewriting
Substituting / Replacing	Replacing original words or phrases in a text with new words or phrases that achieve the desired effect	To refine and clarify the writer's thoughts during revision and/or drafting
TWIST* The AP Vertical Teams Guide for English 167–174	Arriving at a thesis statement that incorporates the following literary elements: tone, word choice (diction), imagery, style and theme	To craft an interpretive thesis in response to a prompt about a text
Webbing	Developing a graphic organizer that consists of a series of circles connected with lines to indicate relationships among ideas	To generate ideas, concepts, or key words that provide a focus and/or establish organization prior to writing an initial draft and/or during the revision process
Writer's Checklist	Using a co-constructed checklist (that could be written on a bookmark and/or displayed on the wall) in order to look for specific features of a writing text and check for accuracy	To focus on key areas of the writing process so that the writer can effectively revise a draft and correct mistake
Writing Groups	A type of discussion group devoted to sharing and responding of student work	To facilitate a collaborative approach to generating ideas for and revising writing.

SPEAKING AND LISTENING STRATEGIES

STRATEGY	DEFINITION	PURPOSE
Choral Reading	Reading text lines aloud in student groups and/or individually to present an interpretation	To develop fluency; differentiate between the reading of statements and questions; practice phrasing, pacing, and reading dialogue; show how a character's emotions are captured through vocal stress and intonation
Note-taking	Creating a record of information while listening to a speaker or reading a text	To facilitate active listening or close reading ; to record and organize ideas that assist in processing information
Oral Reading	Reading aloud one's own text or the texts of others (e.g., echo reading, choral reading, paired readings)	To share one's own work or the work of others; build fluency and increase confidence in presenting to a group
Rehearsal	Encouraging multiple practices of a piece of text prior to a performance	To provide students with an opportunity to clarify the meaning of a text prior to a performance as they refine the use of dramatic conventions (e.g., gestures, vocal interpretations, facial expressions)
Role Playing	Assuming the role or persona of a character	To develop the voice, emotions, and mannerisms of a character to facilitate improved comprehension of a text

COLLABORATIVE STRATEGIES

STRATEGY	DEFINITION	PURPOSE
Discussion Groups	Engaging in an interactive, small group discussion, often with an assigned role; to consider a topic, text or question	To gain new understanding of or insight into a text from multiple perspectives
Think-Pair-Share	Pairing with a peer to share ideas; before sharing ideas and discussion with a larger group	To construct meaning about a topic or question; to test thinking in relation to the ideas of others; to prepare for a discussion with a larger group

Glossary / Glosario

A

advertising: the use of print, graphics, or videos to persuade people to buy a product or use a service
publicidad: uso de impresos, gráfica o videos para persuadir a las personas a comprar un producto o usar un servicio

allegory: a story in which the characters, objects, or actions have a meaning beyond the surface of the story
alegoría: cuento en el que los personajes, objetos o acciones tienen un significado que va más allá de la superficie de la historia

alliteration: the repetition of consonant sounds at the beginnings of words that are close together
aliteración: repetición de sonidos consonánticos al comienzo de palabras que están cercanas

allusion: a reference to a well-known person, place, event, literary work, or work of art
alusión: referencia a una persona, lugar, obra literaria u obra de arte muy conocidos

analogy: a comparison of the similarity of two things; for example, comparing a *part to a whole* or the *whole to a part*
analogía: comparación de la semejanza de dos cosas; por ejemplo, comparar una *parte con un todo* o el *todo con una parte*

analysis (literary): to study details of a work to identify essential features or meaning
análisis (literario): estudio de los detalles de una obra para identificar características o significados esenciales

anecdote: a brief, entertaining account of an incident or event
anécdota: breve relato entretenido de un incidente o suceso

antonyms: words with opposite meanings
antónimos: palabras con significados opuestos

archetype: a character, symbol, story pattern, or other element that is common to human experience across cultures and that occurs frequently in literature, myth, and folklore
arquetipo: personaje, símbolo, patrón de un cuento u otro elemento que es común a la experiencia humana a través de diversas culturas y que aparece con frecuencia en literatura, mitos y folclor

argument: facts or reasoning offered to support a position as being true
argumento: hechos o razonamiento entregados para apoyar una posición como verdadera

artifact: an object made by a human being, typically an item that has cultural or historical significance
artefacto: objeto hecho por un ser humano, habitualmente un objeto que tiene significación cultural o histórica

assonance: the repetition of similar vowel sounds in accented syllables, followed by different consonant sounds, in words that are close together
asonancia: repetición de sonidos vocálicos similares en sílabas tónicas, seguida de diferentes sonidos consonánticos, en palabras que están próximas

atmosphere: the feeling created by a literary work or passage
atmósfera: sentimiento creado por una obra o pasaje literario

audience: the intended readers of specific types of texts or the viewers of a program or performance
público: lectores objetivo de tipos específicos de textos o espectadores de un programa o actuación

B

balanced sentence: a sentence that presents ideas of equal weight in similar grammatical form to emphasize the similarity or difference between the ideas
oración balanceada: oración que presenta ideas de igual peso en forma gramatical similar para enfatizar la semejanza o diferencia entre las ideas

body paragraph: a paragraph that contains a topic sentence, supporting details and commentary, and a concluding sentence and that is usually part of a longer text
párrafo representativo: párrafo que contiene una oración principal, detalles de apoyo y comentarios, y una oración concluyente que normalmente forma parte de un texto más extenso

C

caricature: a visual or verbal representation in which characteristics or traits are distorted for emphasis
caricatura: representación visual o verbal en la que las características o rasgos son distorsionados para dar énfasis

cause: an initial action; an event that makes something else happen
causa: acción inicial; suceso que hace que otra cosa ocurra

character: a person or animal that takes part in the action of a literary work
personaje: persona o animal que participa en la acción de una obra literaria

characterization: the methods a writer uses to develop characters; for example, through description, actions, and dialogue
caracterización: métodos que usa un escritor para desarrollar personajes; por ejemplo, a través de descripción, acciones y diálogo

citation: giving credit to the authors of source information
cita: dar crédito a los autores de información usada como fuente

claim: a position statement (or thesis) that asserts an idea or makes an argument
afirmación: declaración de una posición (o tesis) que afirma una idea o propone un argumento

cliché: an overused expression or idea
cliché: expresión o idea usada en exceso

climax: the turning point or the high point of a story
clímax: punto de inflexión o momento culminante de un cuento

coherence: the clear and orderly presentation of ideas in a paragraph or essay
coherencia: presentación clara y ordenada de ideas en un párrafo o ensayo; la coherencia interna se refiere a la coherencia dentro de un párrafo; la coherencia externa se refiere a la coherencia entre párrafos y se relaciona con el ensayo total

comedy: an entertainment that is amusing or humorous
comedia: espectáculo que es divertido o cómico

commentary: explanation of the way the facts, details and/or examples in a paragraph or essay support the topic sentence
comentario: explicación de la manera en que los hechos, detalles y ejemplos de un párrafo o ensayo apoyan la oración principal

commercialism: an emphasis on gaining profits through advertising or sponsorship
mercantilismo: énfasis en obtener utilidades por medio de la publicidad o el auspicio

communication: the process of giving or exchanging information
comunicación: proceso de dar o intercambiar información

compare: to identify similarities in two or more items
comparar: identificar semejanzas en dos o más elementos

concluding sentence: a final sentence that pulls together the ideas in a paragraph by restating the main idea or by summarizing or commenting on the ideas in the paragraph
oración concluyente: oración final que reúne las ideas de un párrafo, reformulando la idea principal o resumiendo o comentando las ideas del párrafo

conclusion: the ending of a paragraph or essay, which brings it to a close and leaves an impression with the reader
conclusión: fin de un párrafo o ensayo, que lo lleva a su término y deja una impresión en el lector

conflict: a struggle between opposing forces. In an **external conflict**, a character struggles with an outside force, such as another character or something in nature. In an **internal conflict**, the character struggles with his or her own needs, desires, or emotions.
conflicto: lucha entre fuerzas opuestas. En un **conflicto externo**, un personaje lucha contra una fuerza externa, como por ejemplo otro personaje o algo de la naturaleza. En un **conflicto interno**, el personaje lucha contra sus propias necesidades, deseos o emociones.

connotation: the suggested or implied meaning or emotion associated with a word—beyond its literal definition
connotación: significado o emoción sugerida o implícita que se asocia con una palabra—más allá de su definición literal

consensus: an agreement that satisfies everyone in a group
consenso: acuerdo que satisface a todas en un grupo

consequences: something that logically or naturally follows from an action or condition
consecuencias: algo que resulta lógica o naturalmente como resultado de una acción o condición

consonance: the repetition of final consonant sounds in stressed syllables with different vowel sounds
consonancia: repetición de sonidos consonánticos finales en sílabas tónicas con diferentes sonidos vocálicos

consumer: a buyer; a person who acquires goods and services
consumidor: comprador, persona que adquiere bienes y servicios

consumerism: the buying and consuming of goods and products; the belief that it is good to buy and consume goods and services
consumismo: compra y consumo de bienes y productos; creencia de que es bueno comprar y consumir bienes y servicios

context clue: information in words and phrases surrounding an unfamiliar word that hint at the meaning of the unfamiliar word.
clave de contexto: información en las palabras y frases que rodean una palabra no conocida y que dan una pista acerca del significado de esa palabra.

contrast: to identify differences in two or more items
contrastar: identificar las diferencias entre dos o más elementos

copy: the actual text in an advertisement
texto publicitario: información actual en un anuncio publicitario

counterclaim (or counterargument): reasoning or facts given in opposition to an argument
contraargumento: razonamiento o hechos dados en oposición a un argumento

credibility: the quality of being trusted or believed
credibilidad: calidad de ser confiable o creíble

criteria: the facts, rules, or standards on which judgments are based.
criterios: hechos, reglas o estándares sobre las cuales están basadas las opiniones.

D

debate: *n.* a discussion involving opposing points of view; *v.* to present the sides of an argument by discussing opposing points

debate: *s.* discusión que involucra puntos de vista opuestos; *v.* presentar los lados de un argumento discutiendo puntos opuestos

definition: the process of making clear the meaning or nature of something
definición: proceso de aclarar el significado o naturaleza de algo

denotation: the exact, literal meaning of a word
denotación: significado exacto y literal de una palabra

detail: in writing, evidence (facts, statistics, examples) that supports the topic sentence
detalle: en la escritura, evidencia (hechos, estadística, ejemplos) que apoya la oracón principal

diagram: a kind of pictorial representation
diagrama: tipo de representación pictórica

dialogue: conversation between characters
diálogo: conversación entre personajes

diction: a writer's or speaker's choice of words
dicción: selección de palabras por parte del escritor u orador

dissolve: the slow fading away of one image in a film as another fades in to take its place
desvanecimiento: desaparición lenta de una imagen en una película a medida que otra aparece progresivamente para tomar su lugar

documentary film: a nonfiction motion picture intended to document, or record, some aspect of real life, primarily for the purposes of instruction or maintaining a historical record
documental o película de no-ficción: género cinematográfico de no-ficción que documenta o graba algún aspecto de la vida real, con el propósito de instruir o mantener una documentación histórico

drama: a genre of literature that is intended to be performed before an audience; a play
drama: género literario destinado a ser representado ante un público; obra teatral

dystopia: an imagined place or state in which the condition of life is imperfect or bad
distopía: lugar o estado imaginario en el que las condiciones de vida son imperfectas o malas

E

editorial: A short essay in which a publication, or someone speaking for a publication, expresses an opinion or takes a stand on an issue
editorial: ensayo corto en el que una publicación, o alguien que representa una publicación, expresa una opinión o toma partido acerca de un tema

effect: a change that results from a specific action
efecto: un cambio que resulta de una acción específica

effective: producing a desired or intended result
efectivo: que produce un resultado deseado o esperado

epic: a long narrative poem about the deeds of heroes or gods
épica: poema narrativo largo acerca de las proezas de héroes o dioses

epilogue: a section at the end of a book or play that extends or comments on the ending
epílogo: sección al final de un libro u obra teatral, que extiende o comenta el final

essay: a short literary composition on a single subject
ensayo: composición literaria corta acerca de un único tema

ethos: a rhetorical appeal that focuses on the character or qualifications of the speaker
ethos: recurso retórico centrado en el carácter o las capacidades del orador

euphemism: an inoffensive expression that is used in place of one that is considered harsh or blunt
eufemismo: expresión inofensiva usada en lugar de una considerada cruel o ruda

exposition: (*1*) a type of writing that explains, clarifies, defines, or gives information; (*2*) events that give a reader background information needed to understand a story
exposición: (*1*) tipo de escrito que explica, clarifica, define o entrega información; (*2*) sucesos que entregan al lector los antecedentes necesarios para comprender un cuento

expository essay: an essay that makes an assertion and explains it with details, reasons, textual evidence, and commentary
ensayo expositivo: ensayo que hace una afirmación y la explica con detalles, razones, evidencia textual y comentarios

expository paragraph: a paragraph that makes an assertion and supports it with details and commentary
párrafo expositivo: párrafo que hace una afirmación y la apoya con detalles y comentarios

external coherence: unity or logical connection between paragraphs with effective transitions and transitional devices
coherencia externa: enlace o conexión lógica entre párrafos con transiciones efectivas y recursos de transición adecuados

F

fable: a brief story that teaches a lesson or moral, usually through animal characters that take on human qualities
fábula: cuento breve que enseña una lección o moraleja, normalmente por medio de personajes animales que asumen cualidades humanas

fact: a statement that can be proven
hecho: enunciado que puede demostrarse

fairy tale: a story that involves fantasy elements such as witches, goblins, and elves. These stories often involve princes and princesses and today are generally told to entertain children.

cuento de hadas: cuento que involucra elementos fantásticos como brujas, duendes y elfos. A menudo, estos cuentos involucran a príncipes y princesas y hoy se cuentan generalmente para entretener a los niños.

falling action: events after the climax of a story but before the resolution
acción descendente: sucesos posteriores al clímax de un cuento, pero antes de la resolución

fantasy: a story based on things that could not happen in real life
fantasía: cuento basado en cosas que no podrían ocurrir en la vida real

figurative language: imaginative language that is not meant to be interpreted literally
lenguaje figurativo: lenguaje imaginativo que no pretende ser interpretado literalmente

flashback: a sudden and vivid memory of an event in the past; also, an interruption in the sequence of events in the plot of a story to relate events that occurred in the past
narración retrospectiva: recuerdo repentino y vívido de un suceso del pasado; además, interrupción en la secuencia de los sucesos del argumento de un cuento para relatar sucesos ocurridos en el pasado

fluency: the ability to use language clearly and easily
fluidez: capacidad de usar el lenguaje fácilmente y de manera clara

folk literature: the traditional literature of a culture, consisting of a variety of myths and folk tales
literatura folclórica: literatura tradicional de una cultura, consistente en una variedad de mitos y cuentos folclóricos

folklore: the stories, traditions, sayings, and customs of a culture or a society
folclor: historias, tradiciones, dichos y costumbres de una cultura o sociedad

folk tale: an anonymous traditional story passed on orally from one generation to another
cuento folclórico: cuento tradicional anónimo pasada oralmente de generación en generación

foreshadowing: clues or hints signaling events that will occur later in the plot
presagio: claves o pistas que señalan sucesos que ocurrirán mas adelante en el argumento

free verse: a kind of poetry that does not follow any regular pattern, rhythm, or rhyme
verso libre: tipo de poesía que no sigue ningún patrón, ritmo o rima regular

G

genre: a category or type of literature, such as short story, folk tale, poem, novel, play
género: categoría o tipo de literatura, como el cuento corto, cuento folclórico, poema, novela, obra teatral

global revision: the process of deeply revising a text to improve organization, development of ideas, focus, and voice
revisión global: proceso de revisar en profundidad un texto para mejorar su organización, desarrollo de ideas, enfoque y voz

graphic novel: a narrative told through visuals and captions
novela gráfica: narrativa que se cuenta por medio de efectos visuales y leyendas

H

headline: a short piece of text at the top of an article, usually in larger type, designed to be the first words the audience reads
titular: trozo corto de texto en la parte superior de un artículo, habitualmente en letra más grande, diseñado para ser las primeras palabras que el público lea

humor: the quality of being comical or amusing
humor: cualidad de ser cómico o divertido

hook: *n.* a compelling idea or statement designed to get readers' attention in an introduction
gancho: *n.* idea o afirmación atractiva diseñada para captar la atención del lector en una introducción

hyperbole: extreme exaggeration used for emphasis, often used for comic effect
hypérbole: exageración extrema usada para dar énfasis, habitualmente usada para dar efecto cómico

hypothesize: propose an explanation for something or make an assumption or guess
hacer una hipótesis: proponer una explicación de algo, suponer o adivinar algo

I

idiom: a figure of speech that cannot be defined literally
expresión idiomatica: figura del discurso que no puede definirse literalmente

image: a picture, drawing, photograph, illustration, chart, or other graphic that is designed to affect the audience in some purposeful way
imagen: pintura, dibujo, fotografía, ilustración, cuadro u otra gráfica diseñada para producir algún efecto intencional sobre el público

imagery: descriptive or figurative language used to create word pictures; imagery is created by details that appeal to one or more of the five senses
imaginería: lenguaje descriptivo o figurativo utilizado para crear imágenes verbales; la imaginería es creada por detalles que apelan a uno o más de los cinco sentidos

improvise: to respond or perform on the spur of the moment
improvisar: reaccionar o representar impulsivamente

incident: a distinct piece of action as in an episode in a story or a play. More than one incident may make up an event.
incidente: trozo de acción distintivo como un episodio de un cuento o de una obra teatral. Más de un incidente puede conformar un suceso.

inference: a logical guess or conclusion based on observation, prior experience, or textual evidence
inferencia: conjetura o conclusión lógica basada en la observación, experiencias anteriores o evidencia textual

inflection: the emphasis a speaker places on words through change in pitch or volume
inflexión: énfasis que pone un orador en las palabras por medio del cambio de tono o volumen

internal coherence: unity or logical connection within paragraphs
coherencia interna: enlace o conexión lógica en los párrafos

internal rhyme: the rhyming of a word within the line with a word at the end of the line
rima interna: rima de una palabra en un verso con la palabra final de ese verso

interpretation: a writer's or artist's representation of the meaning of a story or idea
interpretación: representación que hace un escritor o artista del significado de un cuento o idea

interview: a meeting between two people in which one, usually a reporter, asks the other questions to get that person's views on a subject
entrevista: reunión entre dos personas, en la que una, normalmente un reportero, hace preguntas a la otra para conocer sus opiniones acerca de un tema

introduction: the opening paragraph of an essay, which must get the reader's attention and indicate the topic
introducción: párrafo inicial de un ensayo, que debe captar la atención del lector e indicar el tema

L

legend: a traditional story believed to be based on actual people and events. Legends, which typically celebrate heroic individuals or significant achievements, tend to express the values of a culture.
leyenda: cuento tradicional que se considera basado en personas y sucesos reales. Las leyendas, que típicamente celebran a individuos heroicos o logros importantes, tienden a expresar los valores de una cultura.

limerick: a light, humorous, nonsensical verse of few lines, usually with a rhyme scheme of a-a-b-b-a
quintilla: verso liviano, humorístico, disparatado y de pocas líneas, normalmente con un esquema a-a-b-b-a

listening: the process of receiving a message and making meaning of it from verbal and nonverbal cues
escuchar: proceso de recibir el mensaje y comprender su significado a partir de claves verbales y no verbales

literary analysis: the process of examining closely and commenting on the elements of a literary work
análisis literario: proceso de examinar atentamente y comentar los elementos de una obra literaria

revisión local: revisar un texto a nivel de palabras o de oraciones
local revision: revising a text on a word or sentence level

logo: a unique design symbol used to identify a company visually
logotipo: símbolo único de diseño, utilizado para identificar visualmente una empresa

logos: a rhetorical appeal to reason or logic through statistics, facts, and reasonable examples
logos: apelación retórica a la razón o la lógica por medio de estadísticas, hechos y ejemplos razonables

M

media: the various means of mass communication, such as radio, television, newspapers, and magazines
medios de comunicación: los diversos medios de comunicación masiva, como radio, televisión, periódicos y revistas

media channel: a type of media, such as television or newspaper
canal mediático: tipo de medios de comunicación, como televisión o periódicos

metaphor: a comparison between two unlike things in which one thing becomes another
metáfora: comparación entre dos cosas diferentes en la que una cosa se convierte en otra

modify: change or alter something
modificar: cambiar o alterar algo

monologue: a speech or written expression of thoughts by a character
monólogo: discurso o expresión escrita de pensamientos por parte de un personaje

mood: the overall emotional quality of a work, which is created by the author's language and tone and the subject matter
carácter: la calidad emocional general de una obra, que es creada por el lenguaje y tono del autor y por el tema

motif: a recurring element, image, or idea in a work of literature
motivo: elemento, imagen o idea recurrente en una obra literaria

multiple intelligences: the variety of learning styles that everyone has in varying degrees. In each individual, different intelligences predominate.
inteligencias múltiples: diversidad de estilos de aprendizaje que todos tienen en diversos grados. En cada individuo predominan diferentes inteligencias.

myth: a traditional story that explains the actions of gods or heroes or the origins of the elements of nature
mito: cuento tradicional que explica las acciones de dioses o héroes o los orígenes de los elementos de la naturaleza

N

narrative: a type of writing that tells a story or describes a sequence of events in an incident
narrativa: tipo de escritura que cuenta un cuento o describe una secuencia de sucesos de un incidente

narrative poem: a story told in verse
poema narrativo: historia contada en verso

news article: an article in a news publication that objectively presents both sides of an issue
artículo noticioso: artículo de una publicación noticiosa que presenta objetivamente ambos lados de un asunto

nonprint text: a text, such as film or graphics, that communicates ideas without print
texto no impreso: texto, como una película o gráfica, que comunica ideas sin imprimir

nonverbal communication: gestures, facial expressions, and inflection that form unspoken communication
comunicación no verbal: gestos, expresiones faciales e inflexión que forman la comunicación no hablada

norm: something that is usual or expected, such as social behavior in a group
norma: algo que es normal o esperado, tal como el comportamiento social en un grupo

novel: a type of literary genre that tells a fictional story
novela: tipo de género literario que cuenta una historia ficticia

O

objective: supported by facts and not influenced by personal opinion
objetivo: apoyado por hechos y no influenciado por la opinión personal

objective camera view: in film, when the camera takes a neutral point of view
visión objetiva de la cámara: en el cine, cuando la cámara toma un punto de vista neutro

omniscient: a third-person point of view in which the narrator is all-knowing
omnisciente: punto de vista de una tercera persona, en la que el narador lo sabe todo

onomatopoeia: the use of words that imitate the sounds of what they describe
onomatopeya: el uso de palabras que imitan los sonidos de lo que describen

one-liner: a short joke or witticism expressed in a single sentence.
agudeza: chiste u comentario ingenioso que se expresa en una sola oración.

opinion: a perspective that can be debated
opinión: perspectiva que es debatible

oral interpretation: reading aloud a literary text with expression
interpretación oral: leer en voz alta un texto literario con expresión

oxymoron: a figure of speech in which the words seem to contradict each other; for example, "jumbo shrimp"
oxímoron: figura del discurso en la que las palabras parecen contradecirse mutuamente; por ejemplo, "audaz cobardía"

P

pantomime: a form of acting without words, in which motions, gestures, and expressions convey emotions or situations
pantomima: forma de actuación sin palabras, en la que los movimientos, gestos y expresiones transmiten emociones o situationes

paraphrase: to restate in one's own words
parafrasear: reformular en nuestras propias palabras

parody: a humorous imitation of a literary work
parodia: imitación humorística de una obra literaria

pathos: a rhetorical appeal to the reader's or listener's senses or emotions through connotative language and imagery
pathos: apelación retórica a los sentidos o emociones del lector u oyente por medio de un lenguaje connotativo y figurado

performance: presenting or staging a play
actuación: presentar o poner en escena una obra teatral

persona: the voice or character speaking or narrating a story
persona: voz o personaje que habla o narra una historia

personal letter: a written communication between friends, relatives, or acquaintances that shares news, thoughts, or feelings
carta personal: comunicación escrita entre amigos, parientes o conocidos, que comparte noticias, pensamientos o sentimientos

personal narrative: a piece of writing that describes an incident and includes a personal response to and reflection on the incident
narrativa personal: texto escrito que describe un incidente e incluye una reacción personal ante el incidente y una reflexión acerca de él

personification: a kind of metaphor that gives objects or abstract ideas human characteristics
personificación: tipo de metáfora que da características humanas a los objetos o ideas abstractas

perspective: the way a specific character views a situation or other characters
perspectiva: manera en que un personaje específico visualiza una situación o a otros personajes

persuasion: the act or skill of causing someone to do or believe something
persuasión: acto o destreza de hacer que alguien haga o crea algo

persuasive essay: an essay that attempts to convince the reader of to take an action or believe an idea
ensayo persuasivo: ensayo que intenta convencer al lector de que realice una acción o crea una idea

phrasing: dividing a speech into smaller parts, adding pauses for emphasis
frasear: dividir un discurso en partes más pequeñas, añadiendo pausas para dar énfasis

pitch: the highness or lowness of a sound, particularly the voice in speaking
tono: altura de un sonido, especialmente de la voz al hablar

plagiarism: taking and using as your own the words and ideas of another
plagio: tomar y usar como propias las palabras e ideas de otro

plot: the sequence of related events that make up a story or novel
trama: secuencia de sucesos relacionados, que conforman un cuento o novela

poetic devices: poetic techniques used for effect
recursos poéticos: técnicas poéticas usadas para crear efectos

point of view: the perspective from which a story is told. In **first-person** point of view, the teller is a character in the story telling what he or she sees or knows. In **third-person** point of view, the narrator is someone outside of the story.
punto de vista: perspectiva desde la cual se cuenta una historia. En el punto de vista de la **primera persona**, el relator es un personaje del cuento que narra lo que ve o sabe. En el punto de vista de la **tercera persona**, el narrador es alguien que está fuera del cuento.

precise: accurate and careful about details
preciso: acertado y detallado

prediction: a logical guess or assumption about something that has not yet happened
predicción: conjetura lógica o suposición acerca de algo que aún no ha ocurrido

presentation: delivery of a formal reading, talk, or performance
presentación: entrega de una lectura, charla o representación formal

primary source: an original document containing firsthand information about a subject
fuente primaria: documento original que contiene información de primera mano acerca de un tema

prose: the ordinary form of written language, using sentences and paragraphs; writing that is not poetry, drama, or song
prosa: forma común del lenguaje escrito, usando oraciones y párrafos; escritura que no es poesía, drama ni canción

pun: the humorous use of a word or words to suggest another word with the same sound or a different meaning
retruécano: uso humorístico de una o varias palabras para sugerir otra palabra que tiene el mismo sonido o un significado diferente

purpose: the reason for writing; what the writer hopes to accomplish
propósito: razón para escribir; lo que el escritor espera lograr

Q

quatrain: a four-line stanza in poetry
cuarteta: en poesía, estrofa de cuatro versos

R

rate: the speed at which a speaker delivers words
rapidez: velocidad a la que el orador pronuncia las palabras

realistic: characterized by a concern for the actual or real
realista: caracterizado por un enfoque en lo real o verdadero

reflection: a kind of thinking and writing which seriously explores the significance of an experience, idea, or observation
reflexión: tipo de pensamiento y escritura que explora seriamente la importancia de una experiencia, idea u observación

reflective essay: an essay in which the writer explores the significance of an experience or observation
ensayo reflexivo: ensayo en que el autor explora la importancia de una experiencia u observación

refrain: a regularly repeated word, phrase, line, or group of lines in a poem or song
estribillo: palabra, frase, verso o grupo de versos de un poema o canción que se repite con regularidad

repetition: the use of the same words or structure over again
repetición: uso de las mismas palabras o estructura una y otra vez

research: (*v.*) the process of locating information from a variety of sources; (*n.*) the information found from investigating a variety of sources
investigar: (*v.*) proceso de buscar información en una variedad de fuentes; *también*, **investigación** (*n.*) información que se halla al investigar una variedad de fuentes

resolution: the outcome of the conflict of a story, when loose ends are wrapped up
resolución: resultado del conflicto de un cuento, cuando se atan los cabos sueltos

revision: a process of evaluating a written piece to improve coherence and use of language; *see also*, local revision, global revision
revisión: proceso de evaluar un texto escrito para mejorar la coherencia y el uso del lenguaje; *ver también*, revisión local, revisión global

rhetoric: the art of using words to persuade in writing or speaking
retórica: el arte de usar las palabras para persuadir en la escritura u oralmente

rhetorical question: a question asked to emphasize a point or create an effect; no answer is expected
pregunta retórica: pregunta que se hace para enfatizar un punto o crear un efecto; no se espera una respuesta

rhyme: the repetition of sounds at the ends of words
rima: repetición de sonidos al final de las palabras

rhyme scheme: a consistent pattern of end rhyme throughout a poem
esquema de la rima: patrón consistente de una rima final a lo largo de un poema

rhythm: the pattern of stressed and unstressed syllables in spoken or written language, especially in poetry
ritmo: patrón de sílabas acentuadas y no acentuadas en lenguaje hablado o escrito, especialmente en poesía

rising action: major events that develop the plot of a story and lead to the climax
acción ascendente: sucesos importantes que desarrollan la trama de un cuento y conducen al clímax

romantic: characterized by an appeal to what is heroic, adventurous, remote, mysterious, or idealized
romántico: caracterizado por apelar a lo heroico, aventurero, remoto, misterioso, o idealizado

S

science fiction: a genre in which the imaginary elements of the story could be scientifically possible
ciencia ficción: género en que los elementos imaginarios del cuento podrían ser científicamente posibles

search term: a single word or short phrase used in a database search
clave de búsqueda: una palabra o frase corta que se usa para investigar en una base de datos

secondary source: discussion about or commentary on a primary source; the key feature of a secondary source is that it offers an interpretation of information gathered from primary sources
fuente secundaria: discusión o comentario acerca de una fuente primaria; la característica principal de una fuente secundaria es que ofrece una interpretación de la información recopilada en las fuentes primarias

sensory details: words or information that appeal to the five senses
detalles sensoriales: palabras o información que apelan a los cinco sentidos

sequence of events: the order in which events happen
secuencia de los sucesos: orden en que ocurren los sucesos

setting: the time and the place in which a narrative occurs
ambiente: tiempo y lugar en que ocurre un relato

short story: a work of fiction that presents a sequence of events, or plot, that deals with a conflict
cuento corto: obra de ficción que presenta una secuencia de sucesos, o trama, que tratan de un conflicto

simile: a comparison between two unlike things, using the words *like* or *as*
símil: comparación entre dos cosas diferentes usando las palabras como o *tan*

slogan: a catchphrase that evokes a particular feeling about a company and its product
eslogan: frase o consigna publicitaria que evoca un sentimiento en particular acerca de una empresa y su producto

speaker: the voice that communicates with the reader of a poem
hablante: la voz que se comunica con el lector de un poema

speaking: the process of sharing information, ideas, and emotions using verbal and nonverbal means communication
hablar: proceso de compartir información, ideas y emociones usando medios de comunicación verbales y no verbales

stage directions: instructions an author places in a script to tell the actors how to perform a scene
direcciones escénicas: las instrucciones que un autor incluye en un guion para decirle al actor cómo interpretar una escena

stanza: a group of lines, usually similar in length and pattern, that form a unit within a poem
estrofa: grupo de versos, normalmente similares en longitud y patrón, que forman una unidad dentro de un poema

stereotype: a fixed, oversimplified image of a person, group, or idea; something conforming to that image
estereotipo: imagen fija y demasiado simplificada de una persona, grupo o idea; algo que cumple esa imagen

structure: the way a literary work is organized; the arrangement of the parts in a literary work
estructura: la manera en que la obra literaria está organizada; la disposicíon de las partes en una obra literaria

subjective: influenced by personal opinions or ideas
subjetivo: influenciado por opiniones o ideas personales

subjective camera view: in film, when the camera seems to show the events through a character's eyes
visión subjetiva de la cámara: en el cine, cuando la cámara parece mostrar los sucesos a través de los ojos de un personaje

subplot: a secondary plot that occurs along with a main plot
trama secundaria: argumento secundario que ocurre conjuntamente con un argumento principal

summarize: to briefly restate the main ideas of a piece of writing
resumir: reformular brevemente las ideas principales de un texto escrito

symbol: an object, a person, or a place that stands for something else
símbolo: objeto, persona o lugar que representa otra cosa

symbolism: the use of symbols
simbolismo: el uso de símbolos

synonyms: words with similar meanings
sinónimos: palabras con significados semejantes

syntax: the arrangement of words and the order of grammatical elements in a sentence; the way in which words are put together to make meaningful elements, such as phrases, clauses, and sentences
sintaxis: la disposición de palabras y el orden de los elementos gramaticales en una oración; la manera en que se organizan las palabras para formar elementos con significado, como frases, cláusulas y oraciones

T

talking points: important points or concepts to be included in a presentation
puntos centrales: puntos o conceptos importantes a incluirse en una presentación

tall tale: a highly exaggerated and often humorous story about folk heroes in local settings
cuento increíble: cuento muy exagerado y normalmente humorístico acerca de héroes folclóricos en ambientes locales

target audience: the specific group of people that advertisers aim to persuade to buy
público objetivo: grupo específico de personas a quienes los publicistas desean persuadir de comprar

tempo: the speed or rate of speaking
ritmo: velocidad o rapidez al hablar

text features: the elements of a text designed to help locate, understand, and organize information
características del texto: los elementos de un texto que están diseñados para ayudar a ubicar, entender y organizar la información

textual evidence: quotations, summaries, or paraphrases from text passages to support a position
evidencia textual: citas, resúmenes o paráfrasis de pasajes de texto para apoyar una position

theme: the central idea, message, or purpose of a literary work
tema: idea, mensaje o propósito central de una obra literaria

thesis statement: a sentence, in the introduction of an essay, that states the writer's position or opinion on the topic of the essay
enunciado de tesis: oración, en la introducción de un ensayo, que plantea el punto de vista u opinión del autor acerca del tema del ensayo

tone: a writer's or speaker's attitude toward a subject
tono: actitud de un escritor u orador hacia un tema

topic sentence: a sentence that states the main idea of a paragraph; in an essay, it also makes a point that supports the thesis statement
oración principal: oración que plantea la idea principal de un párrafo; en un ensayo, también plantea un punto que apoya el enunciado de tesis

transitions: words or phrases that connect ideas, details, or events in writing
transiciones: palabras o frases que conectan ideas, detalles o sucesos de un escrito

TV news story: a report on a news program about a specific event
documental de televisión: reportaje en un programa noticioso acerca de un suceso específico

U

utopia: an ideal or perfect place
utopía: lugar ideal o perfecto

V

valid: believable or truthful
válido: creíble o verídico

verse: a unit of poetry, such as a line or a stanza
verso: unidad de la poesía, como un verso o una estrofa

visual delivery: the way plot, character, and conflict are expressed on stage through gestures, movement, and facial expression
presentación visual: la manera en que el argumento, los personajes y el conflicto se expresan en el escenario a través de los gestos, movimientos y expresiones faciales

voice: a writer's distinctive use of language
voz: uso distintivo del lenguaje por parte de un escritor

vocal delivery: the way words are expressed on stage, through volume, pitch, rate or speed of speech, pauses, pronunciation, and articulation
presentación vocal: la manera en que se expresan las palabras en el escenario, a través del volumen, tono, ritmo o velocidad del discurso, pausas, pronunciación y articulación

voice-over: the voice of an unseen character in film expressing his or her thoughts
voz en off: voz de un personaje de una película, que no se ve pero que expresa sus pensamientos

volume: the degree of loudness of a speaker's voice or other sound
volumen: grado de intensidad sonora de la voz de un orador o de otro sonido

W

wordplay: a witty or clever verbal exchange or a play on words
juego de palabras: intercambio verbal ingenioso u ocurrente o un juego con palabras

Web Organizer

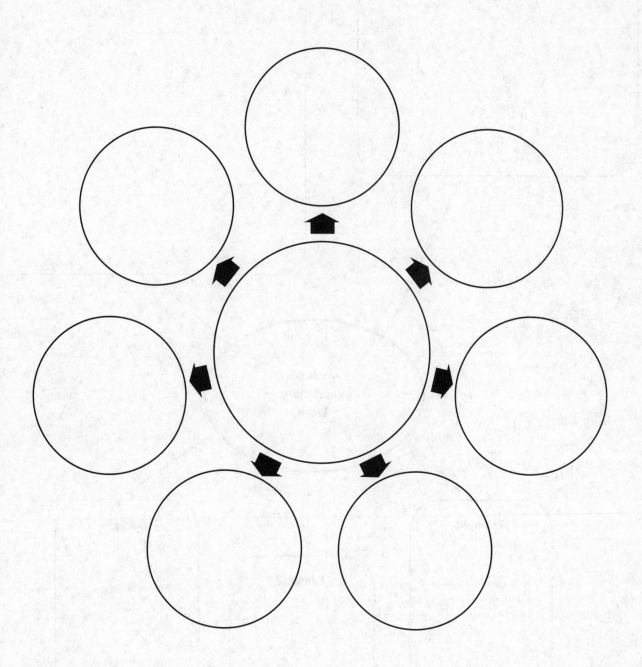

Word Map

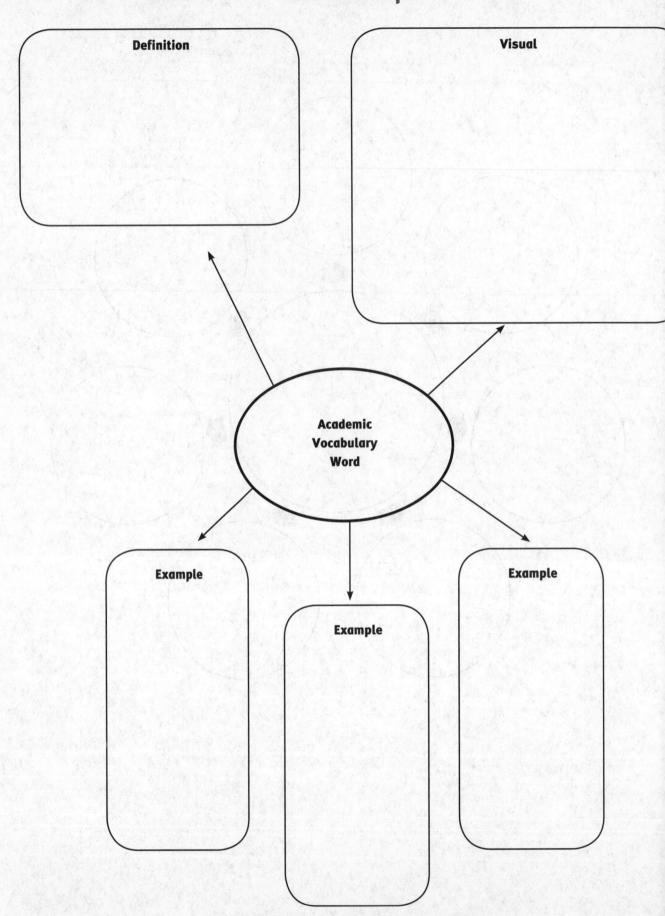

Definition

Visual

Academic Vocabulary Word

Example

Example

Example

Verbal & Visual Word Association

Definition in Your Own Words	Important Elements

Academic Vocabulary Word

Visual Representation	Personal Association

Evaluating Online Sources

The URL

What is its domain?
- .com = a for-profit organization
- .gov, .mil, .us (or other country code) = a government site
- .edu = an educational institution
- .org = a nonprofit organization

- Is this URL someone's personal page?
- Why might using information from a personal page be a problem?
- Do you recognize who is publishing this page?
- If not, you may need to investigate further to determine whether the publisher is an expert on the topic.

Sponsor:
- Does the web site easily give information about the organization or group that sponsors it?
- Does it have a link (often called "About Us") that leads you to that information?
- What do you learn?

Timeliness:
- When was the page last updated (usually this is posted at the top or bottom of the page)?
- How current a page is may indicate how accurate or useful the information in it will be.

Purpose:
- What is the purpose of the page?
- What is its target audience?
- Does it present information or opinion?
- Is it primarily objective or subjective?
- How do you know?

Author:
- What credentials does the author have?
- Is this person or group considered an authority on the topic?

Links
- Does the page provide links?
- Do they work?
- Are they helpful?
- Are they objective or subjective?

SOAPSTone:

SOAPSTone	Analysis	Textual Support
Speaker: What does the reader know about the writer?		
Occasion: What are the circumstances surrounding this text?		
Audience: Who is the target audience?		
Purpose: Why did the author write this text?		
Subject: What is the topic?		
Tone: What is the author's tone, or attitude?		

Index of Skills

Media Skills

Speaking and Listening Skills

Language Skills

Vocabulary Skills

Index of Authors and Titles

Credits

"Choices" from *Cotton Candy on a Rainy Day* by Nikki Giovanni. Copyright © 1978. Reprinted by permission of HarperCollins Publishers/William Morrow.

From *Staying Fat for Sarah Byrnes* by Chris Crutcher. Text copyright © 1991 Chris Crutcher. Used by permission of HarperCollins Publishers.

From *Dust Tracks on a Road* by Zora Neale Hurston. Copyright 1942 by Zora Neale Hurston; renewed © 1970 by John C. Hurston. Reprinted by permission of HarperCollins Publishers.

"Mrs. Conway & Mrs. Lasher" from *Bad Boy* by Walter Dean Myers. Copyright © 1998 by Walter Dean Myers. Used by permission of HarperCollins Publishers.

"Why Couldn't I Have Been Named Ashley?" by Immaculeta Achilike. Used by permission.

"Phaethon" from *Heroes, Gods and Monsters of Greek Mythology* by Bernard Evslin. Published by permission of Writers House, LLC as Agent for the Estate of Bernard Evslin.

"Daedalus and Icarus" from *Greek Myths* by Geraldine McCaughrean. Text copyright © 1992 Geraldine McCaughrean. Reproduced with the permission of Margaret K. McElderry Books, an imprint of Simon & Schuster Childrens Publishing Division.

"Arachne" from *Greek Myths* by Olivia E. Coolidge. Copyright 1949; copyright renewed © 1977 by Olivia E. Coolidge. Reprinted by permission of Houghton Mifflin Harcourt Publishing Company. All rights reserved.

"A Note from the Author" from *In the Beginning: Creation Stories from Around the World* by Virginia Hamilton. Copyright © 1988 by Virginia Hamilton. Reprinted by permission of Houghton Mifflin Harcourt Publishing Company. All rights reserved.

African creation myths from *Voices of the Ancestors: African Myths* by Tony Allan, Fergus Fleming, and Charles Phillips. Copyright © Time-Life Books. Text © 1999 Duncan Baird Publishers.

"Raven and the Sources of Light" by Donna Rosenberg from *World Mythology*. Reproduced by permission of Glencoe/McGraw-Hill Company.

"211 Billion and So Much to Buy—American Youths, the New Big Spenders" from Harris Interactive. Copyright © 2011.

Trends & Tudes from Harris Interactive Youth & Education Research. Copyright © 2010.

"Facts About Marketing to Children" by Betsy Taylor on behalf of the Center for a New American Dream. Reproduced by permission.

"Not Marketing to Children" from Mars. Copyright © Mars

"Marketing to kids gets more savvy with new technologies" by Bruce Horovitz, USA TODAY. Copyright © 2011 by USA TODAY.

"America the Not-So-Beautiful" from *Not That You Asked* by Andrew A. Rooney, copyright © 1989 by Essay Productions, Inc. Used by permission of Random House, Inc.

"Another study highlights the insanity of selling junk food in school vending machines" by Karen Kaplan, *Los Angeles Times*. Copyright © 2010 Los Angeles Times Syndicate.

From "Remarks to the U.N. 4th World Conference on Women Plenary Session" by Hilary Rodham Clinton. Copyright © 1995 American Rhetoric.

"Failure to Ban Violent Video Games Makes Job Harder for Parents" by Tamika Mallory. Copyright © 2011 by newsone.com.

"It's Perverse, But It's Also Pretend" by Cheryl K. Olson, *New York Times*. Copyright © 2011 New York Times, Inc.

"A stunning tale of escape traps its hero in replay" by Harry Brunius. Copyright © 2002 by *The Christian Science Monitor*.

"The Nobel Peace Prize, 1993, Biography of Nelson Mandela" from *Nobel Lectures*, Peace 1991-1995, Editor Irwin Abrams, World Scientific Publishing Co., Singapore, 1999.

From *Long Walk to Freedom: The Autobiography of Nelson Mandela* by Nelson Mandela. Copyright © 1994 by Nelson Rolihlahla Mandela. Published by Little, Brown & Company.

"Landmarks of Nelson Mandela's Life" from *BBC News*. Copyright © 2001 BBC News.

From *Playing the Enemy: Nelson Mandela and the Game That Made a Nation* by John Carlin. Copyright © John Carlin, 2008. Published by Penguin Books, a member of the Penguin Group (USA).

From "Nelson Mandela's Nobel Prize Acceptance Speech" by Nelson Mandela. Copyright © 1993 The Nobel Foundation.

pping by Woods on a Snowy Evening" from *The Poetry of Robert Frost* edited by Edward Connery Lathem. Copyright © 1923, 1969 by Henry Holt and Company. Copyright 1951 by Robert Frost. Reprinted by arrangement with Henry Holt and Company, LLC.

"maggie and milly and molly and may" from *E. E. Cummings: Complete Poems*, 1904-1962, edited by George J. Firmage. Copyright © 1956, 1984, 1991 by the Trustees for the E. E. Cummings Trust. Reprinted by permission of Liveright Publishing Corporation. All rights reserved.

"Mother to Son" from *The Collected Poems of Langston Hughes* by Langston Hughes, edited by Arnold Rampersad with David Roessel, Associate Editor, copyright © 1994 by the Estate of Langston Hughes. Used by permission of Alfred A. Knopf, a division of Random House, Inc.

Haikus by Richard Wright. Copyright © 1998, 2011 by Ellen Wright. Arcade Publishing (registered trademark of Skyhorse Publishing, Inc.).

"It Happened in Montgomery" for Rosa Parks by Phil W. Petrie. Reproduced by permission.

"Eye Contact," "Snob," "Roommate," "Mr. Perfect," "Family Addition," "Too Young for ..." and "Party" from *Teens Have Feelings Too!* by Deborah Karczewski. Copyright © 2000 by Merriwether Publishing Ltd. Used by permission: www.meriwether.com

"Little Red Riding Hood and the Wolf" from *Roald Dahl's Revolting Rhymes* by Roald Dahl and Quentin Blake, illustrator, copyright © 1982 by Roald Dahl Nominee Limited. Used by permission of Alfred A. Knopf, an imprint of Random House, Inc.

Image Credits
Cover: Nick Daly/Stone/Getty Images
1 (t) CWB/Shutterstock; 10 (cr) Nikuwka/Shutterstock; 11 (tr) Charles Knox/Shutterstock; 15 (cr) Venus Angel/Shutterstock; 36 (tl) Chuck Wagner/Shutterstock, (cl) Dennis Donohue/Shutterstock, (bl) Oleg Golovnev/Shutterstock; 37 (tl) ollyy/Shutterstock; 50 (b) wongwean/Shutterstock; 61 (br) Sergey Vasilyev/Shutterstock; 72 (bl) Eric Isselee/Shutterstock, (br) Eric Isselee/Shutterstock; 79 (cr) Daniel Korzeniewski/Shutterstock; 81 (tr) Greg291/Shutterstock; 85 (t) Vaju Ariel/Shutterstock; 91 (tr) Andresr/Shutterstock; 94 (tr) Angela Waye/Shutterstock; 116 (br) Samuel Borges Photography/Shutterstock; 118 (l) Ljupco Smokovski/Shutterstocks; 132 (cr) Svitlana Kazachek/Shutterstock; 133 (br) Darryl Brooks/Shutterstocks; 146 (tr) re_bekka/Shutterstock; 147 (tr) Jose Gil/Shutterstock; 152 (bl) Devin Koob/Shutterstock; 159 (tr) Xiaojia Wang/Shutterstock; 163 (t) RTImages/Shutterstock; 185 (c) justasc/Shutterstock; 226 (c) Louise Gubb/Corbis Saba; 227 (tc) veslivio/Shutterstock., (inset) Denny Allen/Getty Images; 245 (t) Kamira/Shutterstock; 250 (br) Andrei Nekrassov/Shutterstock; 252 (b) Olga Miltsova/Shutterstock; 275 (br) Elya Vatel/Shutterstock; 286 (tl) Clipart deSIGN/Shutterstock; (tcl) Clipart deSIGN/Shutterstock; 298 (bl) Mike Heywood/Shutterstock; 305 (cr) montebasso/Shutterstock